IRON MAIDEN

THE ULTIMATE UNAUTHORIZED
HISTORY OF THE BEAST

by
NEIL DANIELS

with
GAVIN BADDELEY
DANIEL BUKSZPAN
GARRY BUSHELL
IAN CHRISTE
RYAN LAMAR
MARTIN POPOFF
JOHN TUCKER
and
MICK WALL

Voyageur
Press

CONTENTS

INTRODUCTION
MAIDEN ENGLAND

In August 2010, Iron Maiden released their fifteenth studio album, *The Final Frontier*. It hit No. 1 in more than thirty countries. Not only does this accomplishment boldly state that heavy metal is far from dead, but it rather loudly underscores the fact that Iron Maiden is undoubtedly one of the most successful heavy metal bands of all time. There is little argument that, in their thirty-five-year history, Maiden has done more for the metal cause than any other band in history. The band has always been full of charisma and energy, but it is the almost unnerving dedication to their art—and indeed it is art, despite the genre's often frivolous imagery—that has kept them busy for so many years.

Maiden has often been out of vogue, with little help from the mainstream media, but their strict work ethic and tireless drive are to be greatly admired. Unlike a lot of bands, Maiden has a taut relationship with their management and it's the relationship particularly between bassist and Maiden mastermind

Steve Harris and manager Rod Smallwood that evidently has kept the Maiden machine in motion regardless of setbacks. It's often been commented that Maiden is Steve Harris' band, and there's certainly some truth to that statement.

With more than 85 million albums sold, countless awards, and two thousand concerts played to millions around the world, Maiden's legacy is evidently assured for quite some time.

The band formed in London in 1975, and after several lineup changes they cemented their status as pioneers of the now legendary New Wave of British Heavy Metal (NWOBHM) movement that lasted from around 1979 to about 1981. NWOBHM represents a short period of time, but it spawned many bands that garner mention in this book.

While Maiden's first two albums—*Iron Maiden* and *Killers*—are iconic in their own ways, it was not until former Samson singer Bruce Dickinson replaced Paul Di'Anno in 1981 that Maiden's flight to success properly took off. The trilogy

ALL: Mick Hutson/Redferns/Getty Images

comprising *The Number of the Beast* (1982), *Piece of Mind* (1983), and *Powerslave* (1984) gave the band worldwide fame and success in the United States. Those three albums are often included in polls of the "greatest heavy metal albums" and have lost none of their appeal more than twenty years later.

While the band suffered a downward slide in the mid-'90s after the departure of Bruce Dickinson and the hiring of ex-Wolfsbane Blaze Bayley, Maiden made a steady comeback beginning with 2000's "reunion" album, *Brave New World*. Indeed, the band continued rebuilding their career right up to the end of the decade. At this writing, in 2011, they are quite simply a force to be reckoned with.

Iron Maiden is a very British band; their working-class mentality has never diminished and their Britishness is widely known, yet they are extremely popular elsewhere. Their popularity in the United States, while sometimes tumultuous, has not been lost among the countless bands that followed in their wake. The whole Bay Area thrash metal scene of the '80s owes a massive debt to Maiden, as do all the other thrash metal bands that formed not just on the West Coast but elsewhere in the States during that decade. It's a lengthy list that includes such high-profile players as Metallica, Megadeth, Slayer, Anthrax, Annihilator, and Exodus. In addition, several big-name metal bands from the 1990s onward, such as Marilyn Manson, InFlames, and Trivium, have been greatly inspired by Iron Maiden.

Looking at the band's prevalence another way, how many celebrity "it girls" do you see wearing Iron Maiden T-shirts? For them it may not be about the music, but it does show that Maiden has touched many corners of pop culture. Heavy metal is very much an image-led genre, with all the great album covers, T-shirts, and posters. Iron Maiden has always been conscious of that, and while many can claim the visuals are all nonsense, few can argue that such imagery—including Iron Maiden's—has not had a massive impact on popular culture. There are all kinds of Maiden-related multimedia devices and apps, not to mention all the band merchandise. Iron Maiden is more well-known than their peers mostly because they've made more right decisions than wrong.

Not surprisingly, there are many books out there on the history of Iron Maiden. This book is by no means the definitive tale of Iron Maiden, but it is not supposed to be. It is a celebration of their music, a good starting point for newcomers, and an illustrated archive worthy of the attention of longtime fans who argue that Iron Maiden is the most influential heavy metal band of all time. Sure, Metallica and others have sold more albums, but would there be such bands if it weren't for Iron Maiden?

1 BEGINNINGS OF THE BEAST
THE EARLY YEARS, 1975–1978

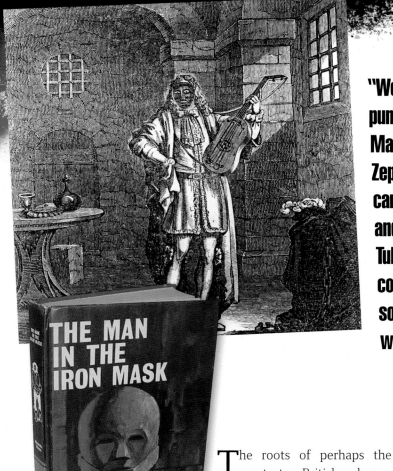

"Well, I didn't start the band as any kind of crusade against punk as people seem to think. I couldn't have because Maiden began in 1975, before all that. . . . It was when Zep and Purple were finishing——a lot of the influences came from them, the twin guitars from Wishbone Ash and Thin Lizzy, the time changes from Yes and Jethro Tull. We wanted to get all the ingredients in there and come up with something different. But after a year or so we realized we weren't getting gigs any more. Then we did 'ate punk."

—Steve Harris, quoted by Phil Sutcliffe,
Q, January 1991

The roots of perhaps the greatest British heavy metal band of all time can be traced back to 1975, when rock music was still popular with the masses and before punk made it seem like an unfashionable and outdated trend. Trailblazing hard-rock bands like Led Zeppelin and Deep Purple were doing good business, and a young East End London lad by the name of Steve Harris wanted in on the action.

Maiden was formed, rather ironically given the band's (misperceived) association with the occult and all things devil-worshipping, on Christmas Day.

Harris had been gigging in a band called Smiler and quit the outfit to form a new band that he would tightly control, something that was his baby, his creation. Harris got the name for his new band after watching *The Man in the Iron Mask*, a film based on an Alexandre Dumas novel in which mention is made of the eighteenth-century torture device known as the iron maiden.

Steve Harris was born Stephen Percy Harris on March 12, 1956, in Leytonstone, London. He originally wanted to be a drummer and was inspired by the Who's Keith Moon and Zeppelin's John Bonham. However, there was simply no room in his small East End London home for something as large as a drum kit, so at seventeen, Harris bought a Fender Precision Bass for £40, a considerable sum in those days, and started plucking away. He began writing songs and got his first gig in a band called Gypsy's Kiss. The band debuted in 1973 (somewhat ironically) at St. Nicholas church in Poplar, London, as part of a talent contest organized by Dave Beazley, who would later become Iron Maiden's lighting and special effects wizard, Dave Lights. Gypsy's Kiss played just a handful of gigs before it folded and Harris joined Smiler.

It was obvious from the get-go that Harris was keen on progressive rock, and the type of songs he penned and the way he played bass were certainly inspired by the likes of King Crimson, ELP, Genesis, and Pink Floyd. But he was also fond of such hard-rock heavyweights as Deep Purple, UFO, Led Zeppelin, and the Who. UFO was especially close to his heart. Perhaps he could somehow combine the progressiveness of, say, early Genesis with the heaviness of UFO?

It was obvious from the get-go that Steve Harris was keen on prog and his record collection included LPs by the likes of Jethro Tull, King Crimson, Genesis, and Nektar. But he was also fond of such hard-rock heavyweights as Deep Purple.

HAMMER

OFFICIAL PROGRAMME
TENPENCE

WEST HAM UNITED

1976-77

Saturday 16 October 1976
KICK-OFF AT 3 p.m.

IPSWICH TOWN

FOOTBALL LEAGUE : First Division

WEST HAM UNITED

Steve Harris is not only a talented musician, but a keen footballer as well, and a rather good one, too. He still famously supports the West Ham club to this day. *Program © M&N/Alamy*

However, those weren't the only bands Harris liked. "I used to listen to early Free, early Sabbath, stuff like that," he told Gueniviere of *Night Rock News* in 1982. "I liked some of the Free bass lines, fairly simple, but really nice technique, you know what I mean? . . . Of course you don't know anything about technique when you're first doing it!"

Harris is not only a talented musician (despite having no formal training), but a keen footballer as well, and a rather good one, too. He was a youth player for the West Ham football team in London, which he (famously) still supports to this day. And when Harris formed Maiden he was an architectural draftsman, though he became so dedicated to the band that he quit his day job to focus fully on it.

Harris' first attempts at starting his own band involved some unknown local musicians whose names have faded in to the mists of time. "When I first started playing we used to muck about in my house," he told Gueniviere. "I used to have a couple of guys comin' over from school, just sort of messin'

about. This guy used to play guitar, and he was a lot better on guitar than I was on bass at the time, and I used to just try and jam in with him. Then we decided, 'Ah, well, we've got to get a drummer!' So we got this guy; anyway, he had this kit. He was pretty useless, but we didn't really know at the time. We thought he was alright, but as we started to progress and get a bit better, we realized he wasn't any good, and we sacked him."

However, the first line-up of the band that became Iron Maiden is known to have included singer Paul Day, guitarists Dave Sullivan and Terry Rance, drummer Ron Matthew, and bassist and bandleader Harris. In spring 1976 Iron Maiden played their first show at the Cart and Horses pub in Stratford, London, with the Day/Sullivan/Rance/Matthew/Harris line-up. But things did not go as planned for Harris and his young cohorts. There was some tension in the band about the way Paul Day handled himself on stage. Simply put, he did not have the energy and enthusiasm that Harris was looking for. Harris, who was a fan of charismatic frontmen like Phil Mogg from UFO and Roger Daltry from the Who, wanted someone with similar vigor. Day just did not fit the bill, so the search was on for a replacement. Enter Dennis Wilcock.

Wilcock was a huge KISS fan and loved the onstage theatrics that made Gene Simmons, Paul Stanley, Ace Frehley, and Peter Criss four of the most talked about musicians in rock history. Maiden's new singer was also a fan of shock rocker Alice Cooper and other stars of rock's darkened theater of devilish delights. In fact he liked them so much he began using fire, makeup, and even fake blood onstage. But

In spring 1976 Iron Maiden played their first show at the Cart and Horses pub in Stratford, London, with the Day/Sullivan/Rance/Matthew/Harris line-up. © Alistair Laming/Alamy

Maiden was envisaged by the band's founder to be a heavy rock outfit with progressive elements that played like lightning onstage but without any frivolous theatrics.

At this time punk was more than just a rumbling in London's inner-city streets, with bands like the Sex Pistols, the Clash, and the Damned singing antiestablishment lyrics, and the Ramones causing equal controversy in New York. Punk was not just a musical movement, but an individualistic and antiauthoritarian subculture—the antithesis of what Harris' hard-rock heroes were singing about. There were no onstage theatrics in punk rock, which touted a DIY approach. Even Led Zeppelin seemed old hat by the end of the 1970s, but some bands soldiered through the punk era remarkably well. Rock music was still played to millions around the world, only

the press and TV did not give it as much or as friendly exposure as they did punk.

In 1976, just two months after Maiden was formed, Wilcock's friend, guitarist Dave Murray, was invited to join the band even though they already had two guitarists. There was something special in Murray's guitar playing that made him standout among his peers—his dexterity on the fretboard certainly raised eyebrows.

Murray was born David Michael Murray on December 23, 1956. His mother was a part-time cleaner, and when she wasn't working she tended to her husband who was disabled. Murray had a hard childhood because of a lack of finances, and like many children raised in poor families he embraced sport, becoming an avid footballer and cricketer. But because his family moved often, he never got the chance to join a sports club where he could truly excel and also make likeminded friends. By the time he reached his teens, Murray had attended several different schools. Rock music came into his life when he was fifteen and heard Jimi Hendrix for the first time. "Voodoo Child (Slight Return)" totally changed Murray's life, and Hendrix's groundbreaking guitar work inspired Murray to buy his first guitar. He also purchased more rock records—Hendrix, Free, the Who, Cream—and played along to them for several hours a day. Murray grew to love the sound of raw and distorted rock. Hearing his favorite bands play live or watching them on TV had a major influence on Murray.

Murray played in some low-key local bands before he joined Maiden, including an outfit called Stone Free, his first band. However, Iron Maiden suffered serious internal friction as a result of his addition, particularly from Sullivan and Rance, who saw no need for a third guitarist. After all, two guitarists worked fine for Wishbone Ash and Judas Priest. Such a hassle ensued that Harris disbanded the first edition of Iron Maiden in 1976 after just a few short months together, and Murray formed a band called Urchin with fellow Stone Free guitarist Adrian Smith. But all was not lost.

Iron Maiden was resurrected before the end of the year with Dave Murray as the band's sole guitarist. It was quite a change from the previous line-up. While in Urchin, Murray recorded a single called "She's a Roller," whereas Iron Maiden had not yet made a recording. Certainly the fact that Murray had made a recording impressed Harris. Murray was working at a mundane nine-to-five job for the Greater London Council, but he still dedicated as much time to Maiden as possible. All of Harris' time and attention went in to the band.

Dave Murray was invited to join the band in 1976 even though they already had two guitarists. Murray's dexterity certainly raised eyebrows among his peers. Rock music came into his life when he was fifteen and heard Jimi Hendrix for the first time. *Virginia Turbett/Redferns/Getty Images*

In 1977 Harris hired guitarist Bob Sawyer to play along-side Murray, but there was friction in the new line-up too, particularly between Murray and singer Dennis Wilcock. Harris made an executive decision and fired both, then hired guitarist Terry Wapram, drummer Barry "Thunderstick" Purkis, and keyboardist Tony Moore. This new, albeit makeshift, version of Iron Maiden played a gig at a London club called Bridgehouse in November but it was a disaster.

In 2009 Barry Purkis spoke about his brief stint in Iron Maiden to U.K. rock writer Joe Geesin (*getreadytorock.com*):

There are a lot of truths behind my time with Iron Maiden. If anyone who reads Wikipedia wants to believe that I fell asleep during the course of a gig whilst playing with them, then it's true! However, as I remember it, my time with Iron Maiden was both pleasurable and enjoyable. The reason I left was the band were going through a transient stage trying desperately to find themselves. Steve couldn't find the formula, and let's make no mistake, it was always Steve's band. He was very directional in what he wanted. He would come to my house,

me behind the kit, he with his bass, and go through the rhythm parts. That was it. That was the way that Steve worked. The material that we were working on was the material that eventually made it onto the first album. For me, it all fell apart when Steve was toying with the idea of going back to college, back to his technical drawing. . . . People were coming and going within the band and it no longer held anything special for me; I should imagine I played in the band for about eight months. We rehearsed a lot and did a couple of gigs.

Indeed—and perhaps unsurprisingly—the latest line-up did not last long. Harris replaced Wapram with the newly reinstated Dave Murray and Purkis was replaced by Doug Sampson, Harris' old mate from Smiler. Wilcock also was let go and went on to form a new outfit with Terry Wapram called V1. Iron Maiden was on the hunt for yet another new singer.

Paul Di'Anno was an interesting choice to replace Dennis Wilcock. Steve Harris had a deep knowledge of prog and metal—Di'Anno was a punk fan through and through. *Virginia Turbett/Redferns/Getty Images*

Harris had met Paul Di'Anno through Doug Sampson at a London pub called the Red Lion in Leytonstone. But it was not the first time Di'Anno had come across the beast known as Iron Maiden.

"It was at school—Leyton County High School in East London in fact—where I was just starting attendance when Steve Harris was leaving," Di'Anno later told Shan Shiva of *battlehelm.com*. "A mutual friend of ours told me that this band called Iron Maiden were looking for a vocalist. I was in a punk band at the time but I went to see them play and basically laughed my ass off and walked away . . . Seriously! After school, the whole situation came about again with them looking again for a vocalist so I went to a rehearsal and did some Deep Purple numbers. We had a good laugh and on Sunday evening Steve came to my house and told me the job was mine. I was sixteen and rest is history!"

Paul Di'Anno was born Paul Andrews in Chingford, London, on May 17, 1958. A tough, street-smart kid who worked as a butcher and a chef, he had raspy vocals that would give Maiden an aggressive punk edge. Di'Anno also had lots of charisma and an attitude that bordered on cocky. He really wasn't scared of anything or anyone.

It was an interesting choice. Bandleader Harris had acquired an in-depth knowledge of rock and heavy metal music whereas Di'Anno was a punk fan through and through who had immersed himself in the '70s London punk scene.

As his most recent line-up began rehearsing, Harris was pleased with the new incarnation. They played gigs in the London area, mostly sticking to the East End. It certainly seemed that this version of Maiden was going to be the most stable thus far in the band's relatively tumultuous history.

On December 30–31, 1978, the Harris/Murray/Di'Anno/Sampson line-up Iron Maiden recorded the demo that would produce *The Soundhouse Tapes*—probably one of the most important EPs in the annals of rock and metal.

1976

By Ryan LaMar

05.01	Poplar, GBR
06.09	Stratford, GBR
06.15, 17	Canning Town, GBR
06.24	Stratford, GBR
07.01	Stratford, GBR
07.08	Stratford, GBR
07.22	Stratford, GBR
07.29	Stratford, GBR
08.07	London, GBR
08.19	Stratford, GBR
08.22	Dagenham, GBR
08.27	??, GBR
08.28	London, GBR
08.29	Dagenham, GBR
09.02	Stratford, GBR
09.03	Barking, GBR
09.05	Dagenham, GBR
09.06	Leytonstone, GBR
09.07	Poplar, GBR
09.16	Stratford, GBR
09.23	Stratford, GBR
10.05	Chingford, GBR
10.15–16	Barking, GBR
10.18	Canning Town, GBR
11.05	Stratford, GBR
11.13	Chingford, GBR
11.??	Waltham Forest, GBR
11.18	Walthamstow, GBR
12.21	Stratford, GBR
??.??	Ramsgate, GBR

1977

02.18	Stratford, GBR
Spring	Canning Town, GBR
04.28	Canning Town, GBR
05.05	Canning Town, GBR
05.14	Canning Town, GBR
05.19	Canning Town, GBR
05.29	Canning Town, GBR

06.??	Plumstead, GBR
06.02	Canning Town, GBR
06.23	Camden Town, GBR
06.24–25	Barking, GBR
06.27	Leytonstone, GBR
07.01–02	Barking, GBR
07.04	Canning Town, GBR
07.08	Barking, GBR
07.09	Leytonstone, GBR
07.11	Canning Town, GBR
07.12	Tramshed, GBR
07.15–16	Barking, GBR
07.18	Canning Town, GBR
07.29	Canning Town, GBR
11.??	Canning Town, GBR

1978

02.17	Canning Town, GBR
04.06	Plumstead, GBR
04.07	Stratford, GBR
04.08	Canning Town, GBR
12.31	East Ham, GBR

Notes: The location of the August 27, 1976, show is cut off in Harris' journal entry in The History of Iron Maiden, Part 1: The Early Years. *Harris' journal lists August 30 (Bethnal Green), September 4 (Dagenham), and November 14 (Chingford), 1976, gigs as cancelled.*

According to fan club magazine No. 4, the December 21, 1976, show at the Cart and Horses pub was Dave Murray's first with the band.

Paul Stenning's Iron Maiden: 30 Years of the Beast *indicates that the band played the Stars and Stripes pub in Ramsgate (date unknown) when Dennis Wilcock was with the band, placing this show, if it occurred, in late 1976 or early 1977.*

Stenning's Iron Maiden: 30 Years of the Beast *suggests the additional spring 1977 date in Canning Town. According to Skoog, a March 10, 1977, show at London's Ron Club was cancelled because Harris refused to play a punk club.*

Tony Moore, in an interview cited in Stenning's book, claims his first gig was in November 1977 at the Bridge House in Canning Town. Yet another source has cited two November Canning Town dates.

There likely are many more dates for 1978. However, the band's performances were spotty after their equipment was stolen on February 2 (hence two cancelled London dates, either February 3 and 4 or 4 and 5) and they had to borrow equipment from other bands. Around summer, the band placed an advertisement claiming they were back in full force, but there's very little evidence they played any more gigs in 1978 after this advertisement, save the New Year's Eve show noted here.

Please see "Tourography Methodology" on pages 207–208 for an explanation of the sources used in researching and compiling the tourography.

Clive Burr, Paul Di'Anno, Dennis Stratton, Dave Murray, and Steve Harris in 1980. © *Presselect/Alamy*

2

RUNNING FREE
FLIGHT TO SUCCESS AND THE NWOBHM, 1979–1980

"I reckon we're the only real New Wave HM band. 'Cos we're the only ones who don't give a monkey's. We're an HM band with punk attitudes."

—Paul Di'Anno, quoted by Garry Bushell, *Sounds*, February 23, 1980

Self-funded and released on the band's own Rock House Records label, *The Soundhouse Tapes* EP hit the streets on November 9, 1979, and featured three songs, all culled from the band's demo, dubbed *Spaceward* because it was recorded at Spaceward Studios in Cambridge: "Prowler," "Invasion," and "Iron Maiden." A fourth track called "Strange World" was not included because the band was not enthusiastic about its production quality.

The release marked the start of Iron Maiden's career successes, though they wouldn't have guessed it at the time. Most of the band members were working day jobs and pouring their hard-earned wages back into the band in the form of gear, petrol, and other gigging expenses.

"We couldn't actually afford to buy the master tapes, which would have been nice to have now," Dave Murray told interviewer Gary James (*harbinger.org*). "We just scraped up enough money to do the recording. But, to actually buy the reel of tape would've cost more and we couldn't afford that. So, unfortunately that's gone."

Writing on the website of Spaceward, engineer Mike Kemp confirms: "[W]e were as poor as they were and couldn't afford to keep £60 multitrack tapes for every band either! (A session cost about that I recall.) We did our best—I think for

£5 a week we would hold them until either they were paid for or the band decided not to keep them any longer, e.g. after a remix. Presumably they did not take that option."

The Soundhouse Tapes were named in homage to the Soundhouse Club at the Prince of Wales pub in Kingsbury, North West London, where famed rock DJ Neal Kay ran a heavy metal disco. The EP went on to sell five thousand copies via mail order within just a few weeks. "Prowler" even went to No. 1 on Kay's *Heavy Metal Soundhouse* charts in the famed *Sounds* magazine. It seemed that Maiden was on its way up. At last.

Maiden had the talent and drive to succeed in the business, but those traits would only get them so far. What they needed was somebody with a business brain to get them a record deal, which would, of course, give them the financial backing for their first album. Then *The Soundhouse Tapes* landed in the hands of Rod Smallwood, the manager and booking agent for Steve Harley & Cockney Rebel. Smallwood and his partner, Andy Taylor, were impressed and signed on as Maiden's managers. Smallwood was a tough-talking northerner who had the intelligence and fierce wit to get Maiden noticed by record company executives.

The new Maiden line-up was not quite so well settled.

Dave Murray had remained the band's sole guitarist until Paul Cairns joined sometime in 1979. But Cairns lasted just three months. After attempts with two other guitarists, Paul Todd and Tony Parsons, were aborted due to poor chemistry, Dennis Stratton was hired to join Murray in October 1979. The story goes that Stratton was hired only because Murray's mate, Adrian Smith, was still busy with Urchin. However, Harris evidently was impressed by Stratton's work with local band Remus Down Boulevard. Stratton brought with him his friend Clive Burr, who replaced Doug Sampson on drums. There was no way Harris was going to hire any below-par musicians. Now he was comfortable with his band's second guitarist and drummer.

In 2009, former Iron Maiden drummer Barry "Thunderstick" Purkis, who was in Samson by the time of Maiden's 1979 personnel changes, told rock scribe Joe Geesin (*getreadytorock. com*): "They had had trouble with their then drummer, Dougie Sampson, and had decided to part company. I received a phone call over the Christmas period '79–'80, attended a jam with the band a few days after Christmas, did the proposed single 'Running Free' with them, and was asked to rejoin. I spent the whole of the Christmas period deliberating but decided that due to my Thunderstick image taking

Self-funded and released on Maiden's Rock House Records label, *The Soundhouse Tapes* EP hit the streets on November 9, 1979. The seven-inch record featured three songs, all culled from the band's Spaceward demo.

Metal for Muthas tour, the Lyceum, London, February 10, 1980.
Both Virginia Turbett/Redferns/Getty Images

off [Purkis was on a recent front cover of *Sounds*], of which Iron Maiden wanted none of, and the fact that I was due to go back into the studios with Samson to record 'Head On,' decided that I had taken a different direction. Steve Harris agreed. Imagine my surprise on finding out that the drummer that had been offered the job was none other than Clive Burr. Clive obviously being Samson's original drummer!"

In December 1979 the band finally landed a record deal, hooking up with EMI. The band's first appearance on an LP, however, came in February 1980, when "Sanctuary" and "Wrathchild" were included on the now legendary *Metal for Muthas* compilation that also featured contributions from Samson, Sledgehammer, and others. Maiden also committed to a support slot on the equally legendary *Metal for Muthas* tour, which began at Aberdeen University on February 1 and featured bands from said compilation, as well as Mötörhead and Saxon.

Guitarist Brian Tatler, co-founder of Black Country metallers Diamond Head, remembers the tour's February 10 London date featuring Maiden and Praying Mantis (both regulars at Neal Kay's Soundhouse) and his own band, which opened with a short set. "This was an important gig for Diamond Head," Tatler told me in 2011. "First off, it was in London and, secondly, we knew there would be press there. We arrived at the Lyceum about 6 p.m. and hung around getting worked up and frustrated waiting for Maiden to finish soundchecking. They seemed to take ages doodling our precious time away. At 7:30 the stage manager shouted, 'The doors are opening' and Maiden quickly quit the stage and then said to us, 'OK lads, you can set up now.' Neither Iron Maiden nor Praying Mantis would move their drum risers, leaving us to play in a straight line with Duncan Scott's drum kit behind the PA. 'I was playing to a panel of black wood with jack plugs coming out of it,' said Duncan. We had thirty minutes to impress and squeezed in four of our very long songs."

New Wave of British Heavy Metal (NWOBHM) was in full swing, abetted by Neal Kay at his Soundhouse disco and *Sounds* scribes, such as Alan Lewis and Geoff Barton. At the time, it seemed as though every major U.K. city was producing a healthy—or unhealthy, depending on your musical tastes—number of bands.

(continued on page 22)

Maiden fans rock the Lyceum, London, February 10, 1980. *Virginia Turbett/Redferns/Getty Images*

MAIDEN AND NWOBHM

BY JOHN TUCKER

IN THE EARLY DAYS of the New Wave of British Heavy Metal, a number of bands were seen as the face of the genre: Def Leppard and Saxon, certainly, alongside the likes of Girlschool, Samson, Diamond Head, and others. The list is long and varied, but if any band was to become synonymous with NWOBHM, as it's come to be more commonly referred to, it's Iron Maiden. They were there from the beginning, they embodied its ethos, and they saw it out, riding a wave of much deserved popularity and artistic and commercial success.

NWOBHM got its name from influential music weekly *Sounds*, after Geoff Barton reviewed a three-band bill of up-and-coming metal acts—Angel Witch, Iron Maiden, and Samson—that took place on May 8, 1979, at the Music Machine in Camden, London. Editor Alan Lewis added the tagline "The New Wave of British Heavy Metal" to the feature and a genre was, well, if not born, at least named.

NWOBHM took the punk ethos that if you believed you could do it, you could do it, but added the caveat "so long as you have a modicum of talent." Instead of hanging around and waiting to be signed to a label, bands formed their own labels and self-pressed their singles. First of the big names past the starter's gun was Def Leppard, with Iron Maiden's *The Soundhouse Tapes* following a few months later. With no record-label support, the only way to afford such a venture was to get out there and be seen, then pool the gig profits (and day-job cash and/or unemployment benefits) to fund the recording. Then you had to get out there all over again to sell the record. Because of this approach, the bands were easily accessible to the fans—these weren't Led Zeppelins playing massive arenas and living in a seemingly closed world—these were ordinary people whom you could talk to, shake hands with, and relate to. If they can do it, many fans reasoned, so can we, which gave rise to a second generation of young metal warriors.

Not every band went down this DIY route. Girl was picked up by Jet Records straight away, for example, while Girlschool put their first single out via independent label Cherry Red (the rise of the indie label being another byproduct of punk). But Witchfynde were so impressed

The issue of *Sounds* that gave the world "New Wave of British Heavy Metal."

with Leppard's do-it-yourself approach that they recorded an entire album on their own, even using the same studio as Joe Elliott's crew (although they signed to Rondelet before they could release it themselves). And of course Diamond Head, having issued their debut single "Shoot out the Lights" themselves, almost made a career of DIY before finally signing to MCA in 1982.

Much is made now of the generally poor sound quality of these early self-financed NWOBHM recordings. It's true that there was something rough 'n' ready about them, but they were usually rushed and recorded in fairly basic studios to keep costs to a minimum. Thinking ahead (although not far enough!) Steve Harris booked a more expensive studio to record Iron Maiden's first demo. Blowing their budget, they planned to go back at a later date to fix the bum notes and properly mix the demo, but by the time they had the cash to return they discovered that the master tape had been wiped. *The Soundhouse Tapes*, therefore, was pressed from the band's copy of that original demo, warts and all.

Iron Maiden worked damned hard to be seen and heard, to build a fan base and accumulate column inches, and they reaped the rewards. When EMI was looking around to sign a new metal band, there was really only one name in contention. 🇬🇧

Maiden's first appearance on an LP came in February 1980 when "Sanctuary" and "Wrathchild" were included on the now legendary *Metal for Muthas* compilation.

(continued from page 19)

"Well I coined [NWOBHM] as a front-page headline," Lewis told me in 2010. "But it was sort of an in-joke. We were always hailing something or other as 'The New Wave of'—it was part of the sense of humor, a bit tongue in cheek. But there is no doubt that we helped to get that whole scene going, and the credit for that goes to Geoff Barton who, along with Pete Makowski, Mick Wall, and Garry Bushell, were celebrating this music when everyone else thought it was a joke. We weren't as snobbish as the other mags. . . . I just knew that from a journalistic point of view it generated great copy and great images and connected with readers, and bugger what the pundits thought. But I have to say that it polarized both readers and writers, and caused a lot of internal strife." With their self-titled debut album, Iron Maiden became one of the genre's leading bands, along with other heavyweights, such as Saxon and Diamond Head. NWOBHM was certainly in some ways a reaction to punk, but like all the punks bands, NWOBHM bands took a very do-it-yourself approach to the music. The period lasted from 1979 to 1981 and produced a lot of bands, including Bitches Sin, Avenger, Raven, Girlschool, Satan, Blitzkrieg, Trespass, Tygers of Pan Tang, Witchfynde, Aragorn, Atomkraft, Angel Witch, Hellanbach—the list goes on. Despite not sounding like a heavy metal band at all, Def Leppard was also rolled into in the NWOBHM movement. "I don't think anyone was really aware of it [NWOBHM] until the press started writing about it, and that pretty much started that whole movement," Steve Harris told Bob Nalbandian in 1998.

Most NWOBHM bands, including Maiden, were inspired by hard rock and heavy metal heavyweights of the early '70s, namely, Black Sabbath, Judas Priest, Deep Purple, Led Zeppelin, Scorpions, Rainbow, and UFO, among others. And of course the NWOBHM bands would play their part in metal history by influencing thrash bands of the 1980s. But what was it about Iron Maiden that appealed to a much larger audience than their NWOBHM peers? Why did their music travel across the Atlantic, leaving most other NWOBHM bands playing to tiny audiences around the U.K.?

"I think of all the NWOBHM bands Iron Maiden probably worked the hardest, toured the most, had the best manager, and the best record label," Brian Tatler told me in 2011. "It's not luck. They had some lucky breaks, but they are consistent with their albums and live shows. They know all about giving the people what they want—you enter into the world of Iron Maiden, it's like supporting a huge football team. They are one of only a few bands who can fill stadiums anywhere in the world—that takes a lot of commitment. In 1980, I was a little jealous that EMI signed Maiden and Phonogram signed Def Leppard, even though they were right to. I knew that two of the biggest and best labels for breaking rock bands had now snapped up a NWOBHM band, and each and the rest of us were left with labels like Arista, Chrysalis, MCA, and RCA. Rod Smallwood has to take some credit for the huge amount of dedication and energy he put into making EMI and *Kerrang!* work on Iron Maiden constantly. Iron Maiden must have been in *Kerrang!* every week for fifteen years!"

In a 2011 interview, original Tygers of Pan Tang singer Jess Cox, from the northeast of England, concurred:

I guess their management was more astute and focused than other NWOBHM managers, who were mostly teachers, postmen, and secondhand car dealers. The press, too, championed them more than any other NWOBHM. Being in London, too, and being local Cockney boys would of helped—they were easily "gottable" by [the] industry, playing the likes of the Marquee as a "local" gig. It was a huge deal to do the Marquee as a Northern band, career-wise and logistically, but Maiden lived in London and were the first NWOBHM band to headline Marquee shows, which was the spiritual home of the NWOBHM.

THE L I V

marquee

90 Wardour St., W.1 | **01-437 6603**

OPEN EVERY NIGHT FROM 7.00 pm to 11.00 pm
REDUCED ADMISSION FOR STUDENTS AND MEMBERS

Wed 17th & Thurs 18th Oct (Adm £1.75)
UK SUBS
Plus support & Jerry Floyd

Fri 19th Oct (Adm £1.00)
Heavy Metal with
IRON MAIDEN
Praying Mantis & Ian Fleming

Sat 20th Oct (Adm £1.00)
BACK TO ZERO
Plus friends Ian Fleming

Sun 21st Oct (Adm £1.50)
TOYAH
Vitas Dance & Mandy H

Mon 22nd Oct (Adm £1.50)
THE PRETENDERS
Plus guests & Jerry Floyd

Tue 23rd & Wed 24th Oct (Adm £1.50)
THE ADVERTS
The Decoys & Jerry Floyd

HAMBURGERS AND OTHER HOT AND COLD SNACKS AVAILABLE

The Decoys & Jerry Floyd
Thurs 25th & Fri 26th
Welcome return of
CLIMAX BLUES BAND
Advance tickets to members £2.00
Non members on the door £2.25

01-261 6153

marquee

90 Wardour St., W.1 | **01-437 6603**

OPEN EVERY NIGHT FROM 7.00 pm to 11.00 pm
REDUCED ADMISSION FOR STUDENTS AND MEMBERS

Wed 2nd & Thur 3rd April (Adm £1.75)
HEAVY METAL
IRON MAIDEN
Tygers of Pang Tang
+ Ian Fleming

Fri 4th April (Adm £2.00)
COME AND HAVE A GOOD TIME
THE BLUES BAND
Plus Friends + Ian Fleming

Sat 5th April (Adm £2.00)
FROM SAN FRANCISCO
PAUL COLLIN'S THE BEAT
Fatal Charm + Ian Fleming

Sun 6th, Mon 7th & Tues 8th April
HEAVY METAL SPECIAL
GIRL
Plus Friends + DJ Ian Fleming
Advance tickets to members £1.75
Non-members on the door £2.00

Wed 9th, Thur 10th, Fri 11th April
RETURN BY PUBLIC DEMAND
ATHLETICO SPIZZ 80
Plus Guests + DJ JERRY FLOYD
Advance tickets to members £1.50

Sat 12th Apr (Adm £1.50)
TENPOLE TUDOR
Plus Support + Ian Fleming

HAMBURGERS AND OTHER HOT AND COLD SNACKS AVAILABLE

Maiden was the first NWOBHM band to headline Marquee shows, the club which, according to original Tygers of Pan Tang singer Jess Cox, was the spiritual home of the NWOBHM.

Also, of course let's not forget their early albums were . . . phenomenal classic heavy metal, which set them up nicely when all the other NWOBHM bands were breaking up and/or being dropped by the major labels. They went on tour for two years promoting the album, cementing them as the "it" band of the genre. The guys then just gave their then-huge fan base what they wanted. Every album after this was a Maiden album musically and visually, with the Eddie graphic and Union Jack easy symbols for metalheads to want to buy into the Maiden brand. Once they became a machine rolling on with album, tour, album, tour, year after year with no competition, they just steamrollered the scenes and mopped up the fans worldwide.

Released in April 1980 in the United Kingdon and in August in the United States, the band's self-titled debut with EMI was produced by Will Malone at London's Kingsway Studios. The story goes that Malone was not totally enthusiastic about the project, and though many longstanding fans continue to like the album's raw, aggressive, and almost punk-like sound, other quarters of the Maiden fan base believe it sounds somewhat amateurish. It has been claimed that Steve Harris took over most of the album's production because of Malone's perceived lack of interest.

The album's influence on subsequent metal bands, particularly in the United States, cannot be overstated. North American thrash and speed metal bands of the 1980s like Metallica and Megadeth owe a huge debt to the *Iron Maiden* LP. The marriage of pulsating riffs, galloping bass lines, aggressive vocals, and progressive elements was extraordinary.

However, the punk element and the band's implied association with the punk scene was not something with which Steve Harris was entirely pleased. "Punk was only important in that we hated it and didn't want anything to do with it," he said in an interview appearing on *musicrooms.net* in 2010. "Punk came out at the time we were doing pub gigs and it was very difficult for us to get work because we didn't look right. We were around before punk, from '75, and then, when punk began to really happen in '77, people started making those comparisons that really annoyed us because we didn't want them."

While Harris sided with hard rock bands, Di'Anno was the band's true punk fan. "We played [heavy metal] 'cause it sounded really fucking good," the band's erstwhile singer told *fanpop.com* in 2009. "We were faster than everybody else's—we were faster and more complicated. But you know, I like punk music and hardcore, yeah, and most of the heavy metal sound I'm not really a fan of."

Maiden's debut album contains some of the band's most cherished songs, including the seven-minute metal epic "Phantom of the Opera," early fan favorite, "Sanctuary," and the instrumental "Transylvania."

Another was "Charlotte the Harlot," about which Di'Anno spoke to *battlehelm.com*. "Her real name is High Hill Lil and

IRON MAIDEN

BY IAN CHRISTE

Nineteen eighty was the year that British heavy metal swarmed over orange-haired punks and bell-bottomed 1970s acid rockers with every broadsword and pole axe in the Tower of London. The hippies and posers were out, and Margaret Thatcher was the next target. Oversized headbanger concert and album-release posters appeared almost daily on London streets, covering the tattered royal parchments warning the public about Jack the Ripper, the Black Plague, and the Beatles. In a span of some months this iron-clad armada of records cleared the path for metal in the 1980s: Mötörhead's notorious *Ace of Spades*, Saxon's triumphant *Wheels of Steel*, Def Leppard's wet-behind-the-ears *On Through the Night*, Judas Priest's landmark *British Steel* . . . and Iron Maiden's horrifying introductory effort.

Alone among that esteemed class of 1980, Iron Maiden tapped into the English fog, the cobblestones, and the fear impulses as seen in the gory new tourist attraction London Dungeon, haunted by the shivery ghosts of centuries of monarchy and a few decades of Hammer horror films. In the real world, serial murderers, mad bombers, and genocidal despots had gleefully terrorized the populace in preceding years, and Maiden mastermind Steve Harris concocted his counterattack with a ravenous suite of songs about bloody floors, bloody whores, knife-wielding perverts, poisonous alien planets, vampires, and mind-destroying all-seeing eyes. KISS and Alice Cooper had donned spooky makeup and played relatively normal-sounding music called shock rock. Iron Maiden may have worn glammy striped pants early on, but their music—and their macabre mascot Eddie—were plenty scary for real.

Early Iron Maiden reeked of comic books and Edgar Allan Poe, but the music was devastating on a higher level. Constant, aggressive attack was the main musical mode, and thug Casanova singer Paul Di'Anno laid down the metal law with hoarse crooning authority. Steve Harris' bass was mixed front and center as if for instructional purposes, but he had little to fear from his droning contemporaries, as few other bands were basing eight-minute songs around bass lines

back then. The uncanny dual guitars of Dave Murray and Dennis Stratton really defined the chilling sound, though, trilling speedy triplets in unison, decorating every flourish with even more flourishes, and eking another spooky moment from every little change-up. Drummer Clive Burr was a steadfast metallian—his pounding performance on the band's theme song, "Iron Maiden," is as close to constant blast beats as heavy metal ventured at the time. And these were just rookies. Yet with "Phantom of the Opera," Maiden also penned a modern masterpiece, as astonishing a milestone as "Black Sabbath" ten years earlier.

The mystery and alchemical creativity of Iron Maiden is as thick and heavy as British meat pie. Dressed up in ruffles and stripes, Iron Maiden pounded the boards in pubs for years, and sing-alongs like "Running Free" called to the working boys and the wayward Oi! fans. Yet the band's early material turned to inner landscapes for breathers like "Remember Tomorrow" and "Strange World." Harris knew the audience could be pleased in a simple fashion, yet he set impossible standards that forced the next generation of metal bands to change the rules to compete. It's hard to imagine the otherworldly transformations that happened one-by-one to early headbangers in packed London rock clubs, tiny venues overloaded with fog machines and as many lights as the breaker box could handle. Yet by the last otherworldly tones of album closer "Iron Maiden," all gateways were certainly open for this band to go anywhere and everywhere. Even today, playing to more people each year than live in greater London, they still carry almost all of these songs with them everywhere.

"Sanctuary" (May 1980). The band asked Derek Riggs to draw British Prime Minister Margaret Thatcher's face on the murder victim as a play on her nickname, "The Iron Lady." The art was, of course, considered offensive and her eyes were covered with a black box to appease the offended.

"Running Free" (February 1980).

she's basically an old prostitute," he told interviewer Shan Siva. "Well, actually she was more of a slut. . . . I mean, if you turned up to her house with some booze or some speed you were more or less guaranteed a lay. She was a legend in Walthamstow, everyone knew her. She was about forty-five but a real rock out bitch. She'd take any guy from fifteen upwards! The song says that she lived on Acacia Avenue but it's actually Markhouse Road, just before you go into Leyton 'cos that's the area where I lived."

The band's first single off the debut LP was the excellent teenage-rebellion song "Running Free," which the band performed on legendary U.K. music program *Top of the Pops*. Maiden was so dedicated to their art that they chose not to lip-synch their performance, becoming the first band to play live on the show since the Who back in 1973.

The sleeve art for both "Running Free" and *Iron Maiden* featured the first appearance of one of rock's great icons, the band's famed mascot Eddie. Interviewed at *getreadytoroll. com* in 2007, former Maiden lighting engineer Dave "Lights" Beazley explained Eddie's background:

Eddie the Ed was a joke that was going around at the time, i.e., a couple had a child, but when the child was born it was only a head—no arms, legs, or anything else. The couple were devastated but the doctor said, "Don't give up hope. When the head's grown to its full size, which will be when the boy is about fourteen years old,

we'll fix him up with a body." So the couple put Eddie on the mantlepiece and looked after him for the next fourteen years. On his fourteenth birthday they said to him, "Eddie, we have a very special present for you," and Eddie replied, "Oh, no . . . not another fuckin' hat!" So yes, the idea for Eddie grew out of that joke! So on the backdrop that we used for the pub gigs, with the help of a friend from art college, I rigged up a mask that was made from a mould of my own face, which coughed up blood in time to those lyrics. The Eddie that was used as the band became more famous was designed from artwork by Derek Riggs, but the original idea started with that joke and that first mask. As to whether I see him as family, yes, in a way I suppose I do!

(continued on page 30)

Maiden or Priest?

BY NEIL DANIELS

THE STONES OR THE BEATLES? Slade or the Sweet? Metallica or Megadeth? Rivalry can often be a healthy thing. There's been something of an ongoing debate among metal fans as to which band is mightier: Iron Maiden or Judas Priest? This rivalry, while later lighthearted, didn't begin that way. It goes back to 1980 when Maiden supported Priest on the latter's *British Steel* U.K. tour.

It probably started when Paul Di'Anno told *Sounds* writer Garry Bushell that they would "blow the bollocks off Priest." Unbeknownst to Rob Halford and his cohorts, Priest's then-manager Jim Dawson invited Maiden to watch them rehearse at a venue in Willesden, North London. The Metal Gods were apparently not pleased. It can be assumed Priest thought Maiden was being arrogant, that they were cocky upstarts with little clue about the business. Judas Priest had been around in various incarnations since 1969, after all, and were the personification of a British heavy metal. They were the second proper heavy metal band after Black Sabbath. Iron Maiden had not yet released their first album. Priest's *British Steel*, meanwhile, had become an instant success story and, in fact, remains one of the greatest metal albums in history.

In 2008, Priest guitarist K. K. Downing told metal writer Joel McIver at *The Quietus*: "I'd never heard of Iron Maiden until we were just finishing the mixes on the record [*British Steel*], and someone told me that they were going to support us on the subsequent tour. I said, 'OK, fine' and then they started to get mouthy in the press, saying they were going to blow the bollocks off Judas Priest and all this sort of stuff. I said, 'I appreciate the attitude, like, but let's fuck 'em off and get somebody who appreciates us!' There was loads of bands who would have wanted that tour and appreciated it, and you just didn't need those sorts of vibes before you go out. Anyway, they did it and it was fine. I'm glad that they emerged and became a force to be reckoned with, and gained their own identity, musically, visually, and in every way possible. All credit to them—they've done a fantastic job to be ambassadors of British metal all around the world."

As told in Mick Wall's Iron Maiden bio, *Run to the Hills*, a booking agent by the name of John Jackson at Cowbell Agency had both bands on his books, yet Priest thought Jackson was biased toward Maiden and reportedly fired him. Jackson went off and formed Fair Warning. His first band? Iron Maiden.

At the time Priest were also somewhat annoyed that Maiden had been copying their style of black leather, silver studs, and various bits of biker attire. There was indeed a striking similarity between Paul Di'Anno and Rob Halford in terms of onstage clothes. Downing told *Soundcheck!* writer Neil Jeffries at the time of Priest's *Defenders of the Faith* album, "It's disappointing when you tour one year with Maiden in support and they come out and wear all your clothes—I have to look at some pictures twice to see if Dave Murray is really me!"

However, bygones were bygones, and Maiden supported Priest again in 1982 on their North American *Screaming for Vengeance* tour.

Maiden went on to become one of the biggest, most successful bands of all time, with album sales over 80 million (Priest's sales are impressive, too, though they linger around the 40 million mark). Certainly Maiden and Priest totally respect each other and both Bruce Dickinson and Rob Halford are two of metal's most iconic and revered frontmen with unique voices. Rob Halford's solo band Halford supported Iron Maiden during the American leg of their 2000 *Brave New World* tour after Dickinson had duetted with Halford on a song called "The One You Love to Hate" from Halford's 2000 acclaimed opus, *Resurrection*. Halford also played at the 2001 Rock in Rio in Brazil, which was headlined by Iron Maiden. One of Priest's downfalls is that they are not as hardworking or energetic as Iron Maiden, both on stage and with their recording output. Indeed in 2011, Priest played their farewell tour (dubbed "Epitaph") but vowed they would not split up; they just wanted an end to the lengthy world tours. 🇬🇧

NWOBHM rumble! Maiden in 1980 and Priest in 1979.
Virginia Turbett/Redferns/Getty Images (top) *and Fin Costello/Redferns/Getty Images* (bottom)

SETLIST SELECTIONS

IRON MAIDEN TOUR

THE IDES OF MARCH
SANCTUARY
PROWLER
WRATHCHILD
REMEMBER TOMORROW
CHARLOTTE THE HARLOT
KILLERS
ANOTHER LIFE
TRANSYLVANIA
STRANGE WORLD
INNOCENT EXILE
PHANTOM OF THE OPERA
IRON MAIDEN
RUNNING FREE
DRIFTER
I'VE GOT THE FIRE (MONTROSE COVER)

OPPOSITE: October 1980, shortly after Dave Murray's old mate, Adrian Smith (center), replaced Dennis Stratton on guitar.
Gered Mankowitz/Redferns/Getty Images

Iron Maiden made their first Reading festival appearance on August 23, 1980. © *Alan Perry*

(continued from page 25)

Even in those early days, Maiden used a lot of backdrops and masks onstage. "I painted the first Eddie backdrop—actually the first three or four—and then I managed to get out of doing them because they were horrible to have to do," Riggs told Scott Hefflon of *lollipop.com*. "You end up getting shipped across London to some lonely, cold, wet warehouse with sheets of canvas and a bucket of paint. [Eddie masks] were specially made. They had a few of them. Some of the masks were made by this bloke who made props for television, and a large puppet was made by a guy who did giants for theater productions."

Graced by Riggs' Eddie artwork and stacked with fan favorites the band had established by touring the British Isles and gigging closer to home in London, *Iron Maiden* was a hit, reaching No. 4 on the U.K. album charts and receiving strong reviews in the rock press. "The record company knew the album was gonna do well because of advance orders," Dennis Stratton told *getreadytoroll.com*'s Jason Ritchie in 2003, "but it was nice to get great support everywhere we went."

Steve Harris was not looking back. There was a lot going on in the band, and a successful future was in the making.

On March 7, 1980, Maiden set out in support of self-proclaimed Metal Gods Judas Priest on the U.K. leg of their *British Steel* tour. The East End lads then launched their own *Iron Maiden* tour on April 1 at London's Rainbow Theatre. The tour saw the band all over the United Kingdom (the live cuts on the flip of "Sanctuary" were recorded at the Marquee on April 3) and included a gig at the Ruskin Arms on April 8 in aid of Dr. Barnardo's, the famous children's charity. The band displayed an incredible amount of charisma and energy that night, and footage was later included in the exhaustive 2004 Maiden documentary *The Early Days*. Notably, Di'Anno's Maiden debut had occurred at the Ruskin back in December 1978. Despite being adored by rock fans the world over, the iconic East End pub closed in 2009.

The tour also brought them to Belgium for their first gig outside of the British Isles, appearing at the Wheel Pop Festival on April 5.

BRUNEL UNIVERSITY STUDENTS UNION
presents in the Sports Barn,
Kingston Lane, Uxbridge

Friday 21st November
IRON MAIDEN

Adm £2.50   8pm

Wednesday 26th November in the Kingdom Room
The Not So Famous Tour

ROCK CITY
FORMERLY HEART OF THE MIDLANDS
TALBOT ST, NOTTINGHAM
Tel 0602 411212
Open 8pm to 2am

Monday 1st December	Adv Tickets £2.50
IRON MAIDEN + Support	
Wednesday 3rd December	Adv Tickets £3.00
HUMAN LEAGUE + Support	
Saturday 6th December	Pay on door £2.00
CLIMAX BLUES BAND + Support	
Thursday 11th December	Adv Tickets £3.00
THE UNDERTONES + Support	
Friday 12th December	Adv Tickets £2.50
SHAKIN' STEVENS + Support	
Saturday 13th December	Adv Tickets £2.00
ECHO & THE BUNNYMEN + Support	
Thursday 18th December	Adv Tickets £2.50
STEVE HARLEY + Support	
Friday 19th December	Adv Tickets £3.00
THE KINKS + Support	
Saturday 20th December	Adv Tickets £3.00
XTC + Support	

Tickets available by post from Rock City — cheques payable to Rock City or from Selectadisc, Virgin Victoria Box Office. Must be over 18 years of age. No dress restrictions. No Membership required

As soon as Maiden's supporting slot on KISS's *Unmasked* European tour came to an end in October 1980, the band carried on with their own headlining tour from November through the end of the year.

RAINBOW THEATRE
OUTLAW & PHIL McINTIRE PRESENT

AN OVER THE TOP HEAVY METAL XMAS
EXTRAVAGANZA
WITH

IRON MAIDEN
+ DJ NEAL KAY

SUNDAY 21st DECEMBER
8pm

Tickets £2.50 and £2.00 from BOX OFFICE AND USUAL AGENTS

Rainbow THEATRE OUTLAW AND PHIL McINTYRE PRESENT
AN OVER THE TOP HEAVY METAL
CHRISTMAS EXTRAVAGANZA

IRON MAIDEN
D.J. NEAL KAY
SUNDAY 21st DECEMBER 8pm

TICKETS £2.50, £2.00
FROM BOX OFFICE, LONDON THEATRE BOOKINGS, PREMIER BOX OFFICE, VIRGIN TICKET UNIT & USUAL AGENTS

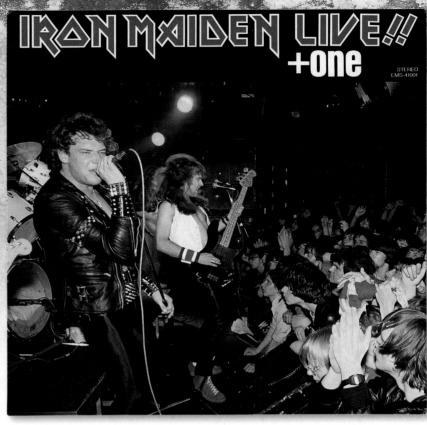

"Women in Uniform" (October 1980).

The Japanese EP *Live!! + one* (November 1980) featured four cuts recorded at the Marquee in London on July 4, 1980.

The *Iron Maiden* tour was split into two halves with the first part winding up in August. After finishing the first half of their own headlining tour, Maiden went out in support of KISS for the New York shock rockers' *Unmasked* European tour, giving Maiden massive exposure outside of the United Kingdom. However, as soon as the KISS tour came to an end in October 1980, Dennis Stratton was out of the band over alleged musical differences. He was replaced by Adrian Smith, Dave Murray's old mate.

Moving into the Maiden camp was a life-changing experience for Smith. "At first, it was all quite new to me because I'd never toured properly," he explained to Chris Vinnicombe of *musicradar.com* in 2009. "I'd played clubs and pubs in England, playing from a couple of hundred people to a man and his dog! In the band I was in before Maiden [Urchin], I was going to gigs on the bus with my guitar and a plastic bag with my wah pedal in it. To go from that to earning a wage every week, having a tour bus, and playing in front of two to three thousand people, it was a huge novelty."

With the KISS obligation complete, Maiden carried on with the second half of their own headlining tour from November through the end of the year. The full tour consisted of more than seventy shows, and the band was quickly building a reputation as a powerful live act.

It had taken the band quite some time to cement a fairly steady line-up. By now, Harris was the only member of the band to have played through every incarnation since their inception. "There's been so many different changes," he reflected in 1982 (*Night Rock News*). "We had so many changes before we actually went professional, 'cause, you know, they didn't want to put money into the band, or they didn't want to spend the time—that sort of thing. . . . Changes are a pain in the ass, but there's no way you can carry on under certain circumstances. When you do make changes, you have to make sure they're for the better. I think the changes we've made have been for the better—but then I'm biased!"

But those changes were far from over. Paul Di'Anno was becoming increasingly erratic and his seemingly out-of-control and wild persona were major causes for concern for Harris. Could Maiden continue with Di'Anno seemingly on a road to self-destruction?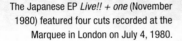

1979 *By Ryan LaMar*

02.15	Canning Town, GBR
02.17	East Ham, GBR
03.03	East Ham, GBR
03.17	East Ham, GBR
04.07	East Ham, GBR
04.09	London, GBR
04.23	Camden, GBR
05.05	East Ham, GBR
05.08	Camden Town, GBR
05.11	East Ham, GBR
05.18	Brighton, GBR
05.19	Kingsbury, GBR
05.25	Cambridge, GBR
05.26	Guildford, GBR
06.01	East Ham, GBR
06.08	East Ham, GBR
06.09	Kingsbury, GBR
06.15	East Ham, GBR
06.18	Canning Town, GBR
06.22	Axminster, GBR
06.29	East Ham, GBR
07.??	Hammersmith, GBR
07.02	Camden Town, GBR
07.03	London, GBR
07.14	Guildford, GBR
07.16	Camden Town, GBR
07.19	Hammersmith, GBR
07.20	Norwich, GBR
07.22	East Ham, GBR
07.28	East Ham, GBR
08.06	Camden Town, GBR
08.10	London, GBR
08.17	Birkenhead, GBR
08.18	Tottenham, GBR
08.19	Newbridge, GBR
08.20	Camden Town, GBR
08.24	London, GBR
08.25	East Ham, GBR
08.30	Swansea, GBR
08.31	Aberavon, GBR
09.01	Tonypandy, GBR

09.03	Camden Town, GBR
09.07–08	East Ham, GBR
09.10	Camden Town, GBR
09.14	London, GBR
09.15	East Ham, GBR
09.17	Camden Town, GBR
09.27	Basildon, GBR
09.28	Wolverhampton, GBR
09.30	Camden Town, GBR
10.03–04	Hammersmith, GBR (rescheduled from 09.06)
10.05	East Ham, GBR
10.06	Nottingham, GBR
10.07	Trent Side, GBR
10.08	London, GBR
10.10	East Ham, GBR
10.12	Gwent, GBR
10.13	Manchester, GBR
10.18	Manchester, GBR
10.19	London, GBR
10.26	Aberavon, GBR
10.27	Tonypandy, GBR
11.01	Aberdeen, GBR
11.02	Blackpool, GBR
11.05	Camden Town, GBR
11.09	Aberavon, GBR
11.10	Stroud, GBR
11.12	Birmingham, GBR
11.14	London, GBR
11.16	Burton on Trent, GBR
11.17	Liverpool, GBR
11.19	London, GBR
11.23	Birkenhead, GBR
11.24	Warrington, GBR
11.30	Middlesbrough, GBR
12.01	Retford, GBR
12.03	Birmingham, GBR
12.04	Swindon, GBR
12.07	London, GBR
12.08	Bristol, GBR
12.09	London, GBR
12.10	Exeter, GBR
12.15	Birmingham, GBR

12.19	Camden Town, GBR
12.21	Liverpool, GBR
12.22	Oldham, GBR

1980

02.01	Aberdeen, GBR
02.02	Glasgow, GBR
02.03	St. Andrews, GBR
02.04	Edinburgh, GBR
02.05	Grimsby, GBR
02.06	Bristol, GBR
02.07	Wakefield, GBR
02.08	Huddersfield, GBR
02.09	Manchester, GBR
02.10	London, GBR
02.11	Mansfield, GBR
03.07	Cardiff, GBR
03.08	Leeds, GBR
03.09	Bristol, GBR
03.10	Manchester, GBR
03.11–12	Sheffield, GBR
03.13	Leicester, GBR
03.14–15	Hammersmith, GBR
03.16	Southampton, GBR
03.18	Aberdeen, GBR
03.19	Edinburgh, GBR
03.20–21	Newcastle, GBR
03.22	Glasgow, GBR
03.23	Deeside, GBR
03.25	Stoke on Trent, GBR
03.26–27	Birmingham, GBR
04.01–03	London, GBR
04.05	Kotrjik, BEL
04.06	London, GBR
04.07	Plymouth, GBR
04.08	East Ham, GBR
04.10	Grimsby, GBR

04.14	East Ham, GBR	06.29	Brighton, GBR	09.24	Lyon, FRA
05.15	Lincoln, GBR	06.30	Poole, GBR	09.27	Paris, FRA
05.16	Newcastle, GBR	07.01	Portsmouth, GBR (possibly	09.28	Basel, SUI
05.17	Dunfermline, GBR		rescheduled from 06.03)	09.30	Cologne, GER
05.18	Ayr, GBR	07.03–05	London, GBR	10.01	Bremen, GER
05.19	Aberdeen, GBR	07.08–09,11–12	London, GBR	10.02	Hannover, GER
05.20	Carlisle, GBR		(these shows may not	10.04	Hamburg, GER
05.21	Bradford, GBR		have happened)	10.05	Leiden, NED
05.22	Withensea, GBR	07.19	Oulu, FIN	10.09	Stockholm, SWE
05.23	Cambridge, GBR	08.10	London, GBR	10.10	Gothenburg, SWE
05.25	Dunstable, GBR	08.21	Cromer, GBR	10.11	Copenhagen, DEN
05.27	Blackburn, GBR	08.23	Reading, GBR	10.13	Drammen, NOR
05.28	Wolverhampton, GBR	08.29	Rome, ITA	10.??	Grimsby, GBR
05.29	Hanley, GBR	08.31	Genova, ITA	11.08	Munich, GER
05.30	Swindon, GBR	09.02	Milan, ITA	11.21	Uxbridge, GBR
05.31	St. Austell, GBR	09.04–05	London, GBR	11.22	Leeds, GBR
06.01	Bristol, GBR	09.11	Nurnberg, GER	11.23	Redcar, GBR
06.02	Malvern, GBR	09.12	Dusseldorf, GER	11.24	Hull, GBR
06.04	Cardiff, GBR	09.13	Frankfurt, GER	11.25	Newcastle, GBR
06.06	Cromer, GBR	09.15	Dortmund, GER	11.26	Birmingham, GBR
06.07	Birmingham, GBR	09.17	Stuttgart, GER	11.27	Derby, GBR
06.08	Sheffield, GBR	09.18	Munich, GER	11.28	Hanley, GBR
06.09	Liverpool, GBR	09.20	Kassel, GER	11.30	Manchester, GBR
06.11	Sunderland, GBR	09.21	Brussels, BEL	12.01	Nottingham, GBR
06.12	Dundee, GBR	09.23	Avignon, FRA	12.19–21	London, GBR
06.13	Glasgow, GBR				
06.14	Middlesborough, GBR				
06.16	Wakefield, GBR				
06.17	Leicester, GBR				
06.18	Chatham, GBR				
06.19	Guildford, GBR				
06.20–21	London, GBR				
06.22	Swansea, GBR				
06.24	Norwich, GBR				
06.25	Derby, GBR				
06.26	Manchester, GBR				
06.27	Bath, GBR				
06.28	Oxford, GBR				

Notes: Six cancelled 1979 dates can be gleaned from Harris' scrapbook in The History of Iron Maiden, Part 1: The Early Years. Per Skoog, a cancelled July 1979 date in London (day unspecified) was the result of an argument between manager Ron Smallwood and the pub owner.

The unidentifiable July 1979 date at Hammersmith is mentioned in Garry Bushell's Running Free.

Seems likely the October 18, 1979, date never occurred but, rather, over the years some have misread the October 13 date as October 18 and perpetuated the latter.

According to the February 2, 1980, issue of Sounds, a string of February and March dates that year were axed so the band could record their debut LP. According to various sources, these numbered seventeen to nineteen from February 13 to March 2.

I have been able to locate absolutely no documenting evidence of the July 8–9 and 11–12, 1980, shows having taken place despite the band receiving excellent media coverage in London by this time.

The September 1980 London dates have been variously reported. Some sources list Maiden as playing on September 4–5 at the Marquee in London, and at least one other as possibly on September 5–6.

Per Gooch's and Suhs' KISS Alive Forever, seven dates of the 1980 KISS European tour were cancelled. One (Drammen, Norway) was rescheduled.

Bushell notes an October 1980 Grimsby date; Wall writes that the band fired Dennis Stratton after the previous Drammen date.

According to the December 6, 1980, Sounds, a November 29 show in Sheffield, England, was cancelled due to Paul Di'Anno's throat infection.

3

666

THE NUMBER OF IRON MAIDEN, 1981–1982

> "[Heavy metal] is a place to dream of adventures: running free through the hills, forever getting girls on their knees, scrapping with Satan, battling with vermin and swimming through space. . . . Monsters, tanks, reptiles, rapists, maniacs, murderers, thugs roam the territory, but it's never *for real*, they're all harmless—HM is an extremely soft land, the monsters and the maniacs are really just teddy bears and dolls."
>
> —Paul Morley, *NME*, May 8, 1982

Songs that Steve Harris had left over from the first album provided the backbone for Maiden's second full studio album, *Killers*. Harris had also been busy writing songs on tour so that by the time recording for *Killers* commenced in November 1980, he only needed to write two more tracks, "Murders in the Rue Morgue" (an homage to Edgar Allan Poe) and "Prodigal Son." Only the title track features a co-credit (with Paul Di'Anno).

Killers was the first Iron Maiden album produced by Martin Birch, who would become an important member of Maiden's extended family. The band hit Battery Studios in London in late 1980 and came out three months later with a brand-new album.

The making of *Killers* is not without its interesting anecdotes, one of them involving former Maiden drummer Barry "Thunderstick" Purkis. *Killers* and Samson's *Head On* (the first Samson LP to feature a certain Bruce Dickinson on vocals) were recorded at separate studios within close proximity of each other. Maiden drummer Clive Burr nipped 'round to Paul Samson's house to have a listen to *Head On* and to play *Killers* for him. The similarities between "Thunderbust," one of the new Samson tracks, and "The Ides of March," an instrumental track on *Killers*, were apparent; both Paul Samson and Clive Burr could not believe it. Could Purkis, Samson's current drummer, be responsible? Indeed, "Ides" had been around in rough format for some time—parts of the song had been used

KILLERS

BY MARTIN POPOFF

NOT QUITE ZEPPELIN IN TRAJECTORY, but certainly as buzz-bandy as Sabbath exactly a decade prior, Iron Maiden was already a potent known quotient by the time *Killers* was released, having made mince-metal of Judas Priest (touring *British Steel*) and KISS (limping through Europe embarrassed by *Unmasked*) as a support act. Hard to call anything by Maiden "forgotten," but the faithful on down overlook *Killers* to varying degrees, even if the album solidified, then expanded the band's rabid punter fan base as a one-for-the-road tie-over until the dramatics of the sacking of punk Paul Di'anno.

Killers deserves more kudos. Sure, the self-titled debut has the heaviness of history, but the ideas here are flashier, brighter, the playing showy and bolder, the impressive package quietly making the first record look a little dodgy, even if blind affection for it bulldozes intellectualized comparison. There's history here as well, with Martin Birch headmastering the role of producer, bringing to the table an emphasis on the warm midrange he knob-jobbed on Blue Öyster Cult's *Cultösaurus Erectus*, less so the bright midrange that made Black Sabbath's *Heaven and Hell* so embraceable. Birch would famously retire from working with other bands and become Maiden's longtime producer, attaining perfection on 1983's *Piece of Mind*. Yet with his first crack at Maiden, the result is not so much remarkable as youthful, energetic, rushed but in a good way, no cringe-able errors to the thing . . . much like we all thought of lovable, thuggable Paul Di'Anno up there at the mic trying to keep up with the growing epic-ness of his soon to be ex-mates. That's the album's tense back story: Di'Anno considered the album too fancy, yet still, he's a tight fit, given the adolescent rollick of songs like "Drifter" and "Murders in the Rue Morgue," even if the latter went uptown through arcane melodic shifts, also offering noodly breaks and switch-ups in speed. Di'Anno is right at the front edge of his reluctant metal persona, while the lads are somewhere in the middle of their potential, operating on fumes and sleep deprivation, but quite sure they can go further, which just adds to the giddiness.

The enduring classics? Not many, but foremost there's "Wrathchild" with its novel bass intro and mournful melodies of the maligned, punched up by Clive Burr's military precision. More of an outlaw classic is the title track, both proto–speed metal and a signature Maiden gallop, again stopping and starting with extreme punctuation built for air drumming between sloshy pints at the Soundhouse. Elsewhere, "Another Life" is the perfect bridge between the dark vibes of the debut and the comical rhythms of something like "Run to the Hills," while "Genghis Khan" is a pomp instrumental, the very idea of an instrumental tacitly proposing that Maiden was a cut above, the prog metal link from Rush to Queensrÿche and Fates Warning. The hidden gem would have to be "Innocent Exile," which is a metaphor for the album as a whole, representing this idea that Maiden was better than Tygers of Pan Tang, Quartz, Fist, Raven, Angel Witch, or even Saxon (let's not forget Dumpy's Rusty Nuts!) because of the quantity of quality riffs. There's another doomful ballad in the form of "Prodigal Son," and even within that you can hear the band locating groove, layering guitars, trying out tones.

This is not the rickety band of one record back. Even if *Killers* is just as frantic (perhaps reaching its frenzied apex in "Purgatory"), there's an impressive getting-across and getting-over roiling that Maiden is going places, that they've grown at a level somewhere between creeps and leaps, closer to leaps than bounds, score one for the underdogs, Up the Irons!, take that, Priest and yer wilted *Point of Entry*. 🇬🇧

who were older than me," he told Shan Siva of *battlehelm. com*. "One minute I was a kid off the street and the next I was expected to handle things like it was sliced bread. Needless to say, I started drinking a lot and I must've done half of Peru up my nose. I screwed up . . . I wasn't happy, both with the album and myself and I really didn't wanna be there."

Released in the U.K. in February 1981 and in the United States in June of that year, *Killers* represented a big step forward from the first album. The band reworked the now classic Maiden track "Wrathchild," which had been featured on the *Metal for Muthas* compilation. Other iconic tracks that *Killers* spawned included the title track and "Purgatory," the latter a remake of an earlier (and slower) Maiden song called "Floating" that they played live in the very early days.

In support of the album, Maiden launched the *Killers* world tour in February 1981, and an extensive road trek that brought the band to the United States for the first time (a territory they were eager to crack) and yielded the live EP *Maiden Japan* later that year. Japan had always been a stronghold for British heavy metal bands, and Maiden was

"Twilight Zone" (March 1981).

as an intro tape at gigs prior to the recording of the album. Thunderstick was summoned to the London headquarters of Maiden's record label, EMI. In 2009, Thunderstick recalled the scene for rock scribe Joe Geesin:

> There was Rod Smallwood, Steve Harris, and Iron Maiden's lawyer/solicitor and an EMI representative sitting opposite me. I was on my own. Samson's then-management had seen fit that I didn't require representation.
>
> It was decided upon that Steve Harris would share fifty/fifty publishing rights on the Samson version and I would get sweet F.A. [f*** all] on the Iron Maiden version. Due to the fact that there are no lyrics on either track there is no true fifty/fifty split required. However on the Samson version there is the singing mask with me going "aaaahaaaa" in the background. Does that constitute vocals? Probably not! Does it leave a sour taste in my mouth? You betcha!"

Thunderstick wasn't the only one with a sour taste. *Killers* did not sit right with Maiden vocalist Paul Di'Anno, either. "[*Killers*] wasn't quite there for me . . . and to be frank, at that age I wasn't also handling things as well as the other guys

"Purgatory" (June 1981).

Killers world tour, Largo, Maryland, July 1, 1981.
Ebet Roberts/Redferns/Getty Images

building up a fan base there. As Steve Harris told *Night Rock News'* Gueniviere the following year, "Everywhere we traveled, there were loads and loads of screaming girls. I mean, it was unbelievable, just screamin'! Guys, as well, would run right down the road and start bangin' on the windows. . . . It was absolutely ridiculous!"

Back in the United Kingdom, Maiden's strongest support was found far from their East End haunts in the north of England and parts of Scotland. "In the early years, it was always Manchester, Glasgow, and Liverpool—those really hardworking areas where football and music meant a lot to people, because they didn't have a lot of prospects then," Adrian Smith told Chris Vinnicombe (*musicradar.com*).

How had Smith settled into the band?

"Well, on the *Killers* album, Adrian was very new and it really wasn't until he'd been with the band about a year and a half that he really felt he was a full member," Harris told Kevin Thompson of *Artist Magazine* in 1983. "He always had been, but he never really seemed to accept that it was happening. [Perhaps] because he went from a local band in the East End to Iron Maiden, which, even at the time, was quite a

SETLIST SELECTIONS

KILLERS TOUR

THE IDES OF MARCH
WRATHCHILD
PURGATORY
SANCTUARY
REMEMBER TOMORROW
ANOTHER LIFE
GENGHIS KHAN
KILLERS
INNOCENT EXILE
MURDERS IN THE RUE MORGUE
TWILIGHT ZONE
PHANTOM OF THE OPERA
IRON MAIDEN
RUNNING FREE
TRANSYLVANIA
DRIFTER
PROWLER
STRANGE WORLD
I'VE GOT THE FIRE (MONTROSE COVER)
22 ACACIA AVENUE
CHILDREN OF THE DAMNED
THE PRISONER
RUN TO THE HILLS

Killers world tour, Asbury Park, New Jersey, July 2, 1981. © *Bob Leafe*

The *Killers* world tour was an extensive road trek that brought Iron Maiden to the United States for the first time. *Frank White Photo Agency*

big act. It took him quite a while to settle in, and it also took both he and Dave a long time to get the right guitar sounds."

But a bigger problem than guitar interplay loomed: Di'Anno was battling his own personal demons on tour, and his backstage antics and alleged lack of passion and drive onstage did not go unnoticed. Harris and manager Rod Smallwood decided to let Di'Anno go in the fall of 1981.

Di'Anno's last live gig with Maiden was on September 10, 1981, in Copenhagen. "Actually, I have good memories of Maiden," Di'Anno reminisced to Shan Siva, "meeting all the people on tours, playing live on *Top of the Pops*, and the fact that we were part of something happening the way we mixed hardcore punk with heavy metal."

Still, Di'Anno continues to refute the long-perceived notion that he was ousted because of drugs. "Where the fuck do you people get this from?" he asked at a press conference in Argentina in 2009 while touring with his RockFellas project. "I left Iron Maiden because they were going too heavy metal, and Iron Maiden is a money-making machine, and I don't give a fuck about it. It was not about drugs—it was nothing like that."

With Di'Anno sacked, Maiden needed somebody committed to the cause and the tough task of touring. A new singer was sought immediately to help fulfill remaining dates on the *Killers* tour. "We had about a thousand tapes sent in, and we had about twelve people come down for the audition," Dave Murray told Gary James in 1999.

One of those twelve hopefuls was a young Bruce Dickinson, who sang "Remember Tomorrow" at his audition, impressing both the band and Smallwood. The former Samson singer made his first appearance as Maiden's new frontman in Bologna on October 26. A new chapter had opened in the Iron Maiden saga.

Eddie at Maiden's opening slot for Judas Priest at the Palladium in New York City, July 23, 1981. © *Larry Marano/Retna Ltd.*

"[Dickinson] suits their style right down to the ground," Di'Anno later told Siva. "Also, I'm too hardcore for Maiden. My attitude is totally different and I'd always rub them up the wrong way—I'm an antagonistic muthafucker 'cos I want a reaction from people. . . . And there's no way you could get me into spandex again man, not for a million fuckin' dollars—it's so *Spinal Tap*."

Bruce Dickinson was born Paul Bruce Dickinson on August 7, 1958, in Worksop, Nottinghamshire. Initially raised by his grandparents, Dickinson moved with his parents to Sheffield, a tough, industrialized working-class city in the northeast of England. After difficulties at his new school, his parents enrolled him at a private school called Sharrow Vale Junior. Still, he felt like an outsider, and many feelings of isolation experienced in Sheffield would surface later in his lyrics, particularly in his solo work.

Dickinson's first band was a local outfit called Styx (which bared no resemblance to the American AOR band of which he was probably not even aware).

"My first excuse for a band was while I was at school," Dickinson reflected in 1983, speaking to Kevin Thompson. "I had a pair of bongos. We did 'Smoke on the Water,' and I used to beat the crap out of those bongos because we didn't have a drum kit. The band realized that the singer couldn't sing, so I got the job—mainly to stop the noise of the bongos! We played in each other's bedrooms, annoying our mums and dads."

Dickinson grew up listening to American rock 'n' roll legends like Chuck Berry and Elvis Presley but he also liked British bands, namely the Beatles and Gerry & the Pacemakers. As he got older, heavy rock bands like Deep Purple and Led Zeppelin attracted his attention.

Sixties Britain was filled with heavy rock bands—male, white, and predominantly working-class—that were inspired by traditional pre- and postwar American blues artists like Buddy Guy, John Lee Hooker, and B. B. King. Bands like the

BOTH: Killers world tour, Palladium, New York City, July 24, 1981.
© *Dean Messina/Frank White Photo Agency* (top)
and © *Frank White* (right)

URIAH HEEP

with Guests SAMSON

LYCEUM
STRAND, W.C.2

WEDNESDAY 3rd DECEMBER 7·30pm

TICKETS £3·00 (INC.VAT) ADVANCE LYCEUM BOX OFFICE, TEL: 836 3715,
LONDON THEATRE BOOKINGS, SHAFTESBURY AVE., TEL: 439 3371; PREMIER BOX OFFICE, TEL: 240 2245,
OR ROCK ON RECORDS, 3 KENTISH TOWN RD., NW1, TEL: 485 5088

STRAIGHT MUSIC PRESENTS

WILD HORSES
GIRLSCHOOL
SAMSON

+ NEIL KAY BANDWAGON ~ HEAVY METAL SOUNDHOUSE

ON THE ROAD

LYCEUM
STRAND, W.C.2

SUNDAY 22nd JULY at 7·30

TICKETS £2·50 (INC.VAT) ADVANCE LYCEUM BOX OFFICE, TEL: 836 3715,
LONDON THEATRE BOOKINGS, SHAFTESBURY AVE., TEL: 439 3371; PREMIER BOX OFFICE, TEL: 240 2245,
OR ROCK ON RECORDS, 3 KENTISH TOWN RD., NW1, TEL: 485 5088

Rainbow THEATRE

MCP presents

JOURNEY

+ Special Guests

Samson

Monday 22nd Sept 8.00pm
Tickets £3.50 £3.00 £2.50

Available from B/O Tel. 263 3148/9, L.T.B., Premier and Virgin Ticket Unit.

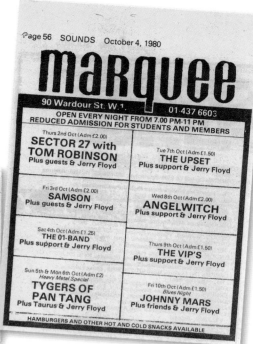

marquee
90 Wardour St. W.1   01-437 6603

OPEN EVERY NIGHT FROM 7.00 PM-11 PM
REDUCED ADMISSION FOR STUDENTS AND MEMBERS

Thurs 2nd Oct (Adm £2.00) **SECTOR 27 with** **TOM ROBINSON** Plus guests & Jerry Floyd	**Tue 7th Oct (Adm £1.50)** **THE UPSET** Plus support & Jerry Floyd
Fri 3rd Oct (Adm £2.00) **SAMSON** Plus guests & Jerry Floyd	**Wed 8th Oct (Adm £2.00)** **ANGELWITCH** Plus support & Jerry Floyd
Sat 4th Oct (Adm £1.25) **THE 01-BAND** Plus support & Jerry Floyd	**Thurs 9th Oct (Adm £1.50)** **THE VIP'S** Plus support & Jerry Floyd
Sun 5th & Mon 6th Oct (Adm £2) *Heavy Metal Special* **TYGERS OF** **PAN TANG** Plus Taurus & Jerry Floyd	**Fri 10th Oct (Adm £1.50)** *Blues Night* **JOHNNY MARS** Plus friends & Jerry Floyd

HAMBURGERS AND OTHER HOT AND COLD SNACKS AVAILABLE

Who, the Yardbirds, and the Kinks, and later Cream and Deep Purple, formed part of the so-called British Invasion that swept through the United States. Dickinson soaked up these new, heavier blues-tinged rock sounds.

Leaving the Territorial Army after six months of service, Dickinson moved to London to study history at Queen Mary College. There he met likeminded musicians and found himself first in a band called Speed in 1977, and later, in 1979, in a band called Shots. However, it was with the hard rock outfit Samson that he made a real impression. By the time Dickinson left Samson in '81, due to the commonly cited musical differences and internal friction, he had witnessed the strict work ethic and taut organization that made the Maiden wheel spin.

"On the first two albums we had a lot of material lying around from before we got signed," Steve Harris told Kevin Purcell of *aquarian.com* years later. "On the third album [*The Number of the Beast*], there was absolutely nothing, and we had a specific period of time to write and a load of pressure to write. It worked great, so that's what we've done ever since. If you were to allow yourself a year to write, you would get distracted and do a lot of other stuff in between. When you're stuck into it, you get to it."

The band began recording *The Number of the Beast* in late 1981 and wrapped it up in January 1982, again with producer Martin Birch at the helm. Asked what it was like working with Birch, in 1982 Adrian Smith told respected rock writer Steven Rosen, "Great. He doesn't try to make it a Martin Birch album. The very first thing he said to us was, 'This is your album. I'm just going to try and bring out what's there.' He's not too pushy or he doesn't try changing the songs. He just gets a good sound and then we just get on with it. If we start slacking, he kicks us then!"

The album featured songwriting credits from Adrian Smith and Clive Burr but not from Dave Murray; and because of contractual obligations with Samson, Dickinson was not able to receive songwriting credits.

The Number of the Beast was released in February 1982 in the United Kingdom, where it hit No. 1 on the album chart and gave the band major exposure around the globe. The album was released in the United States in June of that year. It has since become one of the most talked about albums in heavy metal history and cemented the band's status as one

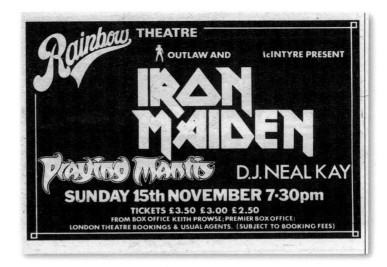

The band wound down 1981 with a new singer and two London shows—one in December and this Rainbow gig in mid-November.

of metal's greatest creations. Indeed, *The Number of the Beast* has sold more than 14 million copies worldwide and continues to shift a healthy number of copies yearly, thanks in part to its frequent inclusion on "greatest albums" lists.

The album's success has also no doubt been abetted by the controversy it incited among some American Christian fundamentalists, who attacked misperceived connections with the occult. Such protests completely missed the point that it was all very tongue-in-cheek. After all, writing about romance and love was not something that interested Iron Maiden.

"I don't think we've ever written anything that is romantic," Harris told *Night Rock News* at the time. "Everyone writes about how they want to love their 'baby' and all that! People write about how hard it is on the road, which it is hard, and how lonely they get, which it is true, what they're saying. . . . But I find that a bit boring. I mean, frankly, it's a bit sort of . . . wimpy, I think. That's not to say I don't sort of have any romance in me at all. It's not that. But I just don't think something like that is what I particularly want to write about."

The same conservatives who objected to Iron Maiden also attacked Ozzy Osbourne and, later, Judas Priest. Many years later, Dave Murray reflected on the controversy with interviewer Joe Matera (2007): "We're definitely not devil worshippers. I think it all started because of *The Number of the Beast* album. When it came out, a lot of the people who didn't like that sort of thing just started gravitating towards that album in particular. And though it became a big issue at the time, it wasn't as big as people made out it to be. But we basically ignored it and left it alone."

By the time Bruce Dickinson left Samson due to the commonly cited "musical differences," he had witnessed the strict work ethic and taut organization that made the Maiden wheel spin. From left: Dickinson, Chris Aylmer, Barry "Thunderstick" Purkis, and Paul Samson. *Fin Costello/Redferns/Getty Images*

THE NUMBER OF THE BEAST

BY DANIEL BUKSZPAN

Replacing a lead singer is a dicey proposition. The voice is the most recognizable sound in any band, and changing it presents the very real risk of alienating fans. Iron Maiden's original singer, Paul Di'Anno, may have had his limitations. Nonetheless, he was the original voice of the group and deserves credit for his role in making *Iron Maiden* and *Killers* the perfect, filler-free albums that they are. Still, the group wanted to graduate from clubs to arenas, and right or wrong, they didn't think Di'Anno was the guy to do it. Luckily for them, former Samson singer Bruce Dickinson was. His phrasing was over the top, his stage persona was flamboyant, and, most importantly, his high-powered voice gave the music wings.

Dickinson's debut was *The Number of the Beast*, released in March 1982. It would go on to become the central pillar of their catalog, and three of its songs—the title track, "Run to the Hills," and "Hallowed Be Thy Name"—are its load-bearing walls. It drags in a couple of spots, in part because any song that follows "Run to the Hills" will suffer by comparison. However, this is nitpicking. The album simply gets too much right to dwell on its flaws.

The Number of the Beast kicks off with "Invaders," a straightforward rocker that has a lot in common with the style presented in the first two albums. However, the vocal performance puts fans on notice that the game has been raised. The first verse ends, Dickinson emits some long, anxiety-provoking high notes, and soon he's relishing words like "fighting" and "marauding" like a scenery-chewing actor playing Iago. New heights of melodrama are wrung out of "Children of the Damned," while "The Prisoner" ventures into anthemic territory that just wouldn't have worked on *Killers*.

After "22 Acacia Avenue," the proggiest song ever written about the healing effects of whorehouses, a spoken-word excerpt from the Book of Revelation that metal fans have committed to memory for decades kicks off the album's title track, which also happens to open the second side. The song's tense, odd-metered opening riff is followed by the most famous scream on an Iron Maiden record. The song also features a brilliant wah-wah guitar solo. However, the real star of the song is band founder Steve Harris, who earns his place in the front line by making the bass a lead instrument without sacrificing one ounce of bottom.

After "The Number of the Beast" slams shut, there's a brief pause before "Run to the Hills," the most famous song on the album. It wholly deserves this status—the song bears repeated listens without becoming tiresome. Anyone claiming otherwise is challenged to sit still while it plays and resist playing imaginary three-fingered bass gallops or refrain from smashing make-believe crash cymbals while Clive Burr kills it on the recording. Go ahead. Try it.

The exuberance gives way to "Gangland" and "Total Eclipse." Neither song really takes off, and the detour costs the album some momentum. Fortunately, the band gets it back on the closer, "Hallowed Be Thy Name." From the song's opening chimes, it's clear that the band means business, and when the serious-as-cancer riffs kick in, a tormented Bruce Dickinson howls from the depths of existential despair. "Hallowed Be Thy Name" is not the sound of a band playing like their lives depend on it. It's the sound of five musicians who are going to be executed in the morning. The song simply cannot be followed, and it's the ideal choice to end the album.

To promote the album the band had launched the Beast on the Road tour in February 1982, which remains one of their longest tours to date with close to two hundred shows played worldwide. "We've never got much radio play at all—we've always made our reputation as a band on the road," Murray told Chris Vinnicombe.

In addition to an important gig at the famed Reading Festival in August, where Dickinson made his presence felt in front of thousands of music fans, Maiden toured extensively around the United States, supporting Rainbow on their *Straight Between the Eyes* tour, the Scorpions on their *Black-out* tour, and Judas Priest on their *Screaming for Vengeance* trek. Maiden also played some headlining shows in the States, further opening a huge market for the band.

Around this time, guitarists Murray and Smith began making a huge impression on the metal scene, and were now often mentioned in the same breath and revered tones as Judas Priest's K. K. Downing and Glenn Tipton.

95½ WMET
WELCOMES

IRON MAIDEN
THE NUMBER OF THE BEAST

CHICAGO CIRCLE PAVILION
JULY 2, 1982

OTTO

IRON MAIDEN

MAIDEN JAPAN

Beast on the Road world tour,
Madison Square Garden, New York City,
October 2, 1982. © *Bob Leafe*

SETLIST SELECTIONS

BEAST ON THE ROAD TOUR

THE IDES OF MARCH
MURDERS IN THE RUE MORGUE
WRATHCHILD
RUN TO THE HILLS
CHILDREN OF THE DAMNED
THE NUMBER OF THE BEAST
ANOTHER LIFE
KILLERS
22 ACACIA AVENUE
TOTAL ECLIPSE
TRANSYLVANIA
THE PRISONER
HALLOWED BE THY NAME
PHANTOM OF THE OPERA
IRON MAIDEN
SANCTUARY
DRIFTER
RUNNING FREE
PROWLER

As Smith told Rosen in 1982, "Dave grew up with a lot of Hendrix. You go down to his house anytime and he'll be playing that. So his approach is wah wah and lots of whammy bar, very, very fast. I tend to, when I do a solo in the studio, I'll just like work it out. Then I'll put it down and maybe I'll keep it. Dave will just rip it out three or four at once."

The year ended with Clive Burr announcing that he had to leave the band due to personal issues and the hectic touring schedule that the band had committed to. Faced with a second consecutive end-of-year personnel change, the band tapped stickman Michael Henry "Nicko" McBrain.

"[Nicko's] drumming is some of the best rock drumming there is," Harris told Kevin Thompson in 1983. "His feel is magic. Nicko toured with us when he played with the French band Trust in 1981 and '82. So he's been on the road with us. Trust and Iron Maiden have always been big friends anyway, and personality-wise there was no problem. He was actually born about a mile and a half from me, and he's just a couple of years older than I am. His drumming, I think, has given us a different dimension. It's tougher, and his timing is perfect. He's a total rock drummer; he's got a great feel and he hits it real hard."

By the time January rolled around, the band was ready to commence work on the new album that would feature the most famous and steady line-up in Maiden's history: singer Bruce Dickinson, bassist Steve Harris, guitarists Dave Murray and Adrian Smith, and drummer Nicko McBrain. 🇬🇧

Iron Maiden were road warriors in 1982, sandwiching three U.K. shows into the middle of their North American tour, including an August 28 appearance at the famed Reading Festival, where they are seen here. Four days later they were playing Long Beach, California. © *Steve Rapport/Retna Ltd.*

1981   *By Ryan LaMar*

02.17	Ipswich, GBR	04.14	Karlsruhe, GER	07.16	Johnstown, USA
02.18	Norwich, GBR	04.15	Stuttgart, GER	07.17	Buffalo, USA
02.19	Oxford, GBR	04.16	Mannheim, GER	07.18	Rochester, USA
02.20	Lancaster, GBR	04.17	Strasbourg, FRA	07.19	Syracuse, USA
02.21	Derby, GBR	04.18	Mulhouse, FRA	07.21	Albany, USA
02.22	Manchester, GBR	04.19	Douvaine, FRA	07.22–24	New York City, USA
02.23	Hanley, GBR	04.21	Colomiers, FRA	07.25	New Haven, USA
02.24	Dunstable, GBR	04.22	Bordeaux, FRA	07.26	Allentown, USA
02.26	Guildford, GBR	04.23	Le Mans, FRA	07.28	Boston, USA
02.27	Bristol, GBR	04.24	Genk, BEL	07.29	Baltimore, USA
02.28	Taunton, GBR	04.25	Antwerp, BEL	07.30	Philadelphia, USA
03.01	Bournemouth, GBR	04.26	Leiden, NED	08.01	San Bernardino, USA
03.02	Southampton, GBR	04.28	Nijmegen, NED	08.04	Long Beach, USA
03.04	Bradford, GBR	04.29	Offenbach, GER (possibly	08.15	Stuttgart, GER
03.05	Liverpool, GBR		rescheduled from 04.09)	08.16	Nuremberg, GER
03.06	Middlesborough, GBR	05.21	Tokyo, JPN	08.23	Darmstadt, GER
03.07	Newcastle, GBR	05.22	Osaka, JPN	08.26	Frejus, FRA
03.08	Glasgow, GBR	05.23	Nagoya, JPN	08.27	Cap d'Agde, FRA
03.09	Edinburgh, GBR	05.24	Tokyo, JPN (two shows)	08.29	Bayonne, FRA
03.10	Sheffield, GBR	06.03	Las Vegas, USA	08.31	Annecy, FRA
03.12	Birmingham, GBR	06.04	Phoenix, USA	09.01	Orange, FRA
03.13	Cambridge, GBR	06.05	El Paso, USA	09.06	Belgrade, YUG
03.14	Bracknell, GBR	06.06	Odessa, USA	09.08	Stockholm, SWE
03.15	Hammersmith, GBR	06.07	Lubbock, USA	09.09	Lund, SWE
03.18	Lille, FRA	06.09	McAllen, USA	09.10	Copenhagen, DEN
03.19	Le Havre, FRA	06.10	Laredo, USA	10.26	Bologna, ITA
03.20	Rheims, FRA	06.11	San Antonio, USA	10.27	Rome, ITA
03.21–22	Paris, FRA	06.13	Dallas, USA	10.28	Firenze, ITA
03.23	Lyon, FRA	06.14	Houston, USA	10.29	Padova, ITA
03.24	Miramar, FRA	06.19	Detroit, USA	10.30	Milan, ITA
03.25	Toulon, FRA	06.21	Toronto, CAN	11.15	London, GBR
03.26	Nice, FRA	06.22	Montreal, CAN	12.23	East Ham, GBR
03.27	Montpellier, FRA	06.26	Milwaukee, USA		
03.30	Milan, ITA (two shows)	06.27	Lynnwood, USA		
03.31	Reggio Emilia, ITA	06.28	Cleveland, USA		
04.01	Brescia, ITA	07.01	Largo, USA		
04.02	Gorizia, ITA	07.02	Asbury Park, USA		
04.03	Turin, ITA	07.03	Salisbury, USA		
04.05	Zurich, SUI	07.04	Norfolk, USA		
04.06	Erlangen, GER	07.07	Pittsburgh, USA		
04.07	Dusseldorf, GER	07.09	Myrtle Beach, USA		
04.10	Hamburg, GER	07.10	Atlanta, USA		
04.11	Bremen, GER	07.11	Johnson City, USA		
04.12	Wertheim, GER	07.12	Memphis, USA		
		07.15	Dayton, USA		

Evidence has shown the following dates, which have appeared elsewhere, including the European tour program, to be unreliable:

03.30	Bologna, ITA
03.31	Milan, ITA
04.01	Udine, ITA
04.02	Bresca, ITA
04.06	Munich, GER
04.07	Frankfurt, GER
04.08	Cologne, GER
04.08	Neu Isenberg, GER
04.09	Kassel, GER

IRON MAIDEN
THE BEAST ON THE ROAD

04.10	Berlin, GER	03.30	Montpellier, FRA	06.09	Tallahassee, USA
04.12	Wurtzburg, GER	03.31	Toulouse, FRA	06.11	Memphis, USA
04.13	Mannheim, GER	04.02	Barcelona, ESP	06.12	Jackson, USA
04.14	Villingen, GER	04.03	Madrid, ESP	06.13	New Orleans, USA
04.15	Karlsruhe, GER	04.04	San Sebastian, ESP	06.15	Little Rock, USA
04.16	Erlangen, GER	04.05	Bergerac, FRA	06.16	Tulsa, USA
04.21	Tolouse, FRA	04.06	Le Mans, FRA	06.18	Shreveport, USA
04.23	Orleans, FRA	04.07	Brest, FRA	06.19	Norman, USA
04.29	Bremen, GER	04.08	Poitiers, FRA	06.22	Ottawa, CAN
04.29	Berlin, GER	04.09	Dijon, FRA	06.23	Toronto, CAN
04.30	Hannover, GER	04.10	Grenoble, FRA	06.24	Kingston, CAN
05.03	Hamburg, GER	04.12	Winterhur, SUI	06.25	Quebec City, CAN
05.22–24	Tokyo, JPN	04.13	Strasbourg, FRA	06.26	Montreal, CAN
05.25	Nagoya, JPN	04.16	Evry, FRA	06.27	Philadelphia, USA
05.29	Sidney, AUS	04.17	Rouen, FRA	06.29	New York City, USA
05.31	Melbourne, AUS	04.18	Brussels, BEL	06.30	Long Island, USA
		04.20	Hannover, GER	07.02	Chicago, USA
		04.21	Hamburg, GER	07.03	Buffalo, USA
		04.22	Bochum, GER	07.04	East Troy, USA

1982

		04.23	Wurzburg, GER	07.06	Danville, USA
02.25	Dunstable, GBR	04.24	Neunkirchen, GER	07.07	Cedar Rapids, USA
02.26	Huddersfield, GBR	04.26	Munich, GER	07.09	St. Louis, USA
02.27	Wolverhampton, GBR	04.27	Eppelheim, GER	07.10	Kansas City, USA
02.28	Hanley, GBR	04.28	Offenbach, GER	07.11	Des Moines, USA
03.01	Bradford, GBR	04.29	Stuttgart, GER	07.14	Salt Lake City, USA
03.03	Liverpool, GBR	04.30	Dusseldorf, GER	07.16	Seattle, USA
03.04	Manchester, GBR	05.01	Amsterdam, NED	07.17	Anaheim, USA
03.05	Leicester, GBR	05.11	Flint, USA	07.18	Oakland, USA
03.06	Birmingham, GBR	05.13	Lansing, USA	07.20	Victoria, CAN
03.08	Portsmouth, GBR	05.14	Detroit, USA	07.21	Vancouver, CAN
03.09	Oxford, GBR	05.15	Kalamazoo, USA	07.23	Edmonton, CAN
03.10	Derby, GBR	05.16	Ft. Wayne, USA	07.24	Calgary, CAN
03.11	Bristol, GBR	05.18	Toledo, USA	07.26	Regina, CAN
03.12	Bracknell, GBR	05.20	Cincinnati, USA	07.27	Winnipeg, CAN
03.14	Glasgow, GBR	05.21	Louisville, USA	07.28	Fargo, USA
03.15	Edinburgh, GBR	05.22	Cleveland, USA	07.30	Minneapolis, USA
03.16	Newcastle, GBR	05.23	Indianapolis, USA	07.31	Springfield, USA
03.17	Sheffield, GBR	05.25	Merillville, USA	08.01	Indianapolis, USA
03.19	Ipswich, GBR	05.26	Davenport, USA	08.03	Cleveland, USA
03.20	Hammersmith, GBR	05.29	Des Moines, USA	08.04	Columbus, USA
03.22	Reims, FRA	06.01	Atlanta, USA	08.05	Chicago, USA
03.23	Lille, FRA	06.02	Nashville, USA	08.06	Louisville, USA
03.24	Paris, FRA	06.04	Birmingham, USA	08.07	Toledo, USA
03.26	Lyon, FRA	06.05	Huntsville, USA	08.08	Memphis, USA
03.27	Clermont-Ferrand, FRA	06.07	Knoxville, USA	08.10	Beaumont, USA
03.28	Nice, FRA	06.08	Columbus, USA	08.11	Corpus Christi, USA
				08.13	Houston, USA
				08.14	Dallas, USA
				08.16	San Antonio, USA

08.17	Odessa, USA	09.29	Columbus, USA	11.26–27	Tokyo, JPN
08.18	El Paso, USA	10.01	Worcester, USA	11.29	Osaka, JPN
08.20	Albuquerque, USA	10.02	New York City, USA	11.30	Kyoto, JPN
08.21	Phoenix, USA	10.03	Harrisburg, USA	12.01	Nagoya, JPN
08.22	Tucson, USA	10.06	Portland, USA	12.02, 04	Tokyo, JPN
08.25	Chippenham, GBR	10.07	Providence, USA	12.07–08	Sapporo, JPN
08.26	Poole, GBR	10.08	Glen Falls, USA	12.10	Nigata, JPN
08.28	Reading, GBR	10.09	New Haven, USA		
09.01	Long Beach, USA	10.11	Binghamton, USA		
09.03	Sacramento, USA	10.12	Philadelphia, USA		*The following dates appeared in fan club magazine No. 3, but were later amended in No. 4 and in the Japanese tour program:*
09.04	Oakland, USA	10.13	Pittsburgh, USA		
09.05	Reno, USA	10.15	Buffalo, USA		
09.07	Boise, USA	10.16	Syracuse, USA		
09.08	Missoula, USA	10.18	Largo, USA	06.03	Birmingham, USA
09.09	Seattle, USA	10.19	Baltimore, USA	06.08	Savannah, USA
09.11–12	Portland, USA	10.20	Salisbury, USA	06.13	Mobile, USA
09.14	St. Louis, USA	10.21	Norfolk, USA	06.19	Oklahoma City, USA
09.15	Kansas City, USA	10.22	East Rutherford, USA	06.22	Buffalo, USA
09.16	Lincoln, USA	10.23	Rochester, USA	06.24	Ottawa, CAN
09.17	Minneapolis, USA	11.07	Sydney, AUS	06.25	Kingston, CAN
09.19	Rockford, USA	11.08	Sydney, AUS	06.28–29	Pittsburgh, USA
09.21	Chicago, USA	11.09	Newcastle, AUS	07.06	Rockford, USA
09.22	Cleveland, USA	11.13	Adelaide, AUS	07.20	Vancouver, CAN
09.23	Dayton, USA	11.14–15	Melbourne, AUS	07.21	Victoria, CAN
09.25	Detroit, USA	11.16	Brisbane, AUS	07.22	Edmonton, CAN
09.26	Kalamazoo, USA	11.19	Canberra, AUS	07.25	Calgary, CAN
09.28	Huntington, USA	11.20–21	Sydney, AUS	08.05	Louisville, USA
				11.12	Adelaide, AUS
				11.13	Melbourne, AUS

Notes: An April 27, 1981, date in Winschoten, Holland, was cancelled due to low ticket sales. A sometimes reported April 29 date in Hannover was likely cancelled due to a conflict with the rescheduled Offenbach show. Additionally, Bushell reports that four German and three Scandinavian dates were cancelled in 1981. These would have been in late April and early May.

Unreliable sources list an April 13, 1981, show in Munich and an August 22, 1981, show in Baarle, Holland.

It is unlikely that the band played a sometimes reported show in Saarbrucken on April 20, 1981, because the distance to Saarbrucken from Douvaine and back to Toulouse is out of character for normal tour travel for that time. Additionally, there is no proof the band played or ever made plans to play a show at this location or on this date. Confusion regarding this date and location stems from a bogus bootleg titled Cross-Eyed Mary, which features official B-sides being passed off of as bootleg tracks.

It's possible the French shows listed from August 26 to 31, 1981, never happened. In 1989 French publication Hard Force released a retrospective of metal shows in France that did not include these dates. Although it should be noted that September 1 in Orange was also not on that list, but it has been confirmed by a ticket scan and an attestment from a fan who attended the gig.

October 26, 1981, marked Dickinson's live debut with the band.

According to the January 30, 1982, Sounds, a February 27 show in Cardiff, Wales, was cancelled because the venue's roof collapsed.

Fan club magazine No. 4 shows an empty spot on a tour list where the April 14 and 15, 1982, dates in Nancy and Mulhouse, France, would have been listed (probably whited out). However, this still doesn't solve a mystery. In magazine No. 3, Bruce claims the band "pulled out" of three gigs in southern France because of a collective band illness. More specifically, Garry Bushell wrote in his book that the band cancelled three gigs along the Cote d'Azur, the southeast coast of France. The band was only scheduled to play one gig in this area: Nice. However, the band's gig in Montpellier was on the southwest coast, and the gig following that—Toulouse—is within reasonable driving distance from the southwest. No other gigs are nearby the Cote d'Azur, so these three might be those which Bushell writes about. One problem: The band did play Nice. A bootleg in circulation has Bruce clearly saying "Bonsoir, Nice." This has caused significant confusion as to which dates were actually cancelled. If the "three dates" were not the two missing in magazine No. 4, then it could be the band postponed the Nice gig until April 1 (the only open date between Toulouse and Barcelona), or the band did play Nice on the originally scheduled date, and then cancelled Montpellier, Toulouse, and an unknown location along the Cote d'Azur. The band did have an open date (March 29) between Nice and Montpellier in which they could have squeezed in a show in Toulon or Marseille.

N075183

ACE PRESENTS

IRON MAIDEN
PALAIS THEATRE
14 NOV 1982 8.00PM

BRACKNELL SPORTS CENTRE
MAXIMUM MUSIC PRESENTS
IRON MAIDEN
PLUS
THE RODS
Friday 12th March 7.30pm
ALL TICKETS £3.50
Management reserve the right to refuse admission
Nº 0718

4 CHILDREN OF THE DAMNED

WORLD DOMINATION, 1983–1985

"See, press and people like that in general misunderstood the whole thing that is heavy rock. They don't comprehend the extent of the dedication of not only the band themselves, but usually the fans that go with the band. To them, pop music means disposable music which sells disposable articles. . . . As far as we're concerned, our music isn't disposable, it isn't designed to sell anything, and all we ask is that people listen to it and enjoy it."

—Bruce Dickinson, quoted by Sylvie Simmons, *CREEM*, October 1983

Iron Maiden's legendary fourth album, *Piece of Mind*, was recorded at Compass Point Studios in the Bahamas in January 1983. The band finished the nine-track album in March as their relationship with Martin Birch continued to prosper.

Steve Harris explained in 1983: "The reason we use Martin is that he puts down the sound that we want, the way we like it. And we think the first three albums were really leading up to this one in terms of quality. In general, bands are being given producers that make the music for them and, in some cases, even co-write it. With Martin, that's not the case at all and never has been. What Martin has always added with us is his expertise in the studio and his great ability at recording our sounds. We've only just come to this point in our drum and guitar sounds, which are exceptional now; it's just a team growing up together. Martin's also become aware, obviously, with the experience of working with us, of the way we want to proceed. The suggestions going both ways are very fluid, so Martin's very much a part of the band in the studio."

On the road for the World Piece tour, 1983. *Chris Walter/WireImage/Getty Images*

Bruce Dickinson and Dave Murray, Capitol Records building, Hollywood, July 1983. *Richard E. Aaron/Redferns/Getty Images*

"The Trooper" flexi disc, Russia.

Piece of Mind has a lot of literary references, including Frank Herbert's *Dune* saga and G. K. Chesterton. Band members were especially keen on science fiction and fantasy, which continue to be major themes in their work. Books and films filled up a lot of time for the band during those long tours. Dickinson was especially well read and harbored some thoughts of becoming an author himself, which became a reality with 1990's *The Adventures of Lord Iffy's Boatrace*. The second track on *Piece*, Dickinson's "Revelations," was inspired by the singer's fascination with the deceased English occultist Aleister Crowley, who was also a source of fascination for musicians including the Beatles, the Stones, Led Zeppelin, and Ozzy Osbourne. In 2009, Dickinson would further his publishing career by cowriting an eponymous book treatment about Crowley.

Released in May, *Piece of Mind* has since become one of the most acclaimed heavy metal albums in history, with rollicking tracks like "The Trooper" and "Flight of Icarus" on offer. *Kerrang!*, the British heavy metal bible of the '80s, with whom Iron Maiden had a close relationship, rated *Piece of Mind* at No. 1 in a 1983 poll of the best heavy metal albums in history (*The Number of the Beast* came in at No. 2). Such was the popularity of *Piece of Mind* that it appeared in *Kerrang!* reader's polls throughout the decade. Additionally, *Piece of Mind* was the band's first Top 20 album in the United States, and sales have since reached more than 13 million worldwide.

Adrian Smith said in 2000, "It's great to be praised by the critics. . . . It's kind of amazing, really, to think that they hold [*Piece of Mind*] in such high regard. What we were doing is just going in and trying to make good music. I think it's just part of the legend of Iron Maiden—a phenomenon. But it's great. It's great that people feel that way."

The band hit the road for the relatively short (by Maiden standards) World Piece tour in April and wound up in December; the tour included a fairly extensive jaunt around North America.

Maiden's former lighting engineer Dave "Lights" Beazley recalled the band's famed set design. "By the time Iron Maiden were promoting the *Piece of Mind* album," he said, "the tours were running into months rather than weeks. We'd previously hired all the lighting equipment, but with a 10- to 12-month tour coming up it was obvious that it would be

(continued on page 60)

"The Trooper" (June 1983).

"Flight of Icarus" (April 1983).

PIECE OF MIND

BY MICK WALL

OF ALL THE BIG CORNERSTONE Iron Maiden albums—the eponymous debut, *The Number of the Beast, Seventh Son...*, etc.—the one that gets the least mentions yet remains one of Steve Harris' all-time personal favorites is *Piece of Mind*.

Released in 1983, *Piece* was also the first Maiden album to feature the classic '80s line-up of Harris, Dave Murray, Adrian Smith, Bruce Dickinson, and—making his recorded debut with the band—Nicko McBrain. As if to announce this fact, track one, "Where Eagles Dare," explodes into life with big percussive flourish. Where McBrain's predecessor, Clive Burr, had been a consummate "feel" player, Nicko brought a greater technical finesse that allowed Maiden a much greater capacity to finesse their full-metal-racket sound. As Harris would later say, "It felt like we were on a high and you can hear that mood on the album. I thought we'd really come up with the goods this time."

As always, it was Harris who led the way with "Where Eagles Dare," a typically fist-shaking anthem to the inner-strength it takes to become a leader; "The Trooper," a battle-hymn set in the Crimean War and featuring strafing guitars and galloping bass and drums; "Quest for Fire," inspired by the 1981 movie of the same name in which a caveman's search for fire becomes symbolic of man's quest for knowledge; and closing track "To Tame a Land," its lyrics based on Frank Herbert's labyrinthine sci-fi novel *Dune*. (Originally the track had been called simply "Dune," but when plans to include a spoken-word passage from the book were rejected by the author, a last-minute rethink was needed.)

Of the album's other five tracks, easily the best are "Flight of Icarus," by Dickinson and Smith, and "Revelations," written by Dickinson alone. The former became the band's first U.S. single, its rock-steady beat and Dio-esque vocals gaining them more radio airtime than any other previous Maiden track. The latter, simply one of their best tracks since Dickinson had joined two years before, became one of the big call-and-response highlights of the Maiden live show for years to come.

Almost inevitably, certain Christian fundamentalist groups in America took offense at the use on the sleeve of a quote from the Bible's Book of Revelation, chapter 21, verse 4: *And God shall wipe away all the tears from their eyes; and there shall be no more Death. Neither sorrow, nor crying. Neither shall there be any more Brain; for the former things are passed away* (except for the word "pain," which was replaced by "'Brain," a pun on the album title).

Already branded in some quarters as satanists after *Number of the Beast*, some in the American South urged the burning of Maiden records. The band couldn't resist making fun, though. Anticipating the response they jokingly included a backward-masked message between "The Trooper" and "Still Life"—a drunken McBrain doing an impression of infamous African dictator Idi Amin: "Don't meddle wi'd t'ings yo don't understand."

The rest of the album was fairly standard Maiden fare: Dickinson's and Smith's "Sun and Steel" is a romping musketeer tale with suitably duelling guitars. "Still Life" is the by now obligatory Harris and Murray number, moody but lacking in true magnificence. And "Die with Your Boots On" is a Dickinson/Smith idea augmented by Harris that would sound grand live but didn't need more than one listen on vinyl.

Another sizeable hit in the U.K. despite lukewarm critical response, *Piece of Mind* became the first Maiden album to penetrate the U.S. Top 20, reaching No. 14 and selling more than a million copies and earning Maiden their first platinum record. ✳

World Piece tour, Uniondale, New York, August 25, 1983.
All © Bob Leafe

LIVE &
HEAVY EXPRESS

IRON MAIDEN

World   Piece Tour '83

SPECIAL GUEST
THE MICHAEL SCHENKER
GROUP

SUNRISE

4.12. Philipshalle
DÜSSELDORF

Einlaß: 19.00 Uhr
Beginn: 20.00 Uhr

Örtliche Durchführung: alpha Konzertbüro, Köln.

Tel. Kartenbestellservice Theaterkasse im Hause Saturn, (0221) 12 19 12

The relatively short (by Maiden standards) World Piece tour began in April 1983 and wound up in December. This Dusseldorf show was rescheduled from November 19.

IRON MAIDEN

MICHAEL SCHENKER GROUP

ROUEN
MARDI 15 NOVEMBRE
PARC DES EXPOSITIONS. 21H.

BESANÇON
VENDREDI 18 NOVEMBRE
PALAIS DES SPORTS. 21H.

PARIS
JEUDI 17 NOVEMBRE
ESPACE BALARD. 20H.

CLERMONT-FERRAND
SAMEDI 19 NOVEMBRE
MAISON DES SPORTS. 21H.

LYON
DIMANCHE 20 NOVEMBRE
PALAIS D'HIVER. 18H.

LE COMBAT HARD DE L'AUTOMNE

PATHÉ MARCONI EMI

Chrysalis
DISTRIBUTION ariola

World Piece tour, November 1983.

(continued from page 55)

easier to design and build a set that we could take with us on the road. Not only would this be cheaper in the long run than hiring, but it also meant that everywhere we went, the fans could see the same show."

The tour, however, was not without controversy. On August 7, a model who had recently won a radio competition was invited onstage at Market Square Arena in Indianapolis during "22 Acacia Avenue." The scantily clad contest winner, appropriately known as "Miss Model," danced around Bruce Dickinson during the song, but the frontman ripped off her top, leaving her topless in front of the thousands in attendance. Dickinson was arrested and reportedly sued by the woman, though the case was settled out of court.

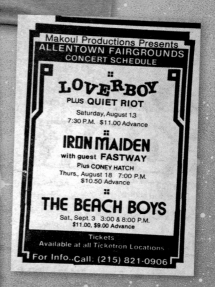

BOTH: Courtesy Wyco Vintage/wycovintage.com

SETLIST SELECTIONS

PIECE OF MIND TOUR

WHERE EAGLES DARE MOVIE THEME
(ENTRANCE)
WHERE EAGLES DARE
WRATHCHILD
THE TROOPER
REVELATIONS
FLIGHT OF ICARUS
DIE WITH YOUR BOOTS ON
22 ACACIA AVENUE
THE NUMBER OF THE BEAST
STILL LIFE
TO TAME A LAND
PHANTOM OF THE OPERA
HALLOWED BE THY NAME
IRON MAIDEN
RUN TO THE HILLS
SANCTUARY
DRIFTER
PROWLER

BOTH: World Piece tour, 1983.
John T. Comerford III collection/Frank White Photo Agency

World Piece tour, somewhere in the United States or Canada, September 1983.
Both Michael Ochs Archives/Getty Images

Dave Murray keeps one eye over his shoulder on the World Piece tour, somewhere on the U.S. East Coast, 1983. *Ebet Roberts/Redferns/Getty Images*

World Piece tour, Madison Square Garden, New York City, October 8, 1983. © *Frank White*

Powerslave includes the bonafide metal classic "Aces High." *Courtesy Wyco Vintage/wycovintage.com*

"Aces High" (October 1984), France.

"2 Minutes to Midnight" (August 1984), France.

In early 1984, the band returned to Compass Point with Martin Birch to record their new album, *Powerslave*. Despite a strong work ethic, the band knew how to have fun and party, and indeed, by most accounts, that's what they did during the recording of the album, enjoying tropical island offerings such as banana daiquiris.

Powerslave includes the band's longest song to date, "Rime of the Ancient Mariner," a retelling of the Samuel Taylor Coleridge poem that clocks in at almost fourteen minutes. The eight-track album also includes bonafide metal classics "Aces High" and "2 Minutes to Midnight."

Released in September 1984, *Powerslave* was a huge hit for the band, eventually reaching platinum status in the United States and Canada and being certified gold in the United Kingdom and Germany. To promote its release, the band committed to an eleven-month tour. By now, Maiden was a force to be reckoned with on the live scene, and the World Slavery tour was even more extensive than the Beast on the Road tour, logging 190 dates in 24 countries. Support acts included Accept, Waysted, Mötley Crüe, and Twisted Sister. In fact, the tour went into the annals of rock history as one of the longest of all time and one of the most iconic, too, thanks to a large Egyptian-themed stage set. Beginning in Poland in August 1984 and winding up in California in July 1985, the tour included such highlights as a slot at

(continued on page 68)

Powerslave includes the band's longest song to date, "Rime of the Ancient Mariner," a retelling of the Samuel Taylor Coleridge poem that clocks in at almost fourteen minutes.

CHILDREN OF THE DAMNED · 63

IRON MAIDEN 4
WORLD SLAVERY TOUR 84/85

IRON MAIDEN 1
WORLD SLAVERY TOUR 84/85

IRON MAIDEN 4
WORLD SLAVERY TOUR 84/85

IRON MAIDEN 4
WORLD SLAVERY TOUR 84/85

IRON MAIDEN 5
WORLD SLAVERY TOUR 84/85

IRON MAIDEN
PHOTO/TV

66 IRON MAIDEN

World Slavery tour, New York City.

POWERSLAVE

BY DANIEL BUKSZPAN

I'LL JUST COME RIGHT OUT AND SAY IT: 1984's *Powerslave* is Iron Maiden's best album. The first two (self-titled and *Killers*) are classic slabs of NWOBHM. *The Number of the Beast* is a cornerstone of heavy metal, and *Piece of Mind* has "The Trooper," which is worth the price of the album all by itself. But *Powerslave* is where it all comes together. It was their first album to use the same line-up that played on the last one, giving the band a chance to develop cohesion and perfect their sound. As a result, all of the band's signature elements solidify here, from galloping rhythms to harmonized guitars to soaring vocal melodies and then some. It also expanded their popularity outside of the Unites States and the United Kingdom—the accompanying tour saw them play South America and also Poland, marking the first time a western heavy metal band had ever officially performed behind the Iron Curtain. If any album deserves to have its lyrics shouted off-mic by Steve Harris while he plays bass with his foot firmly mounted atop a monitor, this is it.

Powerslave opens with "Aces High," the strongest track on the album and an impossible one about which to feign indifference (at least for this writer). The song either confirms your conviction as an Iron Maiden lifer or it forever makes you claim that they sucked after Paul Di'Anno left. Regardless, it's followed by "2 Minutes to Midnight," still a fixture in the band's live sets today and a song with zero fat despite its six-minute length. After the instrumental "Losfer Words (Big 'Orra)" comes "Flash of the Blade." One of the band's most underrated songs, it opens on a highly original note with guitar hammer-ons and sustained bass chords before launching into full chug. Its highlight is the breakdown after the guitar solo, which sounds like ten Brian Mays playing over screeching guitar string harmonics, a detail that is always wonderful to geek out over.

"The Duellists," which ends side one, and "Back in the Village," the side-two opener, are the only questionable moves on the album. The former seems a little long and the latter sounds a bit fussy, but they're not egregious and they don't take you out of the album. "Back in the Village" is also amusing for its ending, which features Dickinson singing so fast that you can almost imagine Tom Araya calling up Jeff Hanneman and saying, "Hey, let's have a whole career based on this." The title track is next, a travelogue down the banks of the Nile and the Euphrates. The album could have effectively ended on this exotic note. Instead it goes into extra innings with "Rime of the Ancient Mariner," a thirteen-odd-minute retelling of Samuel Taylor Coleridge's epic poem of albatross revenge. It can be debated whether it really needed to be extended to infomercial length, or if it really needed to have a narration, bass, and volume pedal jam in the breakdown section. However, the excesses suggest a band that wanted to push things, and somehow, despite its length, the song never bores.

Twenty-five years after *Powerslave*, Iron Maiden remains relevant and still comes up with good albums. However, this is the kind of album that a band can only produce once in their career, and then only if they're lucky. It was their most melodic and accessible album to still showcase the aggression of their early days, and it did so for the very last time. It also featured a band that took risks with no fear of losing either their audience or their record label. Anyone who wants to know what this band was capable of at its creative pinnacle needs to look no further than this. 🏴󠁧󠁢󠁥󠁮󠁧󠁿

The 1984–1985 World Slavery tour went into the annals of rock history as one of the longest of all time and one of the most iconic, too. *Courtesy Wyco Vintage/ wycovintage.com*

(continued on page 63)

the famous Rock in Rio Festival that was headlined by Queen and a five-night residency at New York City's Radio City Music Hall. Some South African dates, however, were cancelled when objections arose to the use of the word *slavery*.

The World Slavery tour spawned the band's first live album *Live After Death*, released in October 1985. Recorded during a run of dates at London's Hammersmith Odeon in October 1984 and at four shows at California's Long Beach Arena in March 1985, it is one of the most acclaimed heavy metal live albums of all time. In October 1985, *Kerrang!* awarded *Live After Death* five Ks (their equivalent of five stars). It was also one of their Albums of the Year in 1985; in the naughties, *Kerrang!* named it one of their 100 Greatest Heavy Metal Albums of All Time. Music writer Greg Prato wrote in his review for *AllMusic*, "*Live After Death* is easily one of heavy metal's best live albums."

Since the *Metal for Muthas* tour in February 1980, Iron Maiden had played more than seven hundred live shows. Plans for a tour to promote *Live After Death* were scrapped, and for the first time in their history, the band took a six-month break. Boy, did they need it. 🇬🇧

SETLIST SELECTIONS

POWERSLAVE TOUR

CHURCHILL'S "WE SHALL FIGHT. . ."
SPEECH (ENTRANCE)
ACES HIGH
2 MINUTES TO MIDNIGHT
THE TROOPER
REVELATIONS
FLIGHT OF ICARUS
RIME OF THE ANCIENT MARINER
POWERSLAVE
THE NUMBER OF THE BEAST
HALLOWED BE THY NAME
IRON MAIDEN
RUN TO THE HILLS
RUNNING FREE
SANCTUARY

Live After Death counter display, October 1985.

"Run to the Hills" (live) (December 1985).

"Running Free" (live) (September 1985).

The World Slavery tour was even more extensive than the Beast on the Road tour, logging 190 dates in 24 countries, including this show in Peoria, Illinois.

1983 *By Ryan LaMar*

04.28	Stuttgart, GER
05.02	Hull, GBR
05.03	Preston, GBR
05.05	Oxford, GBR
05.06	Leicester, GBR
05.07	Southampton, GBR
05.08	Ipswich, GBR
05.10	Nottingham, GBR
05.11	Bradford, GBR
05.12	Glasgow, GBR
05.13	Edinburgh, GBR
05.15	Cardiff, GBR
05.16	Sheffield, GBR
05.17	Newcastle, GBR
05.18	Hanely, GBR
05.20	Bristol, GBR
05.21–22	Birmingham, GBR
05.23	Manchester, GBR
05.25–28	London, GBR
06.01	Helsinki, FIN
06.03	Gothenburg, SWE
06.04	Drammen, NOR
06.05	Stockholm, SWE
06.07	Copenhagen, DEN
06.12	Amsterdam, NED
06.21	Casper, USA
06.22	Salt Lake City, USA
06.23	Boise, USA
06.24	Spokane, USA
06.27	Portland, USA
06.28	Seattle, USA
06.29	Vancouver, CAN
07.02	San Francisco, USA
07.03	Sacramento, USA
07.05	Fresno, USA
07.07	San Bernardino, USA
07.08	San Diego, USA
07.09	Long Beach, USA
07.11	Tucson, USA
07.12	Phoenix, USA

07.13	Albuquerque, USA		09.15	Fargo, USA
07.14	Denver, USA		09.17	Winnipeg, CAN
07.16	Lubbock, USA		09.19	Calgary, CAN
07.17	Amarillo, USA		09.20	Edmonton, CAN
07.20	El Paso, USA		09.29	Peoria, USA
07.22	Norman, USA		09.30	Chicago, USA
07.23	Dallas, USA		10.02	Columbus, USA
07.24	Houston, USA		10.04	Baltimore, USA
07.26	Corpus Christi, USA		10.08	New York City, USA
07.27	San Antonio, USA		10.09	Norfolk, USA
07.29	Shreveport, USA		10.10	Charleston, USA
07.30	Memphis, USA		10.12	Columbia, USA
07.31	Little Rock, USA		10.14	Miami, USA
08.01	Nashville, USA		10.15	Jacksonville, USA
08.02	Louisville, USA		10.16	Lakeland, USA
08.06	East Troy, USA		10.19	Knoxville, USA
08.07	Indianapolis, USA		10.20	Charlotte, USA
08.09	Ft. Wayne, USA		10.21	Atlanta, USA
08.10	Kalamazoo, USA		10.23	Lincoln, USA (rescheduled from 09.25)
08.11	Detroit, USA			
08.13	Erie, USA		10.24	Kansas City, USA (rescheduled from 09.26)
08.14	Cleveland, USA			
08.15	Buffalo, USA		10.25	St. Louis, USA (rescheduled from 09.27)
08.16	Pittsburgh, USA			
08.18	Allentown, USA		11.05	Kerkrade, NED (rescheduled from 06.09 and 11.11)
08.19	Philadelphia, USA			
08.20	Largo, USA		11.07	Hannover, GER
08.23	Glen Falls, USA		11.08	Hamburg, GER
08.24	Syracuse, USA		11.09	Kiel, GER
08.25	Uniondale, USA		11.10	Bremen, GER
08.26	New Haven, USA		11.14	Brussels, BEL (rescheduled from 06.11)
08.27	South Yarmouth, USA			
08.29	Portland, USA		11.15	Rouen, FRA
08.30	Providence, USA		11.17	Paris, FRA
08.31	Poughkeepsie, USA		11.18	Besancon, FRA
09.01	Rochester, USA		11.19	Clermont-Ferrand, FRA
09.05	Toronto, CAN		11.20	Lyon, FRA
09.06	Montreal, CAN		11.22	Barcelona, ESP
09.07	Chicoutimi, CAN		11.24–25	Madrid, ESP
09.08	Quebec City, CAN		11.27	San Sebastian, ESP
09.10	Toledo, USA		11.30	Munich, GER
09.11	Lansing, USA		12.01	Nuremberg, GER (rescheduled from 11.10)
09.13	Madison, USA			
09.14	Minneapolis, USA		12.03	Wurzburg, GER

12.04	Dusseldorf, GER (rescheduled from 11.19)	08.29	San Sebastian, ESP	11.12	Milan, ITA
12.06	Ulm, GER	08.31	Oporto, POR	11.13	Lyon, FRA
12.07	Ludwigshafen, GER	09.01	Cascais, POR	11.14	Basel, SUI
12.08	Stuttgart, GER	09.03	Madrid, ESP	11.24	Halifax, CAN
12.09	Dortmund, GER	09.05	Barcelona, ESP	11.26	Quebec City, CAN
12.10	Russelheim, GER	09.07	Toulouse, FRA	11.27	Montreal, CAN
12.11	Lausanne, SUI	09.08	Bordeaux, FRA	11.28	Ottawa, CAN
12.13	Vienna, AUT	09.11	Glasgow, GBR	11.30	Toronto, CAN
12.14	Linz, AUT	09.12	Aberdeen, GBR	12.01	Sudbury, CAN
12.17–18	Dortmund, GER	09.13	Edinburgh, GBR	12.03	Winnipeg, CAN
		09.15–16	Newcastle, GBR	12.04	Regina, CAN
		09.17	Sheffield, GBR	12.06	Edmonton, CAN
		09.18	Ipswich, GBR	12.07	Calgary, CAN
		09.20	Leicester, GBR	12.09	Vancouver, CAN
		09.21	Oxford, GBR	12.10	Seattle, USA
		09.22	St. Austell, GBR	12.11	Portland, USA
		09.23	Bristol, GBR	12.13	Salt Lake City, USA
		09.25–26	Manchester, GBR	12.15	Denver, USA
		09.27	Hanley, GBR	12.17	Kansas City, USA
		09.29	Nottingham, GBR	12.18	St. Louis, USA
		09.30	Cardiff, GBR	12.19	Milwaukee, USA
		10.02–03	Birmingham, GBR	12.20	Minneapolis, USA
		10.05	Southampton, GBR	12.21	Chicago, USA
		10.07	Cardiff, GBR		

The following dates were listed in fan club magazine No. 6, but do not appear in subsequent tour programs:

07.18	Odessa, USA
08.21	Binghamton, USA
09.22	Saskatoon, CAN
09.24	Sioux City, USA
10.01	Cincinnati, USA
10.04	Knoxville, USA
10.05	Greensboro, USA
10.19	Johnson City, USA

The following dates were listed in fan club magazine No. 7, but do not appear on the subsequent tour shirt:

11.15	Nancy, FRA
11.16	Paris, FRA
12.02	Nuremberg, GER

1984

08.09	Warsaw, POL
08.10	Lodz, POL
08.11	Poznan, POL
08.12	Wroclaw, POL
08.14	Katowice, POL
08.16	Zeltweg, AUT
08.17	Budapest, HUN
08.18	Belgrade, YUG
08.19	Ljublijana, YUG
08.22	Arma di Taggia, ITA
08.25	Annecy, FRA
08.26	Palavas, FRA

10.08–10,12	Hammersmith, GBR
10.15	Cologne, GER
10.16	Stuttgart, GER
10.17	Heidelberg, GER
10.19	Wurzburg, GER
10.20	Brussels, BEL
10.21	Nancy, FRA
10.23	Freiberg, GER
10.24	Munich, GER
10.26	Essen, GER
10.27	Bremen, GER
10.28	Zwolle, NED
10.29	Paris, FRA
11.01	Copenhagen, DEN
11.02	Stockholm, SWE
11.03	Gothenburg, SWE
11.05	Helsinki, FIN
11.08	Russelsheim, GER
11.09	Nuremberg, GER
11.11	Bologna, ITA

1985

01.03	Cincinnati, USA
01.04	Detroit, USA
01.05	Columbus, USA
01.06	Cleveland, USA
01.07	Buffalo, USA
01.11	Rio de Janeiro, BRA
01.14	Hartford, USA
01.15	Worcester, USA
01.17–21	New York City, USA
01.28	Landover, USA
01.29	Philadelphia, USA
01.31	Columbia, USA
02.01	Johnson City, USA
02.02	Atlanta, USA
02.03	Memphis, USA
02.05	Nashville, USA
02.08	Charlotte, USA

02.09	Greensboro, USA	04.14 –15,			06.16	Hoffman Estates, USA
02.10	Greenville, USA	17, 19	Tokyo, JPN		06.18	Peoria, USA
02.12	Jacksonville, USA	04.20	Nagoya, JPN		06.19	Cedar Rapids, USA
02.14	Ft. Myers, USA	04.22	Fukuoka, JPN		06.21	Madison, USA
02.15	Miami, USA	04.24	Osaka, JPN		06.22	Green Bay, USA
02.16	Lakeland, USA	04.25	Tokyo, JPN		06.23	Minneapolis, USA
02.17	St. Petersburg, USA	05.02	Canberra, AUS		06.24	Fargo, USA
02.19	Chattanooga, USA	05.03	Melbourne, AUS		06.26	Des Moines, USA
02.20	Birmingham, USA	05.04	Adelaide, AUS		06.27	Omaha, USA
02.21	Huntsville, USA	05.06	Woollongong, AUS		06.29	Denver, USA
02.23	Beaumont, USA	05.07	Sydney, AUS		07.03	San Jose, USA
02.24	Biloxi, USA	05.08	Newcastle, AUS		07.04	Sacramento, USA
02.27	New Orleans, USA	05.10	Brisbane, AUS		07.05	Irvine, USA
02.28	Houston, USA	05.23	Portland, USA		12.15–16	??, GBR (special shows
03.01	Waco, USA	05.24	Uniondale, USA			with Adrian and Nicko with
03.02	Oklahoma City, USA	05.25	Binghamton, USA			encores by the whole band)
03.04	Dallas, USA	05.27	Rochester, USA		12.18–19	London, GBR (special
03.05	San Antonio, USA	05.28	Glen Falls, USA			shows with Adrian and
03.07	Lubbock, USA	05.29	Springfield, USA			Nicko with encores by the
03.08	El Paso, USA	05.31	New Haven, USA			whole band)
03.09	Albuquerque, USA	06.01	Allentown, USA			
03.10	Tucson, USA	06.02	Providence, USA			
03.14–17	Long Beach, USA	06.04	Columbia, USA			
03.19	Reno, USA	06.05	Pittsburgh, USA			
03.20	Fresno, USA	06.07	Dayton, USA			
03.21	San Francisco, USA	06.08	Evansville, USA			
03.23	San Diego, USA	06.09	East Troy, USA			
03.24	Tempe, USA	06.11	Toledo, USA			
03.25	Las Vegas, USA	06.12	Detroit, USA			
03.26	San Bernardino, USA	06.14	Saginaw, USA			
03.31	Honolulu, USA	06.15	Charlevoix, USA			

Notes: The April 1983 Stuttgart show is often incorrectly cited as Stoccarda, Italy. Unreliable sources have listed the following 1983 shows: June 10 at Shifflange, Luxembourg, and December 12 and 13 at Padova and Milan, Italy, respectively.

An August 21, 1984, show in Pordenone, Italy, is listed in the Japanese tour program, but no other evidence of it has turned up. An October 13, 1984, Hammersmith show was noted in a publication that stated five shows were planned. However, since the date is not in the Japanese tour program, it likely did not occur.

A ticket reading October 24, 1983, for Essen, Germany, is known to exist. Interestingly, several of the 1984 German shows have the incorrect year listed.

Two New York City shows (January 23 and 24, 1985), an Allentown, Pennsylvania, show (January 26, 1985), and likely a show in Glen Falls, New York (January 25, 1985), were cancelled due to Bruce being ill. In addition, a February 6, 1985, date in Knoxville, Tennessee, was cancelled by the promoter, and three May 1985 dates in New Zealand were jettisoned due to a dispute with the airline.

Bushell lists the Adelaide date as May 4, 1985. Skoog claims the date is May 5 because of an account from an Australian fan and the fact that Adelaide is quite a distance from Melbourne. The difference between the two dates may be attributable to the International Date Line, i.e., some North American and/or European media outlets or fans may have reported and perpetuated the date the concert occurred on their side of the line.

John Miles claims the band did only two secret gigs in December 1985: on the 18th under the moniker The Sherman Tankers, and on the 19th under the moniker The Entire Population of Hackney. He also says that the entire band came for encores only on the second night. Skoog, however, maintains that there were four secret gigs. Neither can prove their claim, although Skoog says that he got his information from an interview with Adrian Smith.

Maiden performs PR duties while Dickinson tries to remember where he left his trousers, 1987.
© Ross Marino/Retna UK

5 SOMEWHERE IN TIME

A NEW SOUND, 1986–1989

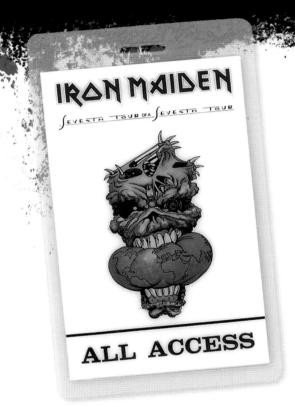

IRON MAIDEN
SEVENTH TOUR OF A SEVENTH TOUR

ALL ACCESS

"I always thought Led Zeppelin were terribly overrated, like Jimi Hendrix, who made a few revolutionary tracks and a lot of s***. Deep Purple was what really moved me. I'd never heard a band play with so much power, so loose and yet so ballsy."

—Bruce Dickinson, quoted by Simon Witter,
***NME*, March 12, 1988**

IRON MAIDEN
SOMEWHERE ... TOUR ... 86/87
PHOTO

Iron Maiden's line-up was finally steady, and on the back of three massively successful albums they justifiably claimed to be one of the most successful and revered heavy metal bands in the world. But Iron Maiden and Steve Harris, in particular, were thirsty to try something new. They did not want to churn out the same-sounding album time after time. Many of Harris' influences were progressive rock bands, and it showed in some of their previous work. Those influences, however, would be even more pronounced on their next release.

Somewhere in Time, which is based around the notion of time travel and features bass and guitar synthesizers, was recorded in early 1986 at Compass Point in the Bahamas and at Wisseloord Studios in the Netherlands. Recording in Holland was a conscious choice to mix things up a bit, but at least one aspect of the Iron Maiden recording process remained constant: producer Martin Birch. "Martin, he is a great character

SOMEWHERE IN TIME

BY MICK WALL

RELEASED IN 1986 at the apex of Iron Maiden's American fame, *Somewhere in Time*, the band's sixth album, should have been the one that sealed their reputation forever. Instead, it became their last platinum-selling album in the United States, and, despite many highlights and more than two million sales, remains one of the most disappointing of their career.

The creation of the album was a troubled one. After the huge success of *Powerslave* and the *Live After Death* double set that followed, Bruce Dickinson felt strongly that Maiden needed to return with something less formulaic for their next album. As he told me, "I thought, well, what would really give me a buzz to go off and do another twelve-month tour would be if we had another fucking record that I really felt was groundbreaking, you know? Like, where's our 'Stairway to Heaven'? So I went off into 'acoustic world' and I wanted to do almost like an unplugged record for the next Iron Maiden album—except this was years before MTV started doing it."

Steve Harris, however, saw things differently and rejected every single idea Dickinson brought with him to Compass Point Studios in the Bahamas. Instead, Harris would take sole credit for four of the album's eight tracks, plus a co-credit on one with Dave Murray. The other three tracks were written alone by Adrian Smith.

Of course, who writes what matters less than whether the songs actually work. The problem this time was that Harris' songs were mostly second-rate, beginning with the tediously long title track and descending into further workmanlike muscle-flexing with "The Loneliness of the Long Distance Runner" (inspired, if that's really the right word, by the British movie of the same name) and, most grating of all, album closer "Alexander the Great" (based on a biography Harris had recently read).

The exception was "Heaven Can Wait," another movie-themed epic that would come into its own live onstage, where it became the custom for the band to be joined on the sing-along chorus by whoever happened to be milling about backstage that night. Tellingly, the only other number from the album that remained in the Maiden live show for any duration was Smith's "Wasted Years," a gloriously anthemic track that fittingly became the first single from the album.

Elsewhere, Smith's equally affecting "Stranger in a Strange Land" (from yet another book) and tail-twisting "Sea of Madness" became the highlights of an exceedingly lugubrious collection, the nadir of which was the Harris/Murray collaboration "Deja-Vu."

Indeed, it says something about the paucity of strong material on offer that the biggest talking point among fans and critics was the band's use of guitar-synthesisers. There were also retrospective suggestions that *Somewhere in Time* was a concept album, the theme: time travel. Again, these were spurious claims—conversation pieces to avoid the elephant in the room, which was the album's complete lack of Dickinson songs and, worse still, anything of real weight to replace them.

Dickinson was left, he says, feeling "squashed inside for a long time." It was a feeling that resulted just a few years later in his acrimonious departure from the band. While the band seemed reduced to relying on the tried and trusted Maiden formula, Dickinson was beginning to crave different musical pleasures and experiences. Time for both singer and band was, in fact, fast running out. 🇬🇧

GREAT PAN

ALAN SILLITOE
author of the sensational
**SATURDAY NIGHT
AND SUNDAY MORNING**

Holds a mirror
to working class
life and morals
in these brilliant
and biting tales

THE LONELINESS OF THE LONG DISTANCE RUNNER

2'6

Somewhere in Time's "The Loneliness of the Long Distance Runner"
was inspired by the book and movie of the same name.

"Wasted Years"
(September 1986),
Netherlands.

"Stranger in a Strange Land"
(November 1986), U.K.

and he's a great producer," Bruce Dickinson explained in 1996 to Matthias Reinholdsson and Henrik Johansson, creators of the Dickinson über-fan site *bookofhours.net*. "He taught me a lot about singing. Martin's philosophy of a good producer is that the producer is just like a mirror that he holds up to the band and he reflects what the band is perfectly."

Much of the album's songwriting was completed by Adrian Smith after the band reportedly overlooked Dickinson's lyrics. Released in September 1986, the album, like its predecessors, was populated with literary references, many of them based around science fiction themes, such as "Stranger in a Strange Land," which takes its title from a famed novel by the American author Robert Heinlein.

Up to this point, Iron Maiden had created their own unique sound, their own identity that was vastly different from any other metal band. Maiden was certainly different from heavy metal originators Black Sabbath, for example. "I think we sound different," Adrian Smith commented on the difference between Maiden and Sabbath to American rock writer Steven Rosen in 1982. "For starters, the bass is very prominent in this band. [Harris] has a very unique sound. He writes a lot

of the songs. He sits down and he works on them, and that's a normal thing that you do on a guitar. So it's just little things like that."

Though Iron Maiden ventured into a new style with *Somewhere in Time*, the album still carried the band's trademark galloping bass lines, robust vocals, and twin-guitar attack. Still, the album's new multilayered sound was criticized in some quarters that yearned for Maiden's trademark heavy metal style. At least it could be said the band was attempting something fresh.

78 · IRON MAIDEN

SETLIST SELECTIONS

SOMEWHERE ON TOUR

BLADE RUNNER MOVIE THEME
(ENTRANCE)
CAUGHT SOMEWHERE IN TIME
2 MINUTES TO MIDNIGHT
SEA OF MADNESS
CHILDREN OF THE DAMNED
STRANGER IN A STRANGE LAND
WASTED YEARS
RIME OF THE ANCIENT MARINER
WHERE EAGLES DARE
HEAVEN CAN WAIT
PHANTOM OF THE OPERA
HALLOWED BE THY NAME
IRON MAIDEN
THE NUMBER OF THE BEAST
RUN TO THE HILLS
RUNNING FREE
SANCTUARY

Somewhere on Tour, Philadelphia, January 13, 1987. © Bob Leafe

Of course the band committed to a world tour to support their new release. The Somewhere on Tour world jaunt began on September 10, 1986, in Belgrade, Yugoslavia, and wound to an end in Japan in May of the following year. To re-create the new album's arrangements on stage, the band invited Steve Harris' tech Michael Kenney to play keyboards on tour. Kenney has remained a touring member ever since. Interestingly, The Somewhere on Tour outing remains the only tour that has not spawned a live commercial recording.

Though *Somewhere in Time* was not a concept album in the strictest sense, there can be no arguments as to its followup, *Seventh Son of a Seventh Son*. Iron Maiden's 1988 release involves a fictional child who has psychic. Harris took his inspiration from the American sci-fi

(continued on page 83)

Somewhere on Tour, East Rutherford, New Jersey, March 28, 1987. © Bob Leafe

The Somewhere on Tour included obligatory dates in the New York metropolitan area. Eddie is dressed in a New York Giants uniform, having soundly defeated a pile of players wearing the orange and blue of the Denver Broncos, whom the Giants had beaten in the Super Bowl earlier that year. *Courtesy Wyco Vintage/wycovintage.com*

Somewhere on Tour, Cleveland, Ohio, 1987.

IRON MAIDEN
Special Guest: WAYSTED
SAT MARCH 14 8 P.M.
Coliseum THEATRE
Reserved Tickets:
$14 Advance, $15 Day of Show

Somewhere on Tour, Minneapolis, Minnesota, April 17, 1987.
Jim Steinfeldt/Michael Ochs Archives/Getty Images

LEFT AND OPPOSITE: The Somewhere on Tour world jaunt began on September 10, 1986, in Belgrade, Yugoslavia, and wound to an end in Japan in May of the following year. *Courtesy Wyco Vintage/ wycovintage.com*

SOMEWHERE IN
NEW YORK

666

MEADOWLANDS ARENA MARCH 28, 1987
MADISON SQUARE GARDEN APRIL 2, 1987

IRON MAIDEN.

IRON MAIDEN.

EDDIE
LIVES

SOMEWHERE ON TOUR '87

YUGOSLAVIA
AUSTRIA
HUNGARY
U.S.A.
JAPAN
POLAND
ENGLAND
WALES
FRANCE
BELGIUM
GERMANY
SWITZERLAND
FINLAND
AUSTRALIA
SWEDEN
NORWAY
ITALY
HOLLAND
NEW ZEALAND

Iron Maiden's 1988 release involves a fictional child who has psychic powers. Harris took his inspiration from the American sci-fi writer Orson Scott Card.

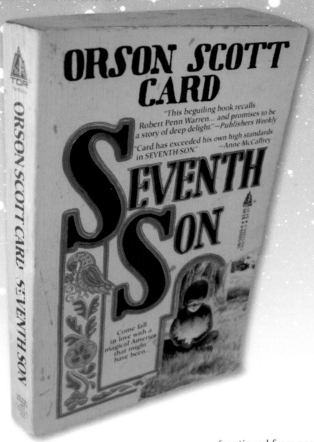

"Can I Play with Madness" (March 1988), U.K.

"The Evil That Men Do" (August 1988), U.K.

"The Clairvoyant" (November 1988).

(continued from page 78)

writer Orson Scott Card. The resulting song cycle intelligently handles such themes as reincarnation, the afterlife, mysticism, psychic phenomena, and prophetic visions. The band recorded the album with Martin Birch at Musicland Studios in Munich throughout the second half of 1987 and into the following year.

Released in April 1988, *Seventh Son of a Seventh Son* was a No. 1 hit for the band in the United Kingdom and peaked at No. 12 in the United States, proving that after the experimentation of *Somewhere in Time* the band had not lost touch with their fan base or their heavy metal roots. While bands like Metallica and Megadeth were setting the metal scene on fire with a new breed of razor-sharp metal, Maiden was still a hot contender and acknowledged originators. Though Metallica and their ilk made a different sort of metal from the traditional style that Maiden pioneered, and were very popular with younger metal fans, Iron Maiden was still atop their game, not to mention the metal scene as a whole.

The band launched the successful Seventh Tour of a Seventh Tour in Cologne in April 1988 and finished in December of the same year. On August 20, Maiden (and that iconic rock

OPPOSITE: Seventh Tour of a Seventh Tour, East Rutherford, New Jersey, July 8, 1988. *Ebet Roberts/Redferns/Getty Images*

"Infinite Dreams" (live) (November 1989).

SEVENTH SON OF A SEVENTH SON

BY GAVIN BADDELEY

ISSUED IN 1988, *Seventh Son of a Seventh Son* was (inevitably) Maiden's seventh full-length studio release. It was also the band's first (and to date only) concept album. Supposedly, the concept album had died out a decade ago during the punk era. But as it turned out, dedicated fans still liked the form, and Maiden had hardly cut their jib to musical fashion on previous releases.

With *Seventh Son of a Seventh Son*, Maiden didn't fall back on a literary inspiration as they had with Coleridge's "Rime of the Ancient Mariner" on 1984's *Powerslave*. Rather, they bound the album together with a story concocted from several sources. The refrain "six, six, six" had helped Maiden break into the big time on *Number of the Beast*, in the process establishing six as the definitive devilish digit (with a little help from Hollywood's *Omen* franchise, which inspired the album's title track.) Seven also holds mystical significance in several folklore traditions—in particular when a seventh son is born of a seventh son, which according to these traditions can imbue a child with strange powers.

This concept inspired American author Orson Scott Card's 1987 fantasy novel *Seventh Son*, which became a successful series of books that in turn inspired Steve Harris to begin his concept album. While Harris was clearly impressed by Card's books, it's not clear how comfortable Card, a devout Mormon, is with the Maiden slant, which contains overt references to the infamous English occultist Aleister Crowley. (Bruce Dickinson's interest in Crowley as a maverick intellectual is well known and was manifested in his 1998 solo album, *The Chemical Wedding*, and his script for the 2008 film of the same name, which was released in the United States as *Crowley*.)

The most obvious evidence of the Crowley influence is "Moonchild." The opening track on *Seventh Son* takes its name from a 1917 Crowley novel in which black and white magicians battle over the fate of an unborn child against the backdrop of World War I. Crowley believed that the creation of a moonchild—a child conceived under ritual conditions to trap the soul of a spirit or demon—was possible.

The third major inspiration for the album was the death of leading British medium Doris Stokes, which led Harris to ask, if she really was psychic, would Stokes have foreseen her own death? It's the sort of speculation that more often manifests itself as a punch line, but in Maiden's case it gave birth to the lyric for the album's penultimate track, "The Clairvoyant."

Of course, the recipe's ingredients are irrelevant if the final dish doesn't work, but *Seventh Son* is a veritable feast. The disparate elements mean that the plot remains vague, but structured enough for Dickinson's visceral vocals to belt through with passion. Crucially, the tracks work individually, as well as form the whole of its saga of a doomed psychic. Card's books are largely set in nineteenth-century America, but *Seventh Son of a Seventh Son* compels the listener to construct their own narrative, in whichever time or place their imagination takes them. "Can I Play with Madness" and "The Evil That Men Do" (the latter inspired by a quote from Shakespeare's *Julius Caesar*) are highlights that saw release as singles along with "The Clairvoyant" (although "Only the Good Die Young" would surely have been a stronger choice). Overall, *Seventh Son of a Seventh Son* is an impressive album worthy of its reputation among some fans as the apex of Bruce Dickinson's first tenure with the band. 🇬🇧

MONSTERS OF ROCK
1988
IRON MAIDEN

SPECIAL GUEST:
DAVID LEE ROTH
HELLOWEEN KISS GUNS'N ROSES
MEGADETH ANTHRAX
GREAT WHITE
TREAT

20. 8. DONINGTON Park	**4. 9. TILBURG** Willem II Stadion
27. 8. SCHWEINFURT Mainwiesen	**10. 9. MODENA** Arena
28. 8. BOCHUM Ruhrstadion	**24./25. 9. PARIS** Berey

On August 20, 1988, Maiden made their first headlining appearance at the famed Monsters of Rock festival in Donington, England, supported by several acts.

MONSTERS OF ROCK
IRON MAIDEN
DONINGTON PARK SATURDAY 20th AUGUST
GUEST
3144
VALID ONLY FOR GUEST AREA

monster Eddie) made their first headlining appearance at the famed Monsters of Rock festival in Donington, England. On the Monsters tour that followed, they were supported by several acts, including David Lee Roth, Metallica, Anthrax, Megadeth, Guns N' Roses, W.A.S.P., Helloween, Killer Dwarfs, Ossian, Trust, Great White, L.A. Guns, Backstreet Girls, and Ace Frehley's Comet. It was yet another Maiden tour that has gone down in the annals of metal history.

In the eight short years since their first tour in 1980, Iron Maiden had established themselves as one of the most exciting, consistent, and entertaining live bands in the world of heavy metal and hard rock. The band also enjoyed a hardcore following in their native country, especially in London.

"There are a lot of different things happening in London," Adrian Smith explained to Steven Rosen. "In England, it changes so quick. You always get a lot of bands coming out with a new style, and you get two or three really good bands and maybe they'll carry on. They're there when everyone else has sort of fallen behind. But as to our music, it never really sinks, like Cream. It has never really sort of gone away. It's always had its fans. It just got pushed in the background for a bit, but there is still a big audience for it."

SETLIST SELECTIONS

SEVENTH TOUR OF A SEVENTH TOUR

MOONCHILD
THE EVIL THAT MEN DO
THE PRISONER
INFINITE DREAMS
THE TROOPER
CAN I PLAY WITH MADNESS
HEAVEN CAN WAIT
WASTED YEARS
THE CLAIRVOYANT
SEVENTH SON OF A SEVENTH SON
THE NUMBER OF THE BEAST
HALLOWED BE THY NAME
IRON MAIDEN
RUN TO THE HILLS
RUNNING FREE
SANCTUARY

Portland, Maine.

East Rutherford, New Jersey.

The London lads had certainly built up a strong fan base in the United States after successful albums and consistent touring. "'Round about 1983 we came over and started headlining," Dave Murray told interviewer Gary James in 1995. "We had a really good run in America from 1983 to 1987. 1987 was probably the peak."

Dickinson reflected on the '80s during an interview with the United Kingdom's *Daily Mirror* tabloid newspaper in 2008: "We were a bunch of 24-year-olds from England going 'round America in the 1980s. What do you think went on? We weren't vicars, but at the same time we're not daft. Nobody was married, nobody got hurt and we're all still here to talk about it."

Maiden managed to balance the big stage production and rock theatrics with well-paced setlists and stunning performances. Sure, each musician proved himself to be a real talent, but the star of the show was almost always frontman Dickinson. He grabbed the audiences' attention with the same charisma and energy as premier frontmen like Freddie Mercury. By the end of the decade Dickinson was on par with great rock frontmen such as Mercury, the late Bon Scott of AC/DC, and the Who's Roger Daltrey.

As the '90s approached, Maiden, by now elder statesmen of the metal world, faced a lot of competition, not from U.K. bands, but from the United States, where they were hugely popular (curiously, their popularity had waned somewhat back home). The thrash movement had spawned heavy bands like Metallica and Slayer, both of which were yet to reach their commercial peak, while the L.A. scene had given rise to Guns N' Roses and a slew of glam metal bands that were doing—or about to do—big business.

After the intensity of 1988, the band took a break, giving Bruce Dickinson time to nip out of the band and work on his first solo album, *Tattooed Millionaire* (released 1990), with ex-Gillan guitarist Janick Gers. Adrian Smith released his first solo album, *Silver and Gold*, in 1989, with his new project, ASAP. "[I]t was a very tense period in the band's career," Smith admitted to Kelley Simms of the metal site *SMNnews.com* in 2010. "Where we went from 1980 with the first album, I came in on the second album, from then, our feet never touched the ground. . . . It was touring and recording."

Was it a sign that all was not well in the Maiden camp?

After the intensity of 1988, the band took a break, giving Dickinson time to nip out and release and tour behind his first solo album, *Tattooed Millionaire*. © Bob Leafe

BRUCE DICKINSON

Tattooed Millionaire

His Debut Single

Available on
7" & Cassette Single (includes exclusive track)
12" Limited edition Poster Bag (plus exclusive bonus track)

EMI

BRUCE DICKINSON

All The Young Dudes

TAKEN FROM THE ALBUM
tattooed millionaire

AVAILABLE ON 7" • GATEFOLD 12" • CASSETTE • CD
ALL WITH EXCLUSIVE B SIDE & 12" PLUS EXCLUSIVE BONUS TRACK

BRUCE DICKINSON ON TOUR 1990

EMI

BRUCE DICKINSON
NEW SINGLE

DIVE! DIVE! DIVE!

PLUS
DIVE! DIVE! LIVE!
SPECIAL 12" & CD

CONTAINING EXCLUSIVE LIVE TOUR VERSIONS OF
'DIVE! DIVE! DIVE!' 'RIDING WITH THE ANGELS'
'SIN CITY' 'BLACK NIGHT'
RECORDED LIVE AT LONDON'S ASTORIA ON JUNE 27TH
12" POSTER BAG WITH EXCLUSIVE LIVE SHOTS AND POSTER
CD WALLET CONTAINING EXCLUSIVE LIVE POSTER

EMI

1986 *By Ryan LaMar*

09.10	Belgrade, YUG
09.11	Zagreb, YUG
09.12	Ljublijana, YUG
09.14	Vienna, AUT
09.15	Graz, AUT
09.17	Budapest, HUN
09.19	Katowice, POL
09.20	Wroclaw, POL
09.21	Poznan, POL
09.23	Gdansk, POL
09.24	Lodz, POL
09.25	Warsaw, POL
10.03	Oxford, GBR
10.04	St. Austell, GBR
10.06–07	Cardiff, GBR
10.08	Bristol, GBR
10.10–11	Manchester, GBR
10.12	Liverpool, GBR
10.14	Leicester, GBR
10.15–16	Sheffield, GBR
10.20	Nottingham, GBR
10.21	Bradford, GBR
10.22	Hanley, GBR
10.24–25	Newcastle, GBR
10.27–28	Edinburgh, GBR
10.30–31,	
11.01	Birmingham, GBR
11.03–05,	
07–09	Hammersmith, GBR
11.12	Helsinki, FIN
11.14	Stockholm, SWE
11.15	Gothenburg, SWE
11.17	Drammen, NOR
11.18	Malmo, SWE
11.20	Offenbach, GER
11.21	Boblingen, GER
11.22	Hannover, GER
11.23	Leiden, NED
11.25	Essen, GER
11.26	Munich, GER
11.28	Brussels, BEL
11.29	Paris, FRA
12.01	Barcelona, ESP
12.02–03	Madrid, ESP
12.05	Cascais, POR
12.07	Toulouse, FRA
12.08	Montpellier, FRA
12.09	Lyon, FRA
12.11	Nuremberg, GER
12.12	Ludwigshafen, GER
12.13	Lausanne, SUI
12.15	Turin, ITA
12.16	Milan, ITA
12.17	Firenze, ITA
12.18	Naples, ITA

1987

01.07	Hampton, USA
01.08	Largo, USA
01.09	Pittsburgh, USA
01.11	Troy, USA
01.12	New Haven, USA
01.13	Philadelphia, USA
01.16	Jacksonville, USA
01.17	Miami, USA
01.18	Lakeland, USA
01.20	Atlanta, USA
01.22	Dallas, USA
01.23	Austin, USA
01.26	Lubbock, USA
01.27	Norman, USA
01.28	Tulsa, USA
01.30	Houston, USA
01.31	San Antonio, USA
02.01	Corpus Christi, USA
02.03	Amarillo, USA
02.04	Wichita, USA
02.06	Denver, USA
02.08	Salt Lake City, USA
02.10	Tacoma, USA
02.11	Portland, USA
02.13	Sacramento, USA
02.14	San Bernardino, USA
02.16–18	Long Beach, USA
02.21	Oakland, USA
02.22	Fresno, USA
02.24	San Diego, USA
02.25	Phoenix, USA
02.26	Tucson, USA
02.27	El Paso, USA
03.01	Ft. Worth, USA
03.03	Albuquerque, USA
03.05	Omaha, USA
03.06	Kansas City, USA
03.07	St. Louis, USA
03.09	Madison, USA
03.10	Milwaukee, USA
03.11	Chicago, USA
03.13	Cincinnati, USA
03.14	Cleveland, USA
03.15	Battle Creek, USA
03.17	Saginaw, USA
03.18	Detroit, USA
03.19	Indianapolis, USA
03.21–22	Toronto, CAN
03.24	Montreal, CAN
03.25	Quebec City, CAN
03.27	Allentown, USA
03.28	East Rutherford, USA
03.30	Providence, USA
03.31	Worcester, USA
04.02	New York City, USA
04.04	Charlotte, USA
04.05	Greensboro, USA
04.07	Baltimore, USA
04.09	Dayton, USA
04.10	Buffalo, USA
04.11	Johnstown, USA
04.13	Rochester, USA
04.14	Toledo, USA
04.15	Columbus, USA
04.17	Minneapolis, USA
04.20	Winnipeg, CAN
04.21	Regina, CAN
04.22	Edmonton, CAN
04.24	Calgary, CAN
04.26	Vancouver, CAN

04.28	Reno, USA	06.14	Albuquerque, USA	08.10	Hampton, USA
04.29	Las Vegas, USA	06.15	Denver, USA	08.17	London, GBR
04.30	San Francisco, USA	06.17	St. Louis, USA	08.20	Donington, GBR
05.01	San Jose, USA	06.18	Kansas City, USA	08.27	Schweinfurt, GER
05.02	Irvine, USA	06.19	Omaha, USA	08.28	Bochum, GER
05.11	Nagoya, JPN	06.21	Minneapolis, USA	08.31	Budapest, HUN
05.13, 15	Tokyo, JPN	06.22	Cedar Rapids, USA	09.02	Innsbruck, AUT
05.17	Kyoto, JPN	06.23	Chicago, USA	09.04	Tilburg, NED
05.18	Hiroshima, JPN	06.25	East Troy, USA	09.08	Lausanne, SUI
05.20–21	Osaka, JPN	06.27	Indianapolis, USA	09.10	Modena, ITA
		06.28	Columbus, USA	09.13	Athens, GRE
		06.29	Cincinnati, USA	09.17	Pamlona, ESP

1988

		07.01	Saginaw, USA	09.18	Madrid, ESP
		07.02	Detroit, USA	09.20	Cascais, POR
04.28–29	Cologne, GER	07.03	Cleveland, USA	09.22	Barcelona, ESP
05.08	Brooklyn, USA	07.05	Pittsburgh, USA	09.24	Paris, FRA
05.13	Moncton, CAN	07.06	Poughkeepsie, USA	09.25	Paris, FRA
05.14	Halifax, CAN	07.08	East Rutherford, USA	09.26	Brussels, BEL
05.16	Quebec City, CAN	07.13	New Haven, USA	09.28	Copenhagen, DEN
05.17	Montreal, CAN	07.15	Uniondale, USA	09.30	Stockholm, SWE
05.18	Ottawa, CAN	07.16	Troy, USA	10.01	Gothenburg, SWE
05.20	Toronto, CAN	07.17	Worcester, USA	10.03	Helsinki, FIN
05.23	Winnipeg, CAN	07.19	Portland, USA	10.05	Drammen, NOR (rescheduled from 10.04)
05.25	Edmonton, CAN	07.20	Providence, USA		
05.27	Calgary, CAN	07.22	Philadelphia, USA	11.18	Newport, GBR
05.30	Vancouver, CAN	07.27	Atlanta, USA	11.20–22	Edinburgh, GBR
05.31	Spokane, USA	07.29	Fort Worth, USA	11.24–25	Whitley Bay, GBR (second date appears unlikely)
06.01	Seattle, USA	07.30	Austin, USA		
06.03	Salt Lake City, USA	07.31	Houston, USA	11.27–28	Birmingham, GBR
06.05	Mountain View, USA	08.02	New Orleans, USA	11.30,	
06.06	Sacramento, USA	08.04	Daytona Beach, USA	12.01	Manchester, GBR
06.08–09	Irvine, USA	08.05	Miami, USA	12.04	Sheffield, GBR
06.10	San Diego, USA	08.06	Tampa, USA	12.06–07	Hammersmith, GBR
06.12	Los Angeles, USA	08.08	Landover, USA	12.10–11	London, GBR
06.13	Phoenix, USA	08.09	Charlotte, USA	12.12	Hammersmith, GBR

Notes: An October 18, 1986, show in Ipswich, England, was cancelled because Bruce had the flu. According to Skoog, December 19, 20, and 21, 1986, dates in Rome, Bologna, and Padova, Italy, which are sometimes cited as taking place, were actually cancelled.

According to Skoog, a January 24, 1987, gig in Beaumont, Texas, was cancelled for poor ticket sales.

According to local media, a July 10, 1988, show in Allentown, Pennsylvania, was cancelled for poor ticket sales.

Fan club magazine No. 25 lists six U.S. dates from July 9 to August 8, 1988, which don't appear in the subsequent tour programs: Utica and Binghamton, New York; Greensboro, North Carolina; Landover, Maryland; Atlanta, Georgia; and Columbia, South Carolina.

Evidence suggests that a sometimes cited August 25, 1988, show in Prague was cancelled. Also, the band planned to tour Australia and the Far East in October and November, 1988, but cancelled before dates and locations were finalized, according to fan club magazine No. 27.

6 BE QUICK OR BE DEAD

THE END OF THE ROAD, 1990–1993

"We'll never cross over, we won't make a nice little pop single, so all we can do is appeal to rock fans. . . . At the end of the day as long as we can play music and have fun we'll keep going and then when the time comes to call it a day we want to go out gracefully."

—Dave Murray, quoted by Phil Sutcliffe, *Q*, January 1991

In 1990 Iron Maiden celebrated ten years of singles releases by issuing the appropriately, if unimaginatively, titled ten-CD box set *The First Ten Years*. The new decade would also bring changes in the band's ranks.

Again produced by Martin Birch, and released in October 1990, *No Prayer for the Dying* was the band's first album recorded at Barnyard Studios in Essex. It was also the first album since 1983's *Piece of Mind* to feature a line-up change. Saying he had grown bored and unenthused with Maiden and their progressive musical direction, Adrian Smith quit and was replaced by Janick Gers, the ex-Gillan guitarist who had appeared on Bruce Dickinson's first solo release, issued earlier that year. Six years later, however, Dickinson offered a different take on Smith's departure. "He wasn't fired but he didn't quit entirely willingly," the singer told Matthias Reinholdsson and Henrik Johansson (*bookofhours.net*). "Adrian is a great guitarist. He sort of agreed to leave. It came to a big discussion one day before *No Prayer for the Dying*. And it started off with him suggesting that maybe we should write more than eight songs per album."

NO PRAYER FOR THE DYING

BY MARTIN POPOFF

MAIDEN MADE IN HAY BALES: I'm paraphrasing Bruce Dickinson there, but yes, the grunting lads recorded 1990's *No Prayer for the Dying* in a farm 'n' barn-ish environment to help fulfill the mission sketched for their eighth studio album: namely to distance themselves from the over-thunk synthesized dreck polluting the last couple o' tiring tries. Maiden's creative drift had been enough to cause Adrian Smith to jump ship prior to the *No Prayer* sessions, replaced by White Spirit/Gillan axeman Janick Gers, or Crazy Legs as we like to call him. Dickinson would last one more bum spin before hugely showing up Steve Harris with a string of fine solo albums, 1998's *The Chemical Wedding*, of course, being a bloody masterpiece.

But back at *No Prayer*, the gesture toward carnality did help jostle the band from jet lag, somewhat, and somewhat admirably, given the industry standard of incredibly slick records at the turn of the decade, essentially the last hurrah for glam before punk apparently broke with Nirvana. Keyboards are kept to a minimum, and, making noises like a guitar-shaped motorbike, Dickinson often goes with an exaggerated, thespian rasp, which is then deftly mixed a bit further back than usual, allowing for the grim metal churn of the record to claim mild victory over a man standing at the mic and wondering why all the good songs went bye-bye.

Yea and verily, *No Prayer for the Dying* was ill-received by fans and critics, but indeed the deliberate NWOBHM grit and spit of the thing helped push a few tracks above and buzzing beyond, one fist-pumpable, the other pint-foisting. Lyrically, smarmy sex romp "Hooks in You" is more Anvil's domain, but this lone Adrian Smith credit is the album's melodic and party-rockin' breath of fresh air (plus it's got cowbell). And if "Tailgunner" sports yet another eye-roller of a job description lyric from Dickinson, musically it's a blustery success, celebrating the band's oft-exploited knack for a sweet 'n' sour and sing-songy stack of chord cakes à la "The Number of the Beast" and arguably

"Murders in the Rue Morgue" before that, although that one's less nose-wrinkling. Advance single "Holy Smoke," marred by a ditzy twin lead, nonetheless succeeds due to a verse that is, freshly, just logical, predictable chords, sorta like "The Boys Are Back in Town." Shoveling coal, Nicko strikes up a decent groove (the charm, of course, is that for Nicko, *Time* is a magazine), while Bruce plays a mischievous blaspheming character somewhere between Christopher Hitchens and Ronnie James Dio. The under-appreciated "Public Enema Number One" and "Fates Warning" keep up the snarling, indie 7-inch vibe of the album (and by the way, no songs over six minutes!), both taut with urgency, each dark and cynical.

All but one of the rest of the long-forgotten songs . . . well, they round the bases, Maiden building shoddy replicas of older anthems that were crafted with purpose, unnecessary rewrites of potent proposals inspired by youth and exploration, worst of these being final track "Mother Russia," an abomination which perpetuates the disastrous tradition of rock bands trying to convert Slav folk melodies into rock talk. Still, if *No Prayer for the Dying* ends upon a horrible song of laughing-out-loud ill consequence, second to merciful end we get the record's uncut gem and its biggest hit, "Bring Your Daughter . . . to the Slaughter," which, like "Hooks in You," leans into that debauched sleaze rock zone, different for Maiden, and questionable, but, man, at this point were we ever bedraggled and begging for some new approaches. 🇬🇧

SHOOT THAT FU KER IRON MAIDEN TAILGUNNER

No Prayer for the Dying promo bumper sticker, 1990.

"Bring Your Daughter . . . to the Slaughter" (December 1990), special edition etched sleeve, U.K.

"I'd been in the band for nine or ten years, it was a very tense period in the band's career," Smith reflected years later with interviewer Kelley Simms (*SMNnews.com*, 2010). "Where we went from 1980 with the first album, I came in on the second album, from then, our feet never touched the ground. . . . It was touring and recording. I suppose I was a little bit burned out. I had no life outside the band. I needed to explore some other things, maybe do a few solo things."

Not that fissures weren't developing between other members. The band could credit much of its success up to that point on a strict work ethic largely put in place by band founder Steve Harris.

Again speaking to Reinholdsson and Johansson in 1996, Dickinson reflected, "Steve is not that flexible a personality, it's just the way he is, you know. He knows pretty much what he wants and I think he tends to exclude a lot of options. He's never taken a drug in his life, he doesn't smoke, he never smoked dope, he's never taken acid or anything that would alter his possibilities. He very rarely gets drunk, even, because he likes to stay in control and I think that's the fundamental difference between me and him."

No Prayer for the Dying represented yet another new sound for the band, which revisited their early influences like Deep Purple, Free, Led Zeppelin, and the Who for a raw, more direct hard rock approach with no synths or progressive elements.

As Janick Gers told Al the Metallian on Sonic Disaster Radio in 1992, "If you have that rock 'n' roll feel in there, which developed on the *No Prayer for the Dying* album, and [Dickinson's] singing—it became less operatic and more what I call rock 'n' roll."

Be that as it may, *No Prayer* was not too well received and was the lowest selling of the band's albums with Dickinson. For many longstanding Maiden fans, *No Prayer* is considered one of the weakest Dickinson-fronted albums. In fact, the band has largely ignored the album since its release, though

"Bring Your Daughter . . . to the Slaughter" (December 1990), 12-inch single, U.K.

they regularly play the single "Bring Your Daughter . . . to the Slaughter," which rose to No. 1 in the United Kingdom (the only Maiden single to do so) on the strength of its appearance on the soundtrack to *A Nightmare on Elm Street 5: The Dream Child*.

In August 1990, the band launched the massive No Prayer on the Road tour, which commenced in August in England and came to an end in France during August of the following year. They continued to shame much younger metal bands when it came to live performances, rarely, if ever, putting in an off night.

Janick Gers had fit into the band rather well, and once the tour wound up he hit the studio for yet another new album. But was the band as a whole showing signs of fatigue?

In 1991, Dickinson embarked on a solo tour before the band began work on their next album, once again at Barnyard Studios. The resulting LP, *Fear of the Dark*, would be the last album produced by Martin Birch, who retired not long after its release. It was also notable as the first Iron Maiden album to feature cover art by someone other than Derek Riggs (instead, the job went to artist Melvyn Grant, although Maiden fans rarely mention Riggs in anything less than revered tones).

No Prayer on the Road tour, East Rutherford, New Jersey, January 21, 1991.
Ebet Roberts/Redferns/Getty Images

SETLIST SELECTIONS

NO PRAYER ON THE ROAD TOUR

633 SQUADRON MOVIE THEME
(ENTRANCE)
TAILGUNNER
PUBLIC ENEMA NUMBER ONE
WRATHCHILD
DIE WITH YOUR BOOTS ON
HALLOWED BE THY NAME
22 ACACIA AVENUE
HOLY SMOKE
THE ASSASSIN
NO PRAYER FOR THE DYING
HOOKS IN YOU
THE CLAIRVOYANT
2 MINUTES TO MIDNIGHT
THE TROOPER
HEAVEN CAN WAIT
IRON MAIDEN
THE NUMBER OF THE BEAST
BRING YOUR DAUGHTER . . . TO THE SLAUGHTER
RUN TO THE HILLS
SANCTUARY

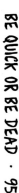

No Prayer on the Road tour, Long Beach, California, February 1991.
Marty Temme/WireImage/Getty Images

In addition to songs like "Be Quick or Be Dead" and the power ballad "Wasting Love," which represent a typically hard rock sound, Fear of the Dark also offered such tracks as "2 Minutes to Midnight" and "Afraid to Shoot Strangers," which are more progressive in an old-school Iron Maiden fashion.

"The identity of Iron Maiden is still there," Dave Murray explained at the time while speaking to Al the Metallian on Sonic Disaster Radio, "and if you put any track on you can tell it's Iron Maiden. But 'Fear of the Dark,' the track itself, probably sums up everything Maiden is about and the whole album is about. For us, this album feels so fresh. It feels like it could be our first album. We are very excited about it."

When *Fear of the Dark* was released in May 1992, it was attacked by some fans and rock scribes as inconsistent while the band was accused of sounding somewhat fatigued or even jaded. Were they simply going through the motions?

MAIDEN'S ARTWORK

BY NEIL DANIELS

IRON MAIDEN IS ALMOST AS WELL-KNOWN for their album and picture-sleeve artwork as they are for their music. Every release features specially commissioned cover art featuring their iconic mascot Eddie. Derek Riggs, who was the band's long-term artist, actually created Eddie for his portfolio. The artwork that appeared on the band's self-titled debut album was made with the intention of placing it with a record label for use on a punk album (hence Eddie's Mohawk). In fact, as Riggs points out, Eddie and the artwork on the debut were created before Iron Maiden even existed as a band.

Riggs subsequently gave Eddie a longer, more metal coif at the band's request and continued to create album and picture-sleeve art for the band through 1990's *No Prayer for the Dying*. In fact, Riggs' art for *The Number of the Beast* is perhaps Maiden's most famous LP cover and has been reprinted on countless T-shirts and posters around the world.

While Riggs had a close relationship with the band in much the same way Roger Dean had a relationship with Yes and Rodney Matthews still has a relationship Magnum, he eventually grew tired of Eddie, so for the *Fear of the Dark*, the band hired Melvyn Grant to design the art. Grant would also go on to create the artwork for the *Virtual XI*, *Death on the Road*, and *The Final Frontier* covers, as well as the "The Reincarnation of Benjamin Breeg" single.

"[N]aturally I wanted to change it and do my version of Eddie," Grant told Mark Morton at *examiner.com*. "But that was stopped by Maiden, who didn't want me to stray too far from the original style, which obviously all of the band's fans like. You get so used to something that it becomes your 'thing,' and you fall in love with that version of Eddie. I did try to change him a bit, in a way that suited me and made me happier with it."

The band later brought even more artists into the fold. Hugh Syme designed the artwork for *The X Factor*, David Pratchett worked on *Dance of Death*, and Tim Bradstreet created the artwork for *A Matter of Life and Death*. Mark Wilkinson—who had previously designed artwork for Marillion and Judas Priest, among others—created the artwork for *Live at Donington*. In an interview with the author for *Fireworks* magazine in 2010, Wilkinson said, "Rod

Record-store counter display. Derek Riggs created the first Eddie artwork with the intention of placing it with a record label for use on a punk album—hence early Eddie's Mohawk-ish 'do.

Smallwood, the band's manager, and Steve Harris were fans of the artwork for Marillion, and Rod liked the poster design I did for the Monsters of Rock festival the year Iron Maiden headlined. He called me in to work on 'The Wicker Man' a few years later when they were struggling to get what they wanted for the illustration of that cover."

Fans eager to see some of Iron Maiden's most iconic artwork should check out the book *Run for Cover: The Art of Derek Riggs*. 🇬🇧

"Be Quick or Be Dead" (April 1992).

"From Here to Eternity" (June 1992), picture disc and plinth.

"Wasting Love" (September 1992).

After all, what was left to prove? It's not uncommon for bands to continue well past their use-by date, while others take lengthy hiatuses and return with fresh material. Others simply call it a day. Regardless of what the critics said about Maiden's new material, the band felt they still had much to say and prove.

Janick Gers defended the album. "The album is consistent in that it has twelve individual songs on it that complement each other," he told Al the Metallian. "We don't want to do twelve songs of the same speed and the same feel just to please the radio or please whomever. We are there to explore different avenues and write different songs. We have explored so many different avenues on this particular album and we are so proud of the songs on there. These are twelve really good tunes."

The band launched a mammoth worldwide trek in support of the album beginning June 3, 1992, in Norwich, England, and ending in November in Tokyo. Supporting bands included the American thrash metal titans Anthrax, as well as Wolfsbane, The Almighty, and King's X.

Not only had the band stripped down their sound for *No Prayer for the Dying*, but they also ditched their outdated spandex on tour in favour of T-shirts and jeans. The tour was more notable, though, for including their first tour of Latin America and a second performance at the Monsters of Rock festival at Donington (later released on CD).

Despite these milestones, *Fear of the Dark* and its supporting tour proved to be the end of an era for the band as Dickinson quit to pursue a solo career, following Rob Halford who had left Judas Priest to go solo.

Dickinson agreed to a farewell outing, the Real Live tour, which kicked off on March 25, 1993, in Portugal and finished in England in August. The final show featuring Dickinson, Harris, Murray, Gers, and McBrain was recorded at Pinewood

(continued on page 106)

Dallas, Texas.

FEAR OF THE DARK

BY JOHN TUCKER

AFTER THE LARGELY DISAPPOINTING *No Prayer for the Dying*, Iron Maiden needed a rethink. Although successful commercially, artistically *No Prayer* cut little new ground and featured nothing of any great merit aside from "Bring Your Daughter . . . to the Slaughter," which Bruce Dickinson had written for a solo project. Some kind of change was needed, and the impetus supposedly came from a bunch of young pups called Dream Theater, whose demos for their groundbreaking *Images and Words* album convinced Dickinson that his band needed to raise their game. The result was *Fear of the Dark*, today regarded as one of the strongest albums in the band's catalog.

Released in May 1992, the band's ninth studio album was the first to credit Steve Harris as co-producer alongside longtime collaborator Martin Birch. Its release was preceded by a generic Maiden single, "Be Quick or Be Dead," which went straight into the U.K. singles charts at No. 2, a sure sign the band had a winner on their hands. The album itself topped that, becoming their third No. 1 after *The Number of the Beast* and *Seventh Son. . .* (like its predecessors, it slammed straight into the top spot) and peaking at a not unrespectable No. 12 in the States. Only *Somewhere in Time* did any better in the United States, peaking at No. 11.

Fear of the Dark's strength is its clever balance of conventional trademarks and inspired embellishments to the band's armory. Whereas things kick off with the traditional (i.e., completely interchangeable) Maiden opener "Be Quick or Be Dead" and the vaguely puerile chest-beater "From Here to Eternity," the more evocative "Afraid to Shoot Strangers" is the first song since "Seventh Son of a Seventh Son" to make you sit up and take notice. "Fear Is the Key" is the first of the album's two epics, nodding its head in time and in deference to "Kashmir," as a quite unexpected—which you come to expect with this band—time-change is pulled off with Maiden panache. "Childhood's End" and "The Fugitive" keep the pot on the boil nicely, and in "Wasting Love" Dickinson and Janick

Gers deliver the band's first real power ballad, perhaps another indication that Dickinson and Harris were now on two separate tracks.

The album is not without its failings. The opening pair (both singles, coincidentally) are pretty standard Maiden fare, and toward the end of the running order things drag terribly. Edit out "The Apparition," "Judas Be My Guide," and "Weekend Warrior" and you end up with a punchier album. With "Chains of Misery," however, Dickinson and Dave Murray take a trip back in time and return with a NWOBHM masterpiece, and in the title track Harris rounds the album off with a work of creative genius. An inventive yet stylistically simple tour de force, the title track and album closer builds from an undemanding refrain into the ultimate neck-wrenching workout. Perhaps the ultimate crowd-pleaser, the song has become an enduring piece of the band's live canon—something that just has to be played, no matter how much the rest of the set around it may be chopped and changed.

Together with its predecessor, *No Prayer for the Dying*, *Fear of the Dark* marked the end of the beginning for Iron Maiden. The final album recorded by the steady hand of Martin Birch (the band's producer since their second album in 1981) was also the last before Dickinson's exit. There wouldn't be another studio album until October 1995, and there wouldn't be another U.K. No. 1 until 2010. Things would never be the same again.

Or would they? 🇬🇧

MONSTERS OF ROCK
IRON MAIDEN
SKID ROW
THUNDER   W.A.S.P.
SLAYER
THE ALMIGHTY

DONINGTON PARK
22 AUGUST
1992

Fear of the Dark and its supporting
tour proved to be the end of an era for
the band as Dickinson quit to pursue
a solo career. *Jeff Kravitz/FilmMagic/
Getty Images*

In 1993, Bruce Dickinson agreed to a farewell outing, the Real Live tour, which kicked off on March 25 in Portugal and finished in London in August. The strip pasted at the bottom of the poster announces that this Berlin show was a rescheduled date.

Real Live tour, Wembley Arena, London, May 17, 1993. *Mick Hutson/Redferns/Getty Images*

Real Live tour, Wembley Arena, London, May 17, 1993. *Mick Hutson/Redferns/Getty Images*

REAL LIVE TOUR

BE QUICK OR BE DEAD
THE NUMBER OF THE BEAST
PROWLER
TRANSYLVANIA
REMEMBER TOMORROW
WHERE EAGLES DARE
FROM HERE TO ETERNITY
WASTING LOVE
BRING YOUR DAUGHTER . . . TO THE SLAUGHTER
THE EVIL THAT MEN DO
AFRAID TO SHOOT STRANGERS
FEAR OF THE DARK
THE CLAIRVOYANT
HEAVEN CAN WAIT
RUN TO THE HILLS
2 MINUTES TO MIDNIGHT
IRON MAIDEN
HALLOWED BE THY NAME
THE TROOPER
SANCTUARY

"Hallowed Be Thy Name" (live) (October 1993).

(continued from page 98)

Studios on August 28 and released on VHS under the moniker *Raising Hell*.

Two live CDs featuring Dickinson were released after his departure: *A Real Live One*, which featured eleven songs recorded in 1992, and *A Real Dead One*, which included twelve songs recorded in 1992 and 1993. Both releases do a remarkable job of capturing the energy of an Iron Maiden concert. As a live band, they were unstoppable and put every effort into perfecting their live performances. Supporting Iron Maiden in concert was certainly a challenge for any band, regardless of experience.

But those live performances were in the past. Iron Maiden had lost yet another frontman and the search was on for a replacement, raising all sorts of questions. Could they recapture the energy and chemistry of their mid-'80s heyday? Who on earth could replace Bruce Dickinson? How would fans react to the replacement? Would the band simply hire a Dickinson clone or somebody entirely different? Only time would tell.

Advertisement for No Prayer on the Road U.K. dates. The lead singer in the opening act would take on a key role in Maiden a few years hence.

1990 *By Ryan LaMar*

06.28	London, GBR
09.19	Milton Keynes, GBR
09.20	Southampton, GBR
09.21	Oxford, GBR
09.23	Dublin, IRE
09.24	Belfast, GBR
09.26	Newcastle, GBR
09.27	Edinburgh, GBR
09.28	Aberdeen, GBR
09.30	Ayr, GBR
10.01	Preston, GBR
10.02	Leicester, GBR
10.04	Liverpool, GBR
10.05	Hull, GBR
10.07	Newport, GBR
10.08	Cambridge, GBR
10.09	Sheffield, GBR
10.11	Derby, GBR
10.12	Manchester, GBR
10.14	Torbay, GBR
10.15	Poole, GBR
10.16	Hanley, GBR
10.18	London, GBR
10.21	Barcelona, ESP
10.23	Cascais, POR
10.25	Madrid, ESP
10.27	San Sebastian, ESP
10.29–30	Paris, FRA
11.01	Brussels, BEL
11.02–03	Leiden, NED
11.05	Copenhagen, DEN
11.08	Drammen, NOR
11.09	Gothenburg, SWE
11.10	Stockholm, SWE
11.12	Helsinki, FIN
11.15	Berlin, GER
11.18	Milan, ITA
11.19	Firenze, ITA
11.20	Rome, ITA
11.21	Treviso, ITA
11.23	Saarbrucken, GER
12.03	Munich, GER
12.04	Stuttgart, GER
12.05	Wurzburg, GER
12.07	Bremen, GER
12.08	Hannover, GER
12.11	Edinburgh, GBR
12.13	Whitley Bay, GBR
12.14–15	Birmingham, GBR
12.17–18	London, GBR
12.20	Genk, BEL
12.21	Dortmund, GER
12.22	Frankfurt, GER

1991

01.13	Halifax, CAN
01.15	Montreal, CAN
01.16	Quebec City, CAN
01.18	Toronto, CAN
01.19	Rochester, USA
01.21	East Rutherford, USA
01.22	Albany, USA
01.23	Worcester, USA
01.25	Providence, USA
01.26	New Haven, USA
01.28	Uniondale, USA
01.29	Philadelphia, USA
01.31	Pittsburgh, USA
02.01	Fairfax, USA
02.02	Charleston, USA
02.04	Detroit, USA
02.05	Cleveland, USA
02.06	Cincinnati, USA
02.15	Houston, USA
02.16	Dallas, USA
02.17	San Antonio, USA
02.19	San Diego, USA
02.20, 22	Long Beach, USA
02.23	Phoenix, USA
02.24	Albuquerque, USA
02.25	Denver, USA
02.27	Kansas City, USA
02.28	Sioux Falls, USA
03.01	Minneapolis, USA
03.03	St. Louis, USA
03.04	Chicago, USA
03.06	Winnipeg, CAN
03.07	Saskatoon, CAN
03.08	Edmonton, USA
03.10	Salem, USA
03.11	Seattle, USA
03.13	Sacramento, USA
03.14	San Francisco, USA
03.15	Bakersfield, USA
03.17	Irvine, USA
03.19	Salt Lake City, USA
03.28–29	Tokyo, JPN
04.01	Omiya, JPN
04.02	Osaka, JPN
04.03	Yokohama, JPN
04.05	Tokyo, JPN
06.29	Roskilde, DEN
09.05	Bern, SUI (rescheduled from 11.17.90 and 11.24.90)
09.06	Winterhur, SUI
09.21	Bol d'Or, FRA

The following dates were announced in a print ad but were eventually superseded by more reliable sources:

02.02	Richmond, USA
02.03	Charlotte, USA
02.05	Johnson City, USA
02.06	Atlanta, USA
02.12	Chattanooga, USA
02.14	Dayton, USA
02.15	Louisville, USA
02.17	Detroit, USA
02.18	San Antonio, USA
02.18	Toledo, USA
02.19	Columbus, USA
02.21	Cleveland, USA
02.23	St. Louis, USA
02.24	Chicago, USA
02.25	Minneapolis, USA
02.26	Sacramento, USA
02.27	San Francisco, USA
02.28	Reno, USA
02.28	Tulsa, USA
03.02	Albuquerque, USA
03.02	Houston, USA
03.03	Denver, USA

03.03	San Antonio, USA	06.21	Tinley Park, USA	09.04	Lausanne, SUI
03.05	Kansas City, USA	06.24	East Troy, USA	09.05	Paris, FRA
03.05	Dallas, USA	06.25	St. Paul, USA	09.07	Mulhouse, FRA
03.06	Odessa, USA	06.27	Denver, USA	09.08	Annecy, FRA
03.07	El Paso, USA	06.28	Salt Lake City, USA	09.10	Beziers, FRA
03.09	Phoenix, USA	06.30	Sacramento, USA	09.12	Reggio Emilia, ITA
03.10	Albuquerque, USA	07.01	San Francisco, USA	09.14	Barcelona, ESP
03.11	Denver, USA	07.02	Irvine, USA	09.17	San Sebastian, ESP
03.13	Reno, USA	07.05	Phoenix, USA		(rescheduled from 09.15
03.15	Sacramento, USA	07.07	San Antonio, USA		and 09.19)
03.17	Long Beach, USA	07.08	Dallas, USA	09.18	Madrid, ESP
03.18	Long Beach, USA	07.09	Kansas City, USA	09.19	Zaragoza, ESP (rescheduled
03.19	Long Beach, USA	07.11	Atlanta, USA		from 09.16)
03.22	Portland, USA	07.12	Charlotte, USA	09.26	San Juan, PUR
03.23	Vancouver, USA	07.14	St. Louis, USA	10.01–02	Mexico City, MEX
03.25	Seattle, USA	07.15	Nashville, USA		(rescheduled from
		07.17	Miami, USA		09.24–25)
		07.25	Buenos Aires, ARG	10.04	Guadalajara, MEX
1992		07.28	Montevideo, URU		(rescheduled from 09.26)
		07.31	Rio de Janeiro, BRA	10.09	Caracas, VEN
06.02	Norwich, GBR	08.01	Sao Paulo, BRA	10.10	Caracas, VEN
06.05	Reykjavik, ISL	08.04	Porto Alegre, BRA	10.20	Auckland, NZL
06.08	New York City, USA	08.15	Mannheim, GER	10.22	Melbourne, AUS
06.11	Rochester, USA	08.17	Brussels, BEL	10.23	Sydney, AUS
06.13	Quebec City, CAN	08.22	Donington, GBR	10.26	Nagoya, JPN
06.14	Ottawa, CAN	08.25	Copenhagen, DEN	10.28	Fukuoka, JPN
06.16	Montreal, CAN	08.27	Helsinki, FIN	10.30	Hiroshima, JPN
06.17	Toronto, CAN	08.29	Stockholm, SWE	11.01–02	Osaka, JPN
06.19	Cuyahoga Falls, USA	08.31	Oslo, NOR	11.03	Yokohama, JPN
06.20	Clarkston, USA	09.02	Den Bosch, NED	11.04	Tokyo, JPN

Notes: A tour itinerary in fan club magazine No. 31 suggests a November 6, 1990, date in Copenhagen was cancelled.

Per Paul Davies, the June 28, 1990, show was not a Maiden gig but a Bruce solo gig in which Nicko, Dave, and Steve joined onstage with Bruce and Janick to play "The Trooper." Technically, it's a Maiden performance.

November 30 and December 1, 1990, dates in Turin and Udine, Italy, sometimes turn up, though the Italian promoter indicates they never occurred. Also, it is common knowledge that the band cancelled dates between Saarbrucken on November 23 and Munich on December 3 due to Bruce's illness. According to fan club magazine No. 31, the band was scheduled to play Toulouse, France, on November 28. An ad in Metal Hammer indicated forthcoming shows in Paris (October 29–30), Grenoble (November 25), Toulouse (November 28), and Marseille (November 29). Ticket stub evidence indicates the November 28 date was actually rescheduled from the 26th.

The scheduling for the American leg of the No Prayer tour in 1991 was a nightmare. So many different tour schedules were published by the band and media that the only way to verify the dates and locations is by individual artifacts, such as tickets, flyers, local newspaper tour listings, and periodical reviews of shows already played. The chaos of the scheduling was so bad that fan club president Keith Wilfort addressed the problem in fan club magazine No. 33.

We do know, however, that various newspapers reported the cancellation of the following 1991 shows: February 8–10 in Miami, Orlando, and Tampa, Florida, and February 13 in Atlanta, Georgia. The St. Petersburg Times reported Bruce had contracted bronchitis. The Chilean government cancelled a July 21, 1992, show in Santiago due to "religious pressure."

Unreliable sources report a September 17, 1992, date in Caceras, Spain, which conflicts with the San Sebastian date.

1993

03.25	Faro, POR
03.27	Madrid, ESP
03.28	San Sebastian, ESP
03.29	Barcelona, ESP
04.05	Ostrava, CZE
04.06	Bratislava, SVK
04.07	Vienna, AUT
04.09	Arnhem, NED
04.10	Paris, FRA
04.11	Berlin, GER (rescheduled from 03.30)
04.13	Wurzburg, GER
04.15	Hannover, GER
04.16	Bremen, GER
04.17	Essen, GER
04.19	Stuttgart, GER
04.20	Saarbrucken, GER
04.21	Augsburg, GER
04.23	Gothenburg, SWE
04.25	Bourges, FRA
04.27	Turin, ITA
04.28	Maiano, ITA
04.29	Firenze, ITA
04.30–31	Rome, ITA
05.02	Priolo, ITA
05.05	Naples, ITA
05.06	Bologna, ITA
05.08	Genova, ITA
05.09	Milan, ITA
05.11	Toulon, FRA
05.13	Grenoble, FRA
05.14	Nancy, FRA
05.16	Sheffield, GBR
05.17	London, GBR
05.19	Manchester, GBR
05.20	Birmingham, GBR
05.21	Glasgow, GBR
05.23	Dublin, IRE
05.24	Belfast, GBR
05.27	Neuchatel, SUI
06.02–04	Moscow, RUS (rescheduled from 04.02–04)
08.27–28	London, GBR

Note: the band cancelled a May 3 show at Reggio di Calabria, Italy, due to security concerns.

With new singer Blaze Bayley outside Barnyard Studios in Essex, England, where the band recorded *The X Factor*.
Mick Hutson/Redferns/Getty Images

7 MEN ON THE EDGE

THE BEGINNINGS OF THE BLAZE BAYLEY YEARS, 1994–1996

"I really didn't think I would get the job because my voice is so different than Bruce Dickinson's. He's much more of a technical singer and I'm much more of a blood-and-guts singer, ya know? . . . When they chose me, I was very, very surprised that they had chosen somebody with a very different voice."

—Blaze Bayley, quoted by Todd Newton, *blasting-zone.com*, 2007

When Bruce Dickinson left Iron Maiden in 1993, the metal landscape had changed enormously. Rock and metal had reigned supreme during the 1980s, when the biggest bands in the world included Bon Jovi, Def Leppard, AC/DC, Van Halen, and Iron Maiden. By 1992 bands of that ilk suddenly seemed somewhat out of fashion. They still retained large fan bases, but things just weren't the same.

After Nirvana broke huge in the autumn of 1991, angst-ridden and distortion-heavy grunge, led by punk- and indie-inspired bands such as, Pearl Jam, Soundgarden, and Alice in Chains, were suddenly stealing headlines, selling millions of records, and playing to thousands of new fans. It screwed up the whole metal scene—bands were unceremoniously dropped from labels, magazine subscriptions fell, and ticket sales slowed.

"I don't feel that we belong to any genre of music," Janick Gers told David Lee Wilson of *kaos2000.net* in 1999. "People talk about heavy metal coming back—to me it is just music and I don't categorize music. . . . I think that media people do, and they have to in order to write about it, but to me it is

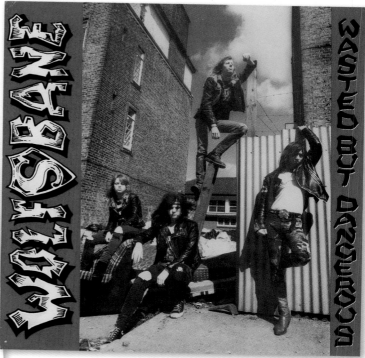

Blaze Bayley had fronted the Midlands band Wolfsbane since 1984. The group had released two LPs on Rick Rubin's Def American label, and three demos prior to that, including 1988's *Wasted But Dangerous*. © Denis O'Regan/CORBIS (left)

either good music or bad music. When I listen to something I think, 'Hey, that is really good.' I don't think 'That is heavy metal so I like it.' I don't see it in those terms. A good song is a good song if it is a good slow song or a good fast song."

Regardless of the 1993 metal landscape, Maiden needed a new singer. But Steve Harris later admitted that he didn't immediately come to that conclusion. "I was a bit down when Bruce left," he later confessed in an interview published at *musicrooms.net* in 2010. "I was going through a divorce, probably at my lowest ebb ever, and for a couple of hours I thought about finishing Iron Maiden. Then I thought, 'What are you doing? Just get out there and bloody do it.'"

The band knew they wanted somebody British. The number of aspiring frontmen they eventually auditioned has been lost to time, but from a lengthy list they picked a chap named Blaze Bayley.

In 2007, Bayley described the audition process to Todd Newton of *blasting-zone.com*: "You have to learn ten of the classic Maiden songs and sing them, and at the second audition you're invited back to sing in the studio as well so they would know what you sound like live and on the record. I really didn't think I would get the job because my voice is so different than Bruce Dickinson's. He's much more of a technical singer and I'm much more of a blood-and-guts singer, ya know? I'm more about the emotion and the passion of the song. When they chose me, I was very, very surprised that they had chosen somebody with a very different voice."

The band takes a break from recording *The X Factor* at Barnyard. They were working not just with a new singer, but also with a different producer—Nigel Green—following the retirement of longtime collaborator Martin Birch. *Mick Hutson/Redferns/Getty Images*

Blaze Bayley was born Bayley Alexander Cooke on May 29, 1963, in Birmingham, England—the natural birthplace of heavy metal. Bayley had fronted the Midlands band Wolfsbane since 1984. Whereas Judas Priest, for example, later hired an American named Tim Owens who sounded exactly like a young Rob Halford and had been fronted a Priest tribute band, Bayley's voice is nothing like Dickinson's.

But would Maiden fans accept and welcome a new frontman?

The X Factor was the first album to feature a new Maiden singer since *Killers* in 1981. Indeed, not only was the band working with a new singer, but also with a different producer following the retirement of the revered Martin Birch. They

hooked up with Nigel Green at Barnyard Studios in Essex in mid-1994. "We wanted to make it sound very 1990s, very modern-sounding but still with the identity of Iron Maiden," Dave Murray explained to Gary James in 1995 (*storyofthestars.com*).

In addition to his writing duties (he receives full credit or shares writing credit on ten of LP's eleven tracks), Harris also took on the bulk of the album's production work with Green. "In studio we were listening to these different takes and each song had this unknown factor to them," Blaze Bayley told Ram Samudrala in 1996, "plus the album itself had unknown factors, you know, new engineer and a new singer, and so we decided to call it *The X Factor*, *X* representing something that is unknown."

(continued on page 116)

THE X FACTOR

BY MICK WALL

WHEN IRON MAIDEN RELEASED *The X Factor* in 1995, the American musical landscape had changed tremendously since they last toured there four years earlier. Musically eclipsed by the heavier, more outrageous metal of thrash-generation giants like Metallica and Megadeth—both of whom enjoyed their first U.S. No. 1 albums during this period—and the ground-zero approach of grunge gods like Nirvana, Pearl Jam, and Soundgarden—who rejected the metal goliaths of the '80s—Iron Maiden was looking old and outdated. Dickinson seemed to agree, walking out on the band in 1993.

The irony was that what Dickinson saw as Maiden's inability to break out of its fantasy metal subcategory was about to be overcome by Steve Harris' sudden need to make his music say more than ever before. Recently divorced from his wife and former childhood sweetheart, Lorraine, after sixteen years together, Harris said the making of *The X Factor* was preceded by "probably the toughest time I've ever faced in my life."

Maiden replaced Dickinson with Wolfsbane frontman Blaze Bayley, who thus found himself singing painfully autobiographical Harris numbers like "Sign of the Cross," the desperately dark eleven-minute opus that opens *The X Factor*, as well as "Fortunes of War" and "Judgement of Heaven," both of which detail not just the bassist's feelings about the disintegration of his marriage but the huge emotional rift he felt within himself and, because of Dickinson's departure, the band itself.

Most wincing of all, "Blood on the World's Hands" speaks specifically of his fears for the future of his four young children. All of this emotion was compounded by some of the most brutal, apocalyptic metal Iron Maiden had ever produced—most of which might have been better balanced had Dickinson still been there to sing it for them. With Bayley's sonorous vocals now driving the numbers forward, the air was one of almost unrelenting gloom and doom.

Even the six tracks Harris co-wrote with Bayley and/or guitarist Janick Gers—including, most powerfully, "Look for the Truth," "The Aftermath," "The Edge of Darkness," "2 A.M.," "Lord of the Flies," and "The Unbeliever"—are monstrous dirges that all seem to be about the same things: isolation, desperation, the end of all things good.

It is no coincidence that the most upbeat track on *The X Factor* was the only one that wasn't written or co-written by Harris: the Bayley/Gers composition "Man on the Edge." And even that, despite being chosen as the first single from the album, sounded bleak and brittle compared to the long string of hits the band had most recently enjoyed in the United Kingdom with Dickinson.

Released worldwide in October 1995, *The X Factor* was largely ignored by the American media, where the album did not even crack the Top 100. Things weren't much better in the United Kingdom, where it received the worst reviews of Iron Maiden's career. Critics either didn't like Bayley's voice or they found the new material "too dark."

Nevertheless, the album reached No. 8 in the band's homeland, and Harris would go on to cite *The X Factor* as one of his three all-time favorite Maiden albums. "I love it that it takes you a bit longer to get into it," he told me. "The best albums are all usually like that." He went on to describe it as "a special album."

It was. But not perhaps in the way Harris had intended.

"Man on the Edge" (September 1995).

(continued from page 113)

In true Maiden form, the album's lyrics made reference to popular culture, mostly films and books, and explored the darker side of human nature. "The Edge of Darkness" references the 1979 Vietnam movie *Apocalypse Now*, and "Man on the Edge" was inspired by the 1993 Michael Douglas movie *Falling Down*. The album also includes the epic "Sign of the Cross," clocking in at eleven minutes—their longest song since the classic "Rime of the Ancient Mariner."

"I suppose one of the biggest things was that we did 'Man on the Edge'," Bayley later said about his songwriting contributions (Newton, 2007), "which was all my lyrics and melodies . . . and that was the song they chose to be the first single from the album. That was absolutely fantastic, ya know? It was a dream come true for me . . . that one of my songs would become a Top 10 single across Europe in the rock charts. . . . It was like a fantasy."

The album was completed in August 1995 and released in October. Many fans did not warm to Bayley's vocal style, and it showed in *The X Factor*'s U.K. sales: the album peaked at No. 8, their lowest showing since *Killers*. Dickinson had acquired such a loyal following that when the band chose to find a replacement, only the most loyal fans stuck around— and even many of them were not keen on the new album.

Nor were the critics. One review in particular, written by Chris Watts and published in *Kerrang!*, got Steve Harris'

temper boiling. The bassist stormed into the magazine's offices looking for Watts. However, the rock scribe was not around (thankfully for Watts), so Harris calmed down and went over to the pub with some of the magazine's other writers.

In 1998 Harris told *Kerrang!*, "When I came in I was really wound up. I'd just spent a year of my life working silly hours doing this album—which I still love and I don't give a fuck what anyone says—and some wanker has completely dismissed it in one sentence. I felt like he was having a joke at our expense. Another time I might have laughed at it, but I thought it was out of order. I wanted to see if he'd say it to my face. He could have been built like a brick shithouse and beat me to a pulp, but I had to have a word. It just ain't right. You know me, that ain't my style. I felt bad afterwards. I thought, fuck, I'm glad he wasn't there, 'cos I probably would have fucking whacked him, or at least got him against a wall or done something stupid, and that gets you nowhere."

The X Factour road jaunt commenced on September 28, 1995, in Israel where the band had never played before,

(continued on page 120)

SETLIST SELECTIONS

THE X FACTOUR

MAN ON THE EDGE
WRATHCHILD
HEAVEN CAN WAIT
LORD OF THE FLIES
FORTUNES OF WAR
BLOOD ON THE WORLD'S HANDS
AFRAID TO SHOOT STRANGERS
THE EVIL THAT MEN DO
THE AFTERMATH
SIGN OF THE CROSS
2 MINUTES TO MIDNIGHT
THE EDGE OF DARKNESS
FEAR OF THE DARK
THE CLAIRVOYANT
IRON MAIDEN
THE NUMBER OF THE BEAST
HALLOWED BE THY NAME
THE TROOPER

BRUCE DICKINSON

ACCIDENT OF BIRTH

THE NEW ALBUM

BRUCE DICKINSON - voices • ADRIAN SMITH - guitar
ROY Z - guitar, mellotron and piano • EDDIE CASILLIAS - bass • DAVID INGRAHAM - drums
PRODUCED BY: ROY Z

OUT 12th May
Limited Edition CD Poster Pack In Slipcase / MC / LP

"Maiden are at a decline big-time now and everything that's associated with that whole era of music is being seen as old and tired and it's had its day," then-solo artist Bruce Dickinson commented in 1996. © Presselect/Alamy

"Shoot All the Clowns" was a single off Dickinson's second solo album, 1994's *Balls to Picasso*. His *Accident of Birth* LP was released in 1997.

BRUCE DICKINSON
THE NEW SINGLE
SHOOT ALL THE CLOWNS

AVAILABLE ON

• 7" CLEAR VINYL WITH EXCLUSIVE TRACK
• LIMITED EDITION 12" GIANT FOLD OUT POSTER PLUS EXCLUSIVE TRACKS
• CD 1 OF A 2 CD SET INCLUDES 4 FREE PRINTS PLUS EXCLUSIVE TRACKS PREVIOUSLY UNRELEASED FROM THE "LOST" KEITH OLSEN ALBUM
• CD 2 TO COMPLETE THE SET WITH FURTHER EXCLUSIVE TRACKS FROM THE "LOST" KEITH OLSEN ALBUM

ON TOUR · OCTOBER
• MONDAY 10TH – BRADFORD · RIOS
• TUESDAY 11TH – GLASGOW · GARAGE
• THURSDAY 13TH – BUCKLEY · TIVOLI
• FRIDAY 14TH NORWICH · OVAL
• SATURDAY 15TH – DUDLEY · JB's
• MONDAY 17TH – BRISTOL · BIERKELLER
• TUESDAY 18TH – LONDON · MARQUEE

The X Factour, Nottingham, England, February 2, 1996. *Mick Hutson/Redferns/Getty Images*

STAMPEDING THRU TEXAS
BRITISH METAL LEGENDS RETURN!!!
SNEAKERS & GREG WILSON Present CMC RECORDS INTERNATIONAL ARTISTS
IRON MAIDEN
"X-FACTOR" TOUR 1996 WARNING: THIS SHOW WILL BE SOLD OUT
Plus Guests FEAR FACTORY
FRI. MARCH 15
SNEAKERS
11431 PERRIN BEITEL * 653 9176
SAN ANTONIO, TEXAS * TICKETS ON SALE NOW at TICKETMASTER
POSTER DESIGN & LAYOUT ©JERRY CLAYWORTH 1996 (P.O. BOX 47655 * SAN ANTONIO, TX 78265)

Venues for The X Factour, Bayley's first tour with Maiden, were noticeably smaller than those from the band's previous tours. The second of these two club shows, on April 2 at Soma in San Diego, was cancelled due to Blaze Bayley's bronchitis.

IRON MAIDEN
THE · X · FACTOUR
SPECIAL GUEST FEAR FACOTRY
TIXS JUST $15
APRIL 2 8:30PM
SOMA LIVE
INFO: 239-SOMA
5305 METRO STREET
ALL AGES!
tickets at the following SOMA outlets only:
OFf the RecoRd (hiLLcreSt & CoLlege).
loU's Records (ENcinitas)
& MUsic traDEr (P.B., pOwaY & eL CajoN)
produced by Big Dummy Productions.

(continued from page 116)

and wound up in Mexico on September 7, 1996. They also journeyed to South Africa and Bulgaria for the first time. The tour included opening performances from Fear Factory, My Dying Bride, and Psycho Hotel.

The venues were noticeably smaller than those to which the band had become accustomed. "Maiden are at a decline big-time now and everything that's associated with that whole era of music is being seen as old and tired and it's had its day," commented Dickinson, now a solo artist, in 1996 (*moshville.co.uk*). "Even if traditional metal ever does come back, it's much more likely to be a *Paradise Lost*–type vibe. You know, something that's new rather than some old hair band from the '80s getting back together."

Indeed, not only was Maiden struggling, but the whole metal scene was collapsing. "We understand that in America, the rock thing has dropped off—there's still fans out there but not as many as ten years ago," observed Murray (James, 1995). "We're over here doing a club tour, trying to rekindle the same interest again. It's incredible how it died, unfortunately. But we're still out there touring and doing it."

Even disregarding what Maiden fans thought of the newly amended line-up and relatively low ticket sales by Maiden's previous standards, it must have been difficult for Bayley to come into a widely established band and step into the shoes of one of heavy metal's most iconic frontmen.

In 2009, Bayley told me about his experiences on tour with Maiden in an interview for *Fireworks* magazine: "A lot of it was so intense because when Maiden starts rolling it's such as huge beast to get on that road and start that when it goes nothing stops it. That's it. You are on the train or you are in its way! Nothing will stop it. That is intense. There's no choice to take it easy—you're just doing it every day. With interviews you talk until you can't speak and you still have to perform at the highest possible level to do the gig. A lot of fantastic experiences—we played some huge venues."

It was reported that at Santiago, Chile, on August 29, 1996, one fan spat at Bayley during the band's performance of "Man on the Edge" and also caused a disruption during "The Trooper." At the end of the song, Harris, along with security, scanned the audience for the offender, who was eventually found and removed from the venue before the band would continue.

That alleged incident proved just how much attention Bayley received from overzealous fans. In their minds Maiden was Maiden only with Bruce Dickinson at the front of the stage. Would their reaction have been different if the band had chosen someone other than Bayley? After all, Sammy Hagar followed in the footsteps of David Lee Roth in Van Halen rather well. And Brian Johnson excelled in the role of AC/DC's frontman after Bon Scott's death.

It was a moot point for Dave Murray. "We ignore negativity," he was quoted as saying on *scritube.com* in 1998. "That's stage one of it. Also, if Blaze had been in the band and if Bruce had joined, I think Bruce would probably [have] had the same thing. Bruce was in the band for a long time and he established himself. It doesn't matter who we had coming in, he would have been hit. Blaze is the best and the right singer for this band."

And how did Blaze Bayley get along with the band's iconic mascot, Eddie?

"Yeah, Eddie's a cunt as far as I'm concerned," he joked with me in 2009. "He's cursed me. That bastard. Fuck him! If I ever see him out on the night time I shall have him. I was doing the last gig of The X Factour tour and it was in France and I'm singing 'Iron Maiden' and that's when Eddie's supposed to walk out and everybody was laughing. I'm looking; I think, 'Are my fly's open?' Then I look behind me: Eddie's only come out, he's tripped, he's gone faced down, and he's being dragged off like a drunk by five or ten crew members. Everybody's in stitches and then I started laughing so much I couldn't sing."

Unfortunately the tour was not as successful as past road jaunts; some shows were cancelled and the North American leg ended sooner than scheduled after Bayley suffered from respiratory allergies.

As the band came off the road, a compilation called *Best of the Beast*, including the new single "Virus," hit store shelves. But it was time for some new material. 🏴󠁧󠁢󠁥󠁮󠁧󠁿

"Virus" (September 1996). The band released three single versions containing different B-sides: one featuring covers of the Who and UFO, one featuring "Sanctuary" and "Wrathchild" from the *Metal for Muthas* compilation, and one featuring "Prowler" and "Invasion" from *The Soundhouse Tapes*. More significantly, it was the first Maiden single since 1980's "Women in Uniform" to not feature on a studio LP.

1995

By Ryan LaMar

09.28	Jerusalem, ISR
09.29	Haifa, ISR
09.30	Tel Aviv, ISR
10.05	Johannesburg, RSA
10.07	Durban, RSA
10.09	Cape Town, RSA
10.14	Athens, GRE
10.15	Salonika, GRE
10.16	Sofia, BUL
10.17	Bucharest, ROU
10.20	Budapest, HUN
10.21	Zilina, SVK
10.22	Prague, CZE
10.24	Warsaw, POL
10.27	Helsinki, FIN
10.29	Stockholm, SWE
10.30	Oslo, NOR
11.01	Gothenburg, SWE
11.02	Copenhagen, DEN
11.04	Wolverhampton, GBR
11.05	Glasgow, GBR
11.06	Manchester, GBR
11.08	Leeds, GBR
11.09	Newport, GBR
11.10	London, GBR
11.12	Cologne, GER
11.13	Deinze, BEL
11.14	Bielefeld, GER
11.16	Paris, FRA
11.18	Pamplona, ESP
11.20	Barcelona, ESP
11.21	Madrid, ESP
11.22	Cascais, POR
11.24	Granada, ESP
11.26	Turin, ITA
11.27	Modena, ITA
11.28	Rome, ITA
11.30	Milan, ITA
12.01	Firenze, ITA
12.02	Pordenone, ITA
12.03	Bolzano, ITA

12.05	Geneva, SUI
12.06	Zurich, SUI
12.07	Furth, GER
12.09	Hannover, GER
12.10	Leipzig, GER
12.12	Bremen, GER
12.13	Hamburg, GER
12.14	Berlin, GER
12.16	Vienna, AUT
12.17	Munich, GER
12.19	Stuttgart, GER
12.20	Neu Isenburg, GER
12.22	Cologne, GER
12.23	Zwolle, NED

1996

01.12–13	Athens, GRE
01.14	Gozo, MLT
01.16	Catania, ITA
01.17	Bari, ITA
01.18	Ancona, ITA
01.19	Montichiari, ITA
01.21	Ljubljana, SLO
01.23	Lyon, FRA
01.24	Nice, FRA
01.26	Montpellier, FRA
01.27	Montluçon, FRA
01.28	Nancy, FRA
01.30	Belfast, GBR
01.31	Dublin, IRE
02.02	Nottingham, GBR
02.08	Quebec City, CAN
02.09	Montreal, CAN
02.11	Toronto, CAN
02.13	Boston, USA
02.14	Providence, USA
02.16	New York City, USA
02.17	Philadelphia, USA
02.19	Baltimore, USA

02.20	Old Bridge, USA
02.21	Harrisburg, USA
02.23	Pittsburgh, USA
02.24	Detroit, USA
02.25	Cleveland, USA
02.27	Cincinnati, USA
02.28	Ft. Wayne, USA
02.29	Chicago, USA
03.02	Milwaukee, USA
03.03	Minneapolis, USA
03.05	St. Louis, USA
03.07	Atlanta, USA
03.08	Orlando, USA
03.09	Ft. Lauderdale, USA
03.10	Jacksonville, USA
03.12	Memphis, USA
03.14	Houston, USA
03.15	San Antonio, USA
03.16	Dallas, USA
03.17	Lubbock, USA
03.19	Albuquerque, USA
03.20	Denver, USA
03.21	Salt Lake City, USA
03.23	Seattle, USA
04.04–05	Hollywood, USA
04.11	Tokyo, JPN
04.12	Nagoya, JPN
04.14	Fukuoka, JPN
04.16	Osaka, JPN
04.17–18	Tokyo, JPN
06.22	Kauhajoki, FIN
06.30	Dessel, BEL

07.06	Ringe, DEN	08.14	Huesca, ESP	08.27	Porto Alegre, BRA
07.13	Weert, NED	08.16	Colmar, FRA	08.29	Santiago, CHI
08.09	Murcia, ESP	08.17	Cunlhat, FRA	08.31,	
08.10	Cadiz, ESP	08.24	Sao Paulo, BRA	09.01	Buenos Aires, ARG
08.11	Caceres, ESP	08.25	Curitiba, BRA	09.04	Mexico City, MEX
08.13	Albacete, ESP	08.26	Rio de Janeiro, BRA	09.07	Monterrey, MEX

Notes: According to one reliable Czech source, 1994 gigs in the Czech Republic, Hungary, and Romania were cancelled three days after they went on sale. It is speculated that this was due to Blaze's motorcycle accident, but that happened long after the first date (February 2) would have passed. The accident is only mentioned in fan club magazine No. 45, which is the last magazine of 1994. Fan club magazine No. 44, which came out in the late summer, did not mention the accident, but it did mention that any rumors for upcoming tour dates or album release parties were false. Chances are that these dates were pushed forth by an overzealous promoter.

The September 28, 1995, show in Jerusalem was Blaze Bayley's first with the band—and Maiden's first in Israel.

The Lebanese government denied the band and their tour entry into that country for a scheduled October 12, 1995, show in Beirut.

Some sources suggest the January 14, 1996, Malta date may have actually occurred on the 15th, and that the March 14, 1996, Houston date may have been on the 13th.

Sources listing a March 12, 1996, New Orleans date are clearly unreliable, as it conflicts with the Memphis date.

U.S. newspapers reported the cancellation of the following 1996 dates due to Blaze's bronchitis: March 24 in Vancouver, British Columbia; March 25 in Portland, Oregon; March 27 and 28 in Sacramento and San Francisco, California; March 30 in Las Vegas, Nevada; March 31 in Riverside, California; April 1 in Phoenix, Arizona; and April 2 in San Diego, California.

Fan club magazine No. 49 listed the August 27, 1996, show at Porto Alegre, Brazil, yet Blaze made no mention of it in an in-depth rundown of the South American shows that appeared in No. 53.

The keen observer realized that Blaze Bayley was not especially well-appreciated by Maiden loyalists. On the other hand, perhaps fans and critics were too loyal to Dickinson. Did they give Bayley a proper chance? *AP Photo/Archiv*

8 LIGHTNING STRIKES TWICE
THE RELEASE OF *VIRTUAL XI,* 1997–1998

"We're not cool. There's other new things going on. The only time we were trendy was in '83, '84. We're not cool 'cos we've been around so long, but I'm proud of *Virtual XI.*"

—Steve Harris, quoted in *Kerrang!,* 1998

Iron Maiden entered Barnyard Studios in Essex with Nigel Green sometime in 1997 to begin work on their second album with Blaze Bayley. The new Maiden frontman had acquired nothing but respect for Steve Harris.

"It's difficult to describe someone you work so close with because he's a friend really," Bayley told *Kerrang!* in 1998. "But it's been a real thrill for me to work and write songs with Steve. He's one of those people that doesn't give up easily, whether his music or on the football field. In my previous band I was forced to make so many compromises and I see now how naive I was. With Iron Maiden, we're fighting exactly the same battles but Steve has the courage to say, 'No, fuck you, I'm not doing it.'"

Released in March 1998, *Virtual XI* included extensive keyboards handled not by the band's usual session player, Michael Kenney, but rather by Harris. The album also featured significantly less songwriting input from Janick Gers than other releases from his previous seven years in the band. *Virtual XI* is also notable for some significantly long songs, namely, the "The Angel and the Gambler" (nine and a half minutes), "The Clansman," (eight and a half minutes), and "Don't Look to the Eyes of a Stranger" (eight minutes).

VIRTUAL XI

BY GARRY BUSHELL

VIRTUAL XI WAS THE MAKE-OR-BREAK ALBUM of Blaze Bayley's tenure.

It broke it.

Released in March 1998, Maiden's eleventh studio effort isn't a bad album, but neither is it a particularly good one, and the band needed a classic after the dross of *The X Factor*. That hellishly gloomy album found Maiden in a dark, brooding place—as cheerful as Ibsen with hemorrhoids. The band called it "melancholic," the sales figures said mediocre. It went Top 10 in the United Kingdom, but peaked at 147 in the United States. It also failed to notch a single gold disc anywhere in the world—a band first.

On the plus side *Virtual XI* boasted two very good songs. "Futureal" kick-started the album with a terrific, driving riff. Although a bit redolent of *Fear of the Dark*'s "Be Quick or Be Dead," this instantly addictive upbeat number boasts a chorus as catchy as razor wire, soaring guitar breaks, and imaginative Bayley lyrics about being hunted in a nightmarish virtual reality.

The album's other standout track is Steve Harris' "The Clansman," a formidable anthem inspired by the frequently ahistorical Mel Gibson movie *Braveheart*. A sweeping, atmospheric masterpiece, the song moves effortlessly between the loneliness of the Highlands and the righteous aggression of the Scottish rebellion. Brilliant live, it features Celtic-tinged guitar solos, handsome harmonies, and a rabble-rousing chorus.

Unfortunately, *Virtual XI* also features Maiden's worst composition of the decade (or ever): "The Angel and the Gambler," a song that sucks like an airplane toilet. The opening riff of this overlong, keyboard-heavy snoozeathon sounds like it's been popping Mogadons, and the chorus is as irritating as thrush. They repeat it a ridiculous twenty-two times—vinyl listeners might swear the needle is stuck. Even the Janick Gers and Dave Murray guitar solos are unexceptional. Maiden aimed for a Who-style epic but missed by a country mile.

Another anemic offering, "When Two Worlds Collide," also repeats on itself like a bad mantra. This compulsion to endlessly reiterate is the album's biggest downfall (the turgid "Educated Fool" also suffers from it).

Virtual XI clearly misses the sure production of Martin Birch. Indeed, the whole sound is wrong; the guitars are too thin, the bass insufficiently urgent. And while the overall mood is lighter than *The X Factor*, the heavy use of keyboards is a side step into another creative cul-de-sac.

A couple of the other numbers fare a little better. "Lightning Strikes Twice" offers a neat, teasing riff, a decent chorus, and sparkling guitar duels, while the eight-minute "Don't Look to the Eyes of a Stranger" has pace but is hamstrung by a will-this-do? riff.

The album ends with "Como Estais Amigos," a tribute to the Falklands War dead on both sides. It's a bold stab at an emotive rock lament that doesn't quite cut it. Nice guitar harmonies, though.

Virtual XI peaked at No. 16 in the United Kingdom and 124 in the United States. Like its predecessor it didn't go gold anywhere—it remains the band's all-time worst-seller. Clearly, the Blaze Bayley experiment wasn't working on record or onstage (for a second time their world tour was cut short due to the singer's "allergic reaction" to stage effects). "Don't you think I can save yer life?" he asked (over and over again) on "The Angel and the Gambler." Well, one thing was for sure: he couldn't save Maiden. The band needed to pull something big out of the bag with their next album or accept that their reign as the living gods of metal was coming to an end. 🏴󠁧󠁢󠁥󠁮󠁧󠁿

Barnyard Studios, Essex, England. *All Mick Hutson/Redferns/Getty Images*

"The Angel and the Gambler" (March 1998).

"We didn't approach this record any differently than we've always done," Harris explained when interviewed by Bob Nalbandian of *hardradio.com*. "We just went in and recorded it and we just wrote whatever felt right during that particular time. 'The Angel and the Gambler' is actually a good example because when I came up with that song idea, I put it on a mini tape recorder while I was driving down the motorway, and I distinctly remember saying to myself . . . 'this reminds me of the Who meets UFO.' So I just took it in that direction."

The album was something of a minor disaster. Initial sales indicated that *Virtual XI* was the poorest selling album in Maiden history, shifting less than one million units worldwide. The reviews were not exactly overwhelming, either. Perhaps, after all, the band had made the wrong decision hiring Bayley. It's certainly true to the keen observer that he was not especially well-liked by Maiden loyalists. On the other hand, perhaps fans and critics were too loyal to Dickinson. Had Maiden fans given Bayley a proper chance? Were they too harsh?

"It's almost like we'd get worried if we got a good review!" Harris explained in *Kerrang!*. "My daughter's homework reports are better than our reviews. I suppose at times you feel like you're up against everything. Every time we do an album we have to prove ourselves again. But in a weird way that works for you, because you fight even harder to show people you can still cut it. It gives you an edge. It's funny. You don't tend to remember the good reviews, but the bad ones you do. It's the bad ones that fire you up and make you think, 'Fuck them, we'll show 'em.' It gives you a bit of an attitude again. It's a challenge."

Despite any motivation provided by two poorly received albums, slipping sales raised all sorts of sordid questions. Had fans moved on to other bands? Should Maiden be left in the past like an historical relic?

"We're not cool," Steve Harris admitted to *Kerrang!*. "There's other new things going on. The only time we were trendy was in '83, '84. We're not cool 'cos we've been around so long, but I'm proud of [*Virtual XI*]. There's no compromise, as usual. We still do what we do. I'm proud of that."

Perhaps the poor sales were due to the fact that metal was no longer in vogue in some parts of the world, particularly in America, where the success of Nirvana earlier in the decade had prompted a major-label bonanza for alt- and indie-rock acts. "In Europe [heavy metal is] still very popular," Murray told Gary James in 1999 (*harbinger.org*). "It's thriving. We've been made to understand in America it's really dropped off.

"The Angel and the Gambler" picture disc.

"Futureal" (July 1998) enhanced CD and 7-inch single. The former featured the video for "The Angel and the Gambler."

On the U.S. leg of the *Virtual XI* tour, Bayley had to face up to boos and heckles, and as with The X Factour, half of the North American leg had to be cancelled when the singer suffered allergic reactions to stage props. The July 18 San Diego date advertised here was played on August 3. Denver (July 22) wasn't rescheduled.

Coors LIGHT
1998 Summer of Stars
UNIVERSAL
UNIVERSAL CONCERTS

METAL MANIA '98
IRON MAIDEN

W.A.S.P.

DIRTY DEEDS

http://www.ironmaiden.com   Artwork taken from ED HUNTER game

July 22 • Paramount Theatre • 7pm

Brought to you by Coors LIGHT   The Silver Bullet
PEPSI

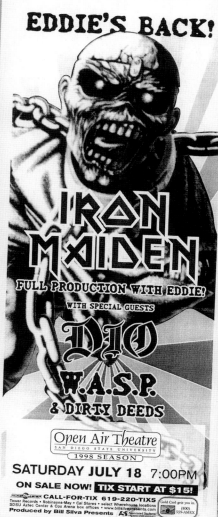

EDDIE'S BACK!

IRON MAIDEN

FULL PRODUCTION WITH EDDIE!

WITH SPECIAL GUESTS

DIO
W.A.S.P.
& DIRTY DEEDS

Open Air Theatre
SAN DIEGO STATE UNIVERSITY
1998 SEASON

SATURDAY JULY 18 7:00PM

ON SALE NOW! TIX START AT $15!

CALL-FOR-TIX 619-220-TIXS
Tower Records • Robinsons-May • Cal Stores • select Wherehouse locations
SDSU Aztec Center & Cox Arena box offices • www.billsilvapresents.com

Gold Card gets you in.
(800) 559-AMEX

Produced by Bill Silva Presents

SETLIST SELECTIONS

VIRTUAL XI TOUR

FUTUREAL
THE ANGEL AND THE GAMBLER
MAN ON THE EDGE
LIGHTNING STRIKES TWICE
HEAVEN CAN WAIT
THE CLANSMAN
WHEN TWO WORLDS COLLIDE
LORD OF THE FLIES
2 MINUTES TO MIDNIGHT
THE EDUCATED FOOL
SIGN OF THE CROSS
HALLOWED BE THY NAME
AFRAID TO SHOOT STRANGERS
THE EVIL THAT MEN DO
THE CLAIRVOYANT
FEAR OF THE DARK
IRON MAIDEN
THE NUMBER OF THE BEAST
THE TROOPER
SANCTUARY

There are still rock fans out there, but not as many as there were ten years ago."

To please the hardcore Maiden enthusiasts and to attract new fans, Harris assisted in the re-release and remastering of the complete Maiden discography up to 1993's *Live at Donington*. It was time for another tour so the band hit the road again.

"*The X Factor* sold about a million copies worldwide and *Virtual XI* is pretty much there too," Murray said (*scritube. co.uk*). "That's still justification to go and tour. Obviously, the mid-'80s were the pinnacle for the band. It's like a wave—it goes up and down and you have to go with the flow. If we sold twenty albums, we'd have to reevaluate, but as far as the album sales go, we can fully justify playing. As long as the fans come to the show, we'll still be there."

And play they did. The *Virtual XI* world tour kicked off with a secret concert at The Oval P.H. (that's "public house,"

or bar, for the uninitiated) in Norwich, England, on April 22, 1998, and finished with a performance at the Monsters of Rock festival in Buenos Aires, Argentina, on December 12 of the same year.

As with the previous tour, the band played much smaller venues than they had with Bruce Dickinson, and ticket sales were certainly not as brisk as they were on past tours. Then there also were some parts of the world that Maiden could not play for economic reasons, such as Australia and New Zealand.

"The logistics to get the equipment over there are very expensive," Murray explained in 1998 (*scritube.co.uk*). "We haven't played over there for years. It seems like the market there is not very receptive for the band at this time. To go there for playing small clubs is not worth it. If the market moves, we'll go there."

DIDI MUSIC - BIG STAR PROMOTION in association with HELTER SKELTER & SANCTUARY

MUSIC presents:

IRON MAIDEN

The ED HUNTER Tour

ΠΑΡΑΣΚΕΥΗ 1 ΟΚΤΩΒΡΙΟΥ 1999
ΓΗΠΕΔΟ ΠΕΡΙΣΤΕΡΙΟΥ
ΚΡΕΣΝΑΣ 82
ΩΡΑ ΕΝΑΡΞΗΣ 20:30
ΕΙΣΙΤΗΡΙΑ ΠΡΟΠΩΛΟΥΝΤΑΙ

www.ironmaiden.com
www.edhunter.com

www.didimusic.gr

Ed Hunter tour, Athens, October 1, 1999.

130 · IRON MAIDEN

SETLIST SELECTIONS

ED HUNTER TOUR

CHURCHILL'S "WE SHALL FIGHT. . ."
SPEECH (ENTRANCE)
ACES HIGH
WRATHCHILD
THE TROOPER
2 MINUTES TO MIDNIGHT
THE CLANSMAN
WASTED YEARS
KILLERS
FUTUREAL
MAN ON THE EDGE
POWERSLAVE
PHANTOM OF THE OPERA
THE EVIL THAT MEN DO
FEAR OF THE DARK
IRON MAIDEN
THE NUMBER OF THE BEAST
HALLOWED BE THY NAME
RUN TO THE HILLS

In the United States, Iron Maiden still struggled to sell their fans on the idea of a new frontman. Bayley had to face up to boos and heckles, and as with The X Factour, half of the North American leg had to be cancelled because Bayley suffered allergic reactions to some stage props.

In February 1999, perhaps inevitably, Bayley announced his departure from the band. "Not the right singer for Iron Maiden at all. Not in the slightest. But his solo stuff is great," opined Paul Di'Anno years later in an interview with Marko Syri. "I think Iron Maiden was a very good experience for him to experience the machine. There is a lot of bullshit that goes on in Iron Maiden."

Looking back on his Maiden years in 2009, Bayley told me: "What's relevant about the Maiden years to me in my life today is that I learned so much and it gave me so much confidence as an artist, as a songwriter, and as a performer. I went from almost a Sunday League to the Premiership in the Champions League in a month! It was an incredible experience but working with Steve Harris, writing songs with him, was such an incredible learning process. I've been in the Top 10 hits in the rock charts all over the world. My voice is on two million albums. I'm on a DVD. I've got six songs on the *Visions of the Beast* DVD and all of that. I look back on those years and there were some absolutely great times." (*Fireworks*)

Bayley continued: "The memories I treasure most—although I don't wanna sound ungrateful for anything that happened to me because I enjoyed it all—were some of the shows where we played smaller gigs like warmup gigs or where there was very limited availability of venues and we had to play somewhere that was like 500 or 5,000 people. It used to make me think, 'Well, this is what Maiden must have been like in the early days when they started.' That felt great to do because I really felt, argh, this is something special. And so did the fans that came to those gigs because you never see Maiden in those small places; it just doesn't happen. I really enjoyed some of those small ones. There's no barrier and you can get to touch the fans and meet people after the show and everything like that. . . . Obviously it's fantastic to play stadiums and all the huge lights and the big sound."

With Bayley's departure, Maiden answered many fans' greatest hope, announcing that Bruce Dickinson would rejoin the band.

"Iron Maiden is an institution and I'm delighted that I'm involved in it, but there was a time that I wasn't delighted, so I quit," Dickinson explained to BBC's Linda Serck and Catherine Turner. "I enjoy making solo albums because over the years it's evolved into more of a genuine personal expression of storytelling and daydreams, and I work in a way that has more control."

Fans received a double shot of good news when it was confirmed that Adrian Smith would return to Iron Maiden as well, giving the band three guitarists and the most revered line-up in Maiden history. "We just try to complement each other so it is not like a battle of who is going to do what," Murray commented to *ultimate-guitar.com*'s Joe Matura regarding the three-guitar attack. "We all feel comfortable enough with each other where we can play how we feel and just enjoy what the other guys are doing. We just want to make music because we enjoy doing that. And what is the point of competing anyway? It's not like you're a soccer player, football player, rugby player, or something like that."

What did the rest of the band have to say?

"To me, this isn't a reunion as such, it is a step forward," Janick Gers explained to David Lee Wilson. "We are moving forward and there is no way that the band is just getting back together for a tour and some money. For starters, this is a new line-up and the second thing is that this is not just a bunch of old farts getting together. I am not against that, and like the Sabbath thing. They are getting together and that is great, but they are not getting together looking forward, they are looking back. . . . We want to go into the studio and make what could possibly be the best Iron Maiden album ever made."

To celebrate the reunion and promote a greatest hits collection named *Ed Hunter* and an *Ed Hunter* PC game, Maiden launched the successful thirty-date *Ed Hunter* tour.

The band rehearsed for several days at Harbour Station in St. John, New Brunswick, Canada, before launching the tour at the same venue on August 11, 1999. Shows in Quebec were followed by appearances in major U.S. markets before the band headed to Europe, where they played to thousands of screaming fans in France, the Netherlands, Germany, Finland, Sweden, Italy, and Spain. The heavily publicized tour finished in Greece on October 1; interestingly, it did not include any U.K. shows.

There would be no stopping Iron Maiden as they entered the new millennium. It would prove to be the most fruitful period of their career.

1998

By Ryan LaMar

04.22	Norwich, GBR
04.26	Lille, FRA
04.27	Nancy, FRA
04.29	Genova, ITA
04.30	Firenze, ITA
05.02	Pesaro, ITA
05.03	Rome, ITA
05.05	Milan, ITA
05.06	Trieste, ITA
05.08	Boblingen, GER
05.09	Hannover, GER
05.10	Dusseldorf, GER
05.12	Paris, FRA
05.13	Leuven, BEL
05.14	Rotterdam, NED
05.16	London, GBR
05.18	Barcelona, ESP
05.19	Madrid, ESP
05.20	Cascais, POR
05.22	Orense, ESP
05.23	Laguna de Duero, ESP
05.24	San Sebastian, ESP
05.26	Valencia, ESP
05.28	Montpellier, FRA
05.30	Ta Qali, MLT
06.26	Chicago, USA
06.27	Columbus, USA
06.28	Hamilton, CAN
06.30	Kalamazoo, USA
07.01	Clarkston, USA
07.02	Cleveland, USA
07.04	Montreal, CAN
07.05	Quebec City, CAN
07.07	New York City, USA
07.10	San Antonio, USA
07.11	McAllen, USA
07.12	Dallas, USA
07.14	Phoenix, USA
07.15	Las Vegas, USA
08.02	Universal City, USA (rescheduled from 07.16)

08.03	San Diego, USA (rescheduled from 07.18)
08.07	Monterrey, MEX
08.09	Mexico City, MEX
09.04	Athens, GRE
09.05	Thessaloniki, GRE
09.07–08	Istanbul, Turkey
09.11	Budapest, HUN
09.12	Katowice, POL
09.13	Prague, CZE
09.15	Munich, GER
09.16	Furth, GER
09.18	Erfurt, GER
09.19	Hamburg, GER
09.20	Copenhagen, DEN
09.23	Helsinki, FIN
09.25	Stockholm, SWE
09.27	Essen, GER
09.28	Berlin, GER
09.29	Leipzig, GER
10.01	Offenbach, GER
10.02	Winterhur, SUI
10.03	Mulhouse, FRA
10.05	Besancon, FRA
10.06	Lyon, FRA
10.08	Zaragoza, ESP
10.09	Albacate, ESP
10.10	Dos Hermanas, ESP
10.13	Nice, FRA
10.14	Pau, FRA (rescheduled from 05.27)
10.15	Clermont-Ferrand, FRA
10.17	Manchester, GBR
10.18	Newcastle, GBR
10.19	Glasgow, GBR
10.21	Nottingham, GBR
10.22	Wolverhampton, GBR
10.23	Newport, GBR
10.25	Sheffield, GBR
10.26	Portsmouth, GBR
11.18	Tokyo, JPN
11.20	Nagoya, JPN
11.21	Osaka, JPN
11.22	Tokyo, JPN

12.02	Rio de Janeiro, BRA
12.05	Sao Paulo, BRA
12.06	Curitiba, BRA
12.12	Buenos Aires, ARG

1999

07.11	St. John, CAN
07.13	Montreal, CAN
07.14	Quebec City, CAN
07.16–17	New York City, USA
07.18	Boston, USA
07.20	Toronto, CAN
07.21	Cleveland, USA
07.23	Milwaukee, USA
07.24	Detroit, USA
07.25	Chicago, USA
07.27	Denver, USA
07.30	Los Angeles, USA
08.05	El Paso, USA
08.07	San Antonio, USA
08.08	Dallas, USA
09.09	Paris, FRA
09.10	Rotterdam, NED
09.12	Hamburg, GER
09.15	Helsinki, FIN
09.17	Stockholm, SWE
09.18	Gothenburg, SWE
09.20	Essen, GER
09.21	Stuttgart, GER
09.23	Milan, ITA
09.25	Barcelona, ESP
09.26	Madrid, ESP
10.01	Athens, GRE

Notes: According to the July 24, 1998, Dynamite Metal News, the band cancelled a string of dates to a throat malady Blaze was suffering: July 19 in San Francisco, California; July 22 in Denver, Colorado; July 24 in Minneapolis, Minnesota; July 25 in Milwaukee, Wisconsin; July 26 in Cincinnati, Ohio; July 28 in Washington, D.C.; July 29 in Baltimore, Maryland; July 31 in Philadelphia, Pennsylvania; August 1 in Hartford, Connecticut; August 2 in Asbury Park, New Jersey; and August 3 in Atlanta, Georgia. Those last two dates were actually taken up by the makeup dates noted.

The band cancelled a December 10, 1998, date due to diplomatic conflict between Chile and the U.K.

Unverifiable sources have indicated that there were December 3 and 4, 1998, shows in Rio de Janeiro and Campinas, Brazil, respectively.

The July 11, 1999, date in St. John, New Brunswick, marked Dickinson's and Smith's returns to the Maiden fold.

Dave Murray's broken finger caused the cancellation of three 1999 U.S. dates: July 31 in San Jose, California; August 2 in Las Vegas, Nevada; and August 3 in Phoenix, Arizona.

Maiden in New York, with Bruce Dickinson and Adrian Smith back in the fold, August 2000. *Mick Hutson/Redferns/Getty Images*

9 WICKER MEN
THE RETURN OF BRUCE DICKINSON AND ADRIAN SMITH, 1999–2002

"As soon as Bruce came down and started singing with the band, and Adrian as well started playing, it was obvious musically it was going to work. Actually we made the decision before we played together. We just got together and said Bruce is going to join, Adrian is going to join, let's go down to the pub, and that was it."

—Dave Murray, quoted by Gary Boole, July 11, 1999

"Metal has changed beyond recognition," said Adrian Smith. The guitarist was quoted by the *Times of India* in 2009. "When I was eighteen, I couldn't think of records. You carried your own equipment, you slept with it. You had a few clubs. Kids now have records at eighteen and they've studios at home! Their exposure to rock is massive. There is talent, and opportunity is certainly more."

In the naughties, metal came back into mainstream vogue, albeit in a far different incarnation than that pioneered by Iron Maiden and their peers during the genre's hedonistic mid-'80s heyday. A short-lived subgenre called nü-metal

that merged rap with metal guitars, and proved very popular among teenagers, did huge business around the world. Although veteran fans often loathed nü-metal, many could not help but appreciate the fact that it was making heavy metal popular again. Bands such as Limp Bizkit, Linkin Park, Korn, and Drowning Pool, to name a few, were themselves fans of seasoned players like Maiden and Priest, as well as Metallica and Anthrax, and in fact helped turn on their adolescent fans to older bands like Maiden and their devilish ilk.

The previous decade had been a bleak time for heavy metal in general and Iron Maiden in particular, but things were about to change, as if a magician had cast a spell and enticed a whole new generation of rock fans to listen to Maiden. "We started a whole new generation of metal bands," Bruce Dickinson opined in *The Mirror*, "and there aren't too many originals around. . . .I'll be very happy if we are still running round like them at sixty-five."

The reunited and extended Iron Maiden line-up set to work on a new album after the *Ed Hunter* tour. "We just thought we'd go straight in fresh off the tour and do a new album," Harris told interviewer Johnny B at *cavemanproductions.com* in 2000. "We could've just gone in and done an album but we thought it best to go and do some shows first. . . . Basically we wanted to go in the studio and add all the vibes, all the freshness of coming off a tour and playing together again."

Brave New World was the band's twelfth studio album and their first with Bruce Dickinson since *Fear of the Dark* in 1993. In hindsight, getting back with Dickinson seemed like a no-brainer. "As soon as Bruce came down and started singing with the band, and Adrian as well started playing, it was obvious musically it was going to work," Murray confessed in an interview with Canadian journalist Gary Boole before the first show of the *Ed Hunter* tour, the band's first with Dickinson and Smith back in the fold. "Actually we made the decision before we played together. We just got together and said Bruce is going to join, Adrian is going to join, let's go down to the pub [*laughs*], and that was it."

Brave New World was recorded at Guillaume Tell Studios in Paris from November 1999 through early 2000. The band had previously done some writing in Belgium at a venue located near Maiden's production manager, Dick Bell. They did a spot of rehearsing there, too, although much of the writing had been done at sporadic times rather than during one intense period. That approach—writing songs, rehearsing them, and repeating the cycle until it was time to record—was new to the band.

For the new album the band decided to team up with the South African–born and California-based producer Kevin "Caveman" Shirley, well-known for his work with Journey and Australian teen grunge sensations Silverchair. It would be the beginning of a prosperous professional relationship.

Shirley enticed the band to play live in the studio for the first time—something Steve Harris was not especially keen on. "They'd never recorded everybody playing at the same time," the famed producer told Bryan Reesman in 2002. "They'd always gone in and done the overdubs in the control room. I said, 'Just try it, see how it goes.' The first day we

were starting, Steve said, 'I don't think it's going to work. We've never made records like this.' I said, 'Well, let's give it a go and see what happens.' We gave it a go, and he came back and said he was actually having a lot of fun. Also, rehearsal was important. They had to be out of England for one reason or another, so they were holed up in France and were rehearsing and writing songs together. . . . They had rehearsed and were ready to go."

Certainly what the band liked about Kevin Shirley was that he was filled with ideas and new methods of recording and producing, similar to Martin Birch. Perhaps the band didn't warm to all of Shirley's ideas, but they had a solid working chemistry.

"I mean it was really great working with him," Harris said in 2000 (Johnny B). "I was a little worried about working with a different person you don't know. I always would be because you don't know what they're going to be like. Obviously, you know what they've done work-wise and their reputation. We met him and he seemed like a nice guy. However, until you get down to it you don't know if you're going to click with somebody or not . . . but it clicked perfectly. It's just the way he works. It's very similar to the way we've been working the last two or three albums anyway, in a lot of ways, There were some things that he was doing that we hadn't been doing before, but it was really good working like that."

How did the three guitarists work together? Surely, there must have been some rivalry between them even if it was only frivolous fun?

As for working with two other guitarists in the studio, Smith told Ed McArdle of *Review*: "Well, I think there has always been a lot of guitar harmonies and solos in Maiden stuff anyway. On albums we tended to put more guitar parts on than just two so we can re-create those more faithfully live now. . . . I think what you have to do is think of it as a team and you have to give each other space, otherwise it's not going to work. Fortunately, we get on well as people. We've got different guitar styles so if the song calls for different styles we can use what we've got. It's working out great."

The bulk of the album's lyrics had been penned during the *Ed Hunter* tour in 1999, though some had apparently been left over from the *Virtual XI* sessions, namely "The Nomad," "Dream of Mirrors," and "The Mercenary." Yet again lyrics reference movies and books: "The Wicker Man" is a reference to the acclaimed British horror movie of the same name starring Edward Woodward; of course the album title is a reference

BRAVE NEW WORLD

BY GARRY BUSHELL

AFTER *Virtual XI*, many feared that Iron Maiden's glory days were over. *Brave New World*, released May 2000, was a triumphant return to form that reinvigorated the band and reversed their global decline. The album smashed into the U.K. Top 10, saw Maiden back in the U.S. Top 40 for the first time in eight years, and went gold in eight countries.

Of course it didn't hurt that Bruce Dickinson was back, or that Adrian Smith had returned on guitar—not replacing Janick Gers, but in addition to.

Maiden plus Dickinson plus *triple* guitars . . . fans were not disappointed.

Brave New World was the band's strongest and most self-assured outing since *Seventh Son of a Seventh Son* twelve years prior—proof positive that the Cockney boys could still deliver. The only thing louder was the collective sigh of relief from metalheads around the planet.

Yet Maiden avoided the obvious temptation to regurgitate the successful formula of their '80s boom years. This is an album that takes chances and expands their musical muscle organically. Old fans were reassured, newer ones intrigued. And the arrival of Kevin Shirley (he of Aerosmith's *Nine Lives*) to co-produce with Steve Harris laid to rest the production problems suffered by *Virtual XI*.

The ten-track album, the band's first recorded live in the studio, clocks in at over an hour, with only a couple of relative duds. Dickinson claimed that the album attained "a level of brutality beyond *A Piece of Mind*," and that isn't hyperbole. *World* has an adolescent energy that finds the band punching like men less than half their age.

The album abounds with melodic riffs and memorable harmonies; it packs more hooks than an angling club outing. Both "Blood Brothers" and the title track boast insanely catchy choruses, but the album opens with the urgent drive of "The Wicker Man," a massively confident, invigorating sing-along anthem full of troubling images of impending death—an instant classic.

Other highlights include the tight and addictive "The Fallen Angel" with its insistent riff, and the moodily dynamic "Ghost of the Navigator," which opens with atmospheric, three-guitar interplay and morphs into a powerful, mostly midtempo stomper that leads into a captivating multispeed chorus before motoring into in a spring-heeled instrumental passage.

The keen-eared might spot at least three songs left over from the *Virtual XI* writing sessions: "The Mercenary," "Dream of Mirrors," and "The Nomad." Bellicose and a touch Maiden-by-numbers, "The Mercenary" is lifted by rip-roaring guitar breaks. "Dream" sounds better with Dickinson than it would have with Bayley, but it's still decidedly more stupor than "Trooper."

"The Nomad" is another long 'un, but it works better, a throwback to essential epics like "Powerslave" and "To Tame a Land," kicking in with a jabbing riff and moving effortlessly between hard-punching power surges and mellower, intricate passages. More instant is "Out of the Silent Planet," the second single, which begins with harmonious guitar interplay before powering into a storming canter.

The weakest link is the closer, "The Thin Line Between Love & Hate," a long and to these ears unnecessary dip into prog, with a relatively dull chorus. A heavy, almost Sabbathy riff speeds up neatly before meandering around the houses like a drunken mailman. But even here the guitar work sparkles.

Overall, *Brave New World* marked a remarkable and welcome renaissance. Dickinson sounds like he never left. Cynics might claim that he and Smith came back only because their post-Maiden projects had failed to catch fire, but who cares? The bottom line is it's what you want an Iron Maiden album to sound like, doffing its cap to the past while looking with renewed confidence to the future. Welcome to the naughties, Maiden. 🇬🇧

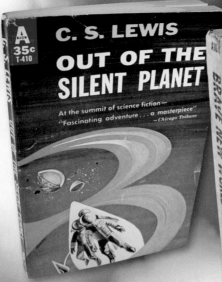

"Out of the Silent Planet" takes its name from a C. S. Lewis sci-fi novel from 1938; and of course the album title is a reference to the classic novel by Aldous Huxley. Nobody can accuse Maiden of not being well-read.

to the classic novel by Aldous Huxley, and "Out of the Silent Planet" takes its name from a C. S. Lewis sci-fi novel from 1938. Nobody can accuse Maiden of not being well-read.

"You see, the thing is when people ask you what the lyrics are, we get asked this question all the time and it's one of the most boring and difficult questions, and you can quote me on that if you want to," Harris said (Johnny B). "You just write at the time whatever you're feeling at the time. You draw your influences from anything at the time—it could be films, books, history, or circumstantial events, whatever. . . . You know, people kind of read into them all sorts of things. Sometimes they get it right, sometimes they don't. I think that's good that they have a bit of imagination. They are thinking what they perceive about the lyrics."

For Adrian Smith, the previous year's *Ed Hunter* tour and the making of *Brave New World* opened up a new chapter in his life, and the future certainly looked exciting. "It was one of the most enjoyable tours of my life—and I've done a few," the guitarist told McArdle. "But the important thing was for us to go back in the studio and do new music. You can only tread on your past for so long and we all felt we had a really good album in us. We wanted to make the best Iron Maiden album we've ever done."

Though *Brave New World* was not a big hit compared to their 1980s output, it did score significantly higher in the charts than the two lackluster Blaze Bayley–era releases. *Brave New World* peaked at No. 7 in the U.K. charts after it was released in May 2000, and reached No. 39 in the United States.

"The Wicker Man" (April 2000). The band opted for a photo on the 7-inch picture sleeve after rejecting the piece by Derek Riggs that was used on the 12-inch picture disc and other merchandise. It would be Riggs' last work for the band until 2007.

Sputnikmusic.com declared, "*Brave New World* sounds like what you would expect an Iron Maiden album to sound like. Great harmonies and melodic riffs can be found all over the album, as they always have, and unless Steve Harris loses it, always will. Bruce sounds like he never left the band, only it's 1988 and not 1992."

Rockzone.com enthused: "The sound of the album is timeless, it meshes so much of the old-style metal, classical works, and various other styles of music that you will have no choice but respect the band's ability and fall in love with the music. Iron Maiden was a pioneer in the late '70s and have been on top of their game for over thirty years. You've got to love the fact that they could stay fresh and continue to progress for that long."

"As far as our audience is concerned, they quite like what we do, so it's irrelevant what people think," Dickinson told Steven Poole of *The Guardian*. "It's either a good Maiden record or a bad Maiden record, and if you don't understand Iron Maiden, then it's irrelevant what you think anyway. Metal is like that, it's a series of little villages, if you like, and music increasingly is becoming like that, unless you're in the big boy band, girl band–type things, which I really know nothing about. I'm probably way out of step with the rest of the population, but then, on the other hand, I am the lead singer of Iron Maiden, so almost by definition I'm out of step with the mass of the population."

Of course, by this time the Internet had become a fundamental tool for bands promoting their music and for fans accessing new sounds. "I think it's great, obviously the fact that it's coming very close the fact that you can already download different songs and stuff like that," Harris told Boole in 1999. "I think that we are going to do various stuff like record live shows or put odd songs on the 'net so that people can download and say, 'Oh I was there two nights ago, I was there.' I think technology's great if you can utilize it in the right way."

With the new album doing reasonably well in the charts, Maiden launched the *Brave New World* tour on June 2, 2000, in France, though the European leg was actually dubbed Metal 2000.

"I think it is challenging and sometimes I even think it's quite brave of us to play the amount of new stuff that we do," Harris commented on Maiden's setlist choices for the tour (Johnny B). "Whenever we go out on tour with a new album, we always play at least six new songs. A lot of people don't do that. They are scared of reactions so they only

SETLIST SELECTIONS

BRAVE NEW WORLD/ METAL 2000 TOUR

THE WICKER MAN
GHOST OF THE NAVIGATOR
BRAVE NEW WORLD
WRATHCHILD
2 MINUTES TO MIDNIGHT
BLOOD BROTHERS
SIGN OF THE CROSS
THE MERCENARY
THE TROOPER
DREAM OF MIRRORS
THE CLANSMAN
THE EVIL THAT MEN DO
FEAR OF THE DARK
IRON MAIDEN
ENCORES:
THE NUMBER OF THE BEAST
HALLOWED BE THY NAME
SANCTUARY

Brave New World tour, Madison Square Garden, New York City, August 5, 2000. *George De Sota/Liaison/Getty Images*

Brave New World tour, San Jose, California, September 16, 2000. *Both Tim Mosenfelder/Getty Images*

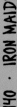
play one new song. They are worried about people bitching about new material but I think it just shows a lack of confidence in their new product."

Iron Maiden performed almost one hundred shows on the *Brave New World* tour, but not without any hitches. Janick Gers fell off stage during a show in Mannehiem, Germany, on July 8, sustaining a concussion and a sprained back. Three shows in Germany, Greece, and Bulgaria were subsequently cancelled.

Maiden's gig at the Air Canada Theatre in Toronto (with support from Halford and Entombed) on August 1 was reviewed by Waspman at the renowned metal fansite *metal-rules.com*: "When Iron Maiden hit the stage, the place just went absolutely crazy! Every single fan in attendance was on their feet for the entire show. Bruce commanded the stage like a true professional, while the rest of the band took up their accustomed places (Adrian/Dave stage right, Janick stage left, and Steve roaming between). . . . This show was true metal heaven, classic songs, great new songs, fire, explosions, a full size Wickerman, and of course, Eddie! Easily a must see show."

The tour wound up with a headlining spot at the famous Rock in Rio festival in Brazil on January 19, 2001, which

"Out of the Silent Planet" (October 2000) featured cover art by Mark Wilkinson.

UNA VEZ MÁS LLEGA LA BESTIA...

IRON MAIDEN
BRAVE NEW WORLD
CON EL REGRESO DE BRUCE DICKINSON
...MÁS FUERTE QUE NUNCA

PRÓXIMAMENTE

EN MÉXICO
EN VIVO...

Disponible en cd y kct   ESPÉRALOS   www.emimx.com.mx EMI

Fans in Mexico were clearly excited about the return of Bruce Dickinson, as this poster
for *Brave New World* attests. The band would treat fans in Mexico City to a show at the
50,000-seat Foro Sol on January 9, 2001.

BOTH: Rock in Rio, January 19, 2001. *Mick Hutson/Redferns/Getty Images*

"Run to the Hills" (live) (March 2002). This marked the third time the band released this fan favorite as a single.

SETLIST SELECTIONS

GIVE ME ED . . . 'TIL I'M DEAD TOUR

THE NUMBER OF THE BEAST
THE TROOPER
DIE WITH YOUR BOOTS ON
REVELATIONS
HALLOWED BE THY NAME
22 ACACIA AVENUE
WILDEST DREAMS
THE WICKER MAN
BRAVE NEW WORLD
THE CLANSMAN
THE CLAIRVOYANT
HEAVEN CAN WAIT
FEAR OF THE DARK
IRON MAIDEN
BRING YOUR DAUGHTER . . . TO THE SLAUGHTER
2 MINUTES TO MIDNIGHT
RUN TO THE HILLS

was issued on CD and DVD. It was the second biggest crowd Maiden had performed for (the largest being 1985's Rock in Rio). However a significant technical glitch resulted in some issues with the PA.

"I don't know if anybody knew—I certainly don't think Maiden knew—but they were playing on a third of the P.A. rig," Shirley explained to Bryan Reesman in 2002. "We didn't redo any parts [on the *Rock in Rio* CD/DVD.]. . . . There are times when Bruce is right in front of the monitors and you can't hear him for the noise that's coming through. He's got a wireless microphone. At those points, in both the DVD and CD mix, I just let him blend into the thing. It's part of what happens live. But the crowd was phenomenal."

Despite the technical hassles, Maiden has always gone down a storm in South America. "One show isn't different from any other in terms of what we put into it, but this passion down here in South America, and like Bruce says the further south you go, the hotter it gets," Nicko McBrain told *metalhammer.co.uk* in 2009. "You don't want to disappoint them so you feel you have to be a little bit more on edge. We don't go on and play any better or worse. It's Iron Maiden and you get what you get. But with the audience, they get so emotionally involved, the cheering and the chanting between songs and five minutes can go by."

By the turn of the new century, some seasoned bands had slowed down with years, but not Maiden. Right after the *Brave New World*/Metal 2000 tour they committed themselves to the Give Me Ed . . . 'Til I'm Dead tour, which commenced May 23, 2003, in Spain and finished in California on August 30. This tour gave fans a chance to hear some of the band's back catalog rather than newer material. One reviewer in attendance at a Maiden show in Oslo, Norway, wrote on *ultimate-guitar.com*, "A very special setlist, they've only played the first four albums 'cause they where [*sic*] going to release a new album next year. So then they wouldn't have time to play these songs again. The audience had a blast on these old classics. The scene with Eddie in 'Iron Maiden' was pretty cool."

With support from Dio and Mötörhead, Maiden's sh DTE Energy Music Theatre in Detroit was reviewed by Da Wilson at the popular website *blistering.com*: "Bruce Dick appeared to be about as hopped up as anyone in the au and spent the first song, '[The] Number of the Beast,' tr over things but pulled it together nicely by the time 'The Tr required him to run waving the Union Jack about. . . . Wh music is this good you can forgive the pretentious goo of bands like KISS and Iron Maiden who claim that the near when they know damned well it is not."

Was it a challenge for the band to prove to younger generations of metal fans that they were not relics of the past? The band members were not exactly spring chickens anymore, but then again, neither were they overweight, unfit, or showing signs of slowing down.

"We've been still selling the albums and doing the ticket sales," explained Harris (Boole). "I suppose in Canada and North America and to a certain degree in the U.K. we lost a lot of ground and it's a challenge to try to win those people back. We've been very lucky that our career hasn't been revolved around North America, so we're lucky we got hardcore fans. It's not dropped so we can't do shows. We still got our hardcore fanbase. It would be nice to get back to where it was."

On the Give Me Ed tour, the band played the new track "Wildest Dreams," which was to appear on their forthcoming studio album. Maiden was steadily building up a bigger fan base, and while they were not as popular as they were in the '80s, things would change. They had a ten-year plan to release new studio albums and to tour the world and perform in countries they had yet to play. They were just overcoming the Blaze Bayley years to build a more extensive fan base in the United States. They knew they had a lot of hard work to put in, but if they could pull off their plan they once again would become the biggest metal band in the world. Iron Maiden wasn't starting from scratch, but they certainly had a lot of work to do if they were to regain their glory years of the mid-'80s. 🇬🇧

2000
By Ryan LaMar

06.02	Strasbourg, FRA
06.03	Nijmegen, NED
06.05	Prague, CZE
06.06	Banska, SVK
06.07	Budapest, HUN
06.09	Izola, SLO
06.10	Monza, ITA
06.13	St. Etienne, FRA
06.14	Paris, FRA
06.16	London, GBR
06.20	Katowice, POL
06.21	Warsaw, POL
06.23	Leipzig, GER
06.24	Dessel, BEL
06.26	Oslo, NOR
06.27	Stockholm, SWE
06.29	Roskilde, DEN
06.30	Turku, FIN
07.02	Tallin, EST
07.04	Vienna, AUT
07.05	Munich, GER
07.06	Zurich, SUI
07.08	Mannheim, GER
07.16	Vilar de Mouros, POR
07.18	San Sebastian, ESP
07.19	Madrid, ESP
07.22	Murcia, ESP
07.23	Barcelona, ESP
08.01	Toronto, CAN
08.02	Montreal, CAN

08.03	Quebec City, CAN
08.05	New York City, USA
08.06	Mansfield, USA
08.08	Hartford, USA
08.09	Portland, USA
08.11	Pittsburgh, USA
08.12	Camden, USA
08.13	Scranton, USA
08.15	Detroit, USA
08.16	Buffalo, USA
08.17	Holmdel, USA
08.19	St. Louis, USA
08.20	Kansas City, USA
08.23	Cleveland, USA
08.25	Chicago, USA
08.26	Milwaukee, USA
08.27	St. Paul, USA
08.29	Colorado Springs, USA
08.30	Denver, USA
09.01	Dallas, USA
09.02	Houston, USA
09.03–04	San Antonio, USA
09.06	El Paso, USA
09.08	Albuquerque, USA
09.09	Phoenix, USA
09.10	Irvine, USA
09.12	San Diego, USA
09.13	Universal City, USA
09.15	Bakersfield, USA
09.16	San Jose, USA
09.17	Las Vegas, USA
09.19	Tacoma, USA

09.20	Vancouver, CAN
10.19	Sendai, JPN
10.21	Tokyo, JPN
10.22	Yokohama, JPN
10.23	Tokyo, JPN
10.25	Osaka, JPN
10.26	Fukuoka, JPN
10.28	Nagoya, JPN
10.29	Tokyo, JPN
11.02	Glasgow, GBR
11.03	Manchester, GBR
11.04	Birmingham, GBR
11.06	Oberhausen, GER (rescheduled from 07.09 in Essen)
11.10	Athens, GRE (rescheduled from 07.14)

2001

01.06–07	London, GBR
01.09	Mexico City, MEX
01.13	Buenos Aires, ARG
01.15	Santiago, CHI
01.19	Rio de Janeiro, BRA

2002

03.19–21	London, GBR

Notes: The March 3, 2000, issue of Iron Maiden News announced the band would play Kiev, Ukraine, June 11, yet I've uncovered no evidence of that date.

The Oberhausen and Athens shows at the end of the 2000 itinerary were made up due to an injury sustained by Janick. A July 12, 2000, show slated for Sofia, Bulgaria, was not rescheduled.

Some sources list a July 21, 2000, show in Mijas, Spain, but a tour diary notes the band had the day off.

The band reported a September 18, 2000, date in Anchorage, Alaska, was cancelled with no reason given. September 23 and 24, 2000, shows in Edmonton and Calgary, Alberta, were also cancelled.

The November 2000 Iron Maiden News announced a January 12, 2001, show in Buenos Aires as well, but subsequent tour diaries note it as an off day.

The band performed live on Top of the Pops before playing their third night, March 21, 2002, at Brixton.

10 JOURNEYMEN

DANCING NEAR DEATH, 2003–2005

"There are an enormous minority extant across the globe who adore the band's singular muse to the virtual exclusion of all other artists. People don't so much own Iron Maiden T-shirts as live in them."

—Ian Fortnam, *Classic Rock*, October 2003

Christened *Dance of Death*, Iron Maiden's thirteenth studio album was recorded at Sarm West Studios in London at the tail end of 2002 with Kevin Shirley. The band used up a good portion of 2003 to work on the new tracks.

Looking back on his experiences working with Maiden, Kevin Shirley told Bryan Reesman of *mixonline.com* in 2002, "Maiden had their idiosyncrasies. Steve Harris is the boss of the band. To his credit, he likes what he likes, and when he doesn't like something, he just says, 'I don't like it.'

As the sun set on 2004, Iron Maiden was celebrating twenty-five years since the release of their debut album. *Mick Hutson/Redferns/Getty Images*

And that's it. I tried to fight some of those battles with Bruce."

The album marked the first songwriting credit for drummer Nicko McBrain, on "New Frontier," and included the full acoustic track "Journeyman," their first such track in twenty-some years. Of course the band peppered the album with their trademark literary and philosophical references, but perhaps these latest references were somewhat more downbeat than those on past albums and conveyed themes that contrasted starkly with those on *Brave New World*. *Dance of Death* was certainly an ambitious project, and one that paid off, resulting in some of the best reviews of their career upon its release in September 2003.

Download Festival, Donington Park, England, May 31, 2003. *Mick Hutson/Redferns/Getty Images*

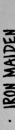

Metal-observer.com declared, "*Dance of Death* has every Maiden ingredient and a few more added in. It will delight the hardcore fan and dismay the critics who will still vilify it and denounce the band and wonder just why Harris and Co. have such staying power and longevity."

Chris Jones wrote on BBC Online: "Maiden have always survived by ignoring fickle fashion and giving their loyal minions exactly what they want," Chris Jones wrote on BBC's website. "With *Dance of Death* they won't have one dissatisfied customer."

Andrew McNiece concluded his mixed review at *melodicrock.com* by writing, "A solid album—that's the best description. Pleasing to some, maybe not as much so to some other Maiden fans. But considering the age of the band and their history, a good effort that is sadly marred by an average production sound. Maybe it's as the band wanted, but to the listener, there's a bit to be desired. Clearer guitar parts would be the best place to start if a fix was possible."

Producers Steve Harris and "Caveman" Shirley certainly got to know each other's strengths and weaknesses as they built a relationship that reflected the Martin Birch years. It remained important to Harris to have a creative, practical, and solid working relationship with a producer who shared his vision but also brought new ideas into the studio.

DANCE OF DEATH

BY GAVIN BADDELEY

Dance of Death, Maiden's thirteenth studio album, emerged in 2003, the second with Bruce Dickinson and Adrian Smith returned to the fold. The less said about the cover the better—the artist disowned the work as an unfinished early draft, and fan discussion of it threatened to eclipse consideration of content. (The band shots on the inside sleeve aren't much better, with band members apparently being visited by spectral strippers—lap dancers of death, perhaps?)

But what of the meat in the sandwich?

If the Blaze Bayley years proved anything, it was the essential contribution of Dickinson's tonsils to Maiden's identity. His vocals soar when he attacks the lyrics as a part in some imaginary play. It's when he's given nothing to get his teeth into that the material lacks conviction and character, and *Dance of Death* is a classic case in point. For this punter's pound, Maiden is always at their strongest when conjuring musical tales to stir the blood or chill the bones. Old-school opener "Wildest Dreams" canters along, a defiant feel-good anthem that never really goes anywhere. It's curiously anonymous, a competent rocker that does its job but not much more.

Several other tracks suffer a similar fate, particularly when the subject matter is unclear. "New Frontier" (genetic engineering?) and "Gates of Tomorrow" (the Internet?) are both okay but hardly rattle the teeth. "Age of Innocence," in which we're treated to a litany of grumpy, pub politics, is a lyrical misfire, while the bloated "No More Lies" rather overstays its welcome with a labored chorus, an accusation that also could be levelled at the acoustic finale "Journeyman." There's a little too much middle-aged flab here, which boded ill for a band already a quarter-century into their career.

Which isn't to say Maiden should abandon the epics. Far from it. The eight-minutes-plus title track is a classic campfire ghost story told Maiden style, and it's enormous fun. It's also one of the more notable examples of the album's occasional Celtic, even folky, slants, reminiscent perhaps of Thin Lizzy or Jethro Tull. (Though, as "Dance of Death" is set in the Everglades, a Cajun flavor might have been more appropriate, the jig rhythm rather suggesting a "Riverdance of Death.") "Rainmaker," the debut single from the album, also justifies its place, courtesy of some irresistible hooks.

To these ears, however, the true standout tracks are the album's two historical epics.

"Montségur" revisits the French site of an infamous massacre of heretics by Crusaders in the thirteenth century. Dickinson had holidayed there and he brings some real viscera to a song that demands a heavy, overblown approach, which Maiden delivers in operatic spades.

Paschendale, Belgium, which witnessed some of the bloodiest fighting of World War I, is the setting and title of *Dance of Death*'s standout track. It's another grim, real-life horror story that demands both gravity and melodrama. Stirring and somber in equal parts, "Paschendale" is a fitting companion to "The Trooper," Maiden's classic, rousing meditation on the futility of war.

Dance of Death occupies a curious place in the Iron Maiden discography. It has its fans but certainly isn't the band's finest hour. Overall there's a little too much self-indulgence on the record, a feeling that quite a few minutes could have been trimmed to good effect. It's routinely compared to *Seventh Son of a Seventh Son*, and there's some virtue to such comparisons. But while *Seventh Son* hangs together better as a package, *Dance of Death* at least offers the maudlin punch of "Paschendale." 🇬🇧

Shirley was certainly a man with vision and insight, having worked with Jimmy Page and various Led Zeppelin projects, as well as with American AOR legends Journey.

"The thing about Martin, and for that fact Kevin Shirley too, is that they both have the same kind of filter," Dave Murray told Joe Matera (*ultimate-guitar.com*). "What I mean is that, they just let the band go in there and do its thing. Martin and Kevin will just enhance it all through the production of the sound. With Martin it was great, as we would go in there with the songs and just play the songs and he would just enhance it through the production side of it all and through the editing process and stuff like that. . . . So you have the identity of the band still in there being the primary focus."

The album peaked at No. 2 in the United Kingdom and No. 18 in the United States—a marked improvement on *Brave New World*. The plan was working.

The *Dance of Death* world tour has certainly gone down in Maiden history as one of their greatest: they played more than fifty shows in front of 750,000 fans in Europe, North America (Montreal, Quebec City, New York, and Los Angeles only), South America, and Asia from October 19, 2003, to February 8, 2004. At Westfalenhalle in Dortmund, Germany, they recorded a CD and DVD that were released under the title *Death on the Road*. Admittedly, some fans began to notice that perhaps the band had issued one too many live albums.

On the subject of the band's extensive touring history, Murray told Gary Boole in 1999, "I think we've probably toured more than most bands. The cycle would be over eighteen months we would do an album and spend ten months on the road. We've done a lot of touring over the last twenty years. . . . We've had a lot of hardcore supporters as well that are still there today, but there is a certain secret you tap into."

By the time 2004 came to a close, Iron Maiden was celebrating twenty-five years since the release of their debut album. To celebrate, they launched the Eddie Rips Up the World tour. The tour was also to promote 2004's DVD release *The Early Days*, which covered the band's early history from their inception in 1975 through 1983's *Piece of Mind*.

Beginning in Prague on May 28, 2005, and finishing in London on September 2, the tour included numerous stadium dates and festival appearances. On the tour Maiden were supported by young acolytes such as Mastodon, DragonForce, Dream Theater, Marilyn Manson, and Turbonegro.

Reviewing the band's July 9 gig at Ullevi Stadium in Gothenburg, Sweden, Mike Sterry wrote in *NME*: "Iron

(continued on page 154)

DANCE
OF DEATH
TOUR 2003
MEDIA
IRON MAIDEN
PHOTO

SETLIST SELECTIONS

DANCE OF DEATH TOUR

WILDEST DREAMS
WRATHCHILD
CAN I PLAY WITH MADNESS
THE TROOPER
DANCE OF DEATH
RAINMAKER
BRAVE NEW WORLD
PASCHENDALE
LORD OF THE FLIES
NO MORE LIES
HALLOWED BE THY NAME
FEAR OF THE DARK
IRON MAIDEN
JOURNEYMAN
THE NUMBER OF THE BEAST

THIS SPREAD: Dance of Death world tour, Milan, October 27, 2003 (upper left), and Madrid, November 2, 2003 (above, below, and opposite bottom). *All Mick Hutson/ Redferns/Getty Images*

"Rainmaker" (November 2003), limited edition colored vinyl. The cover art was taken from the song's Howard Greenhalgh–directed video.

"Wildest Dreams" (September 2003), CD and DVD. The latter featured the "Dance of Death – Behind the Scenes" video.

(continued from page 150)

Maiden never show their age. Bruce Dickinson's voice is in top form and he manages to land a surprising number of wince-free jumps during 'Wrathchild.' There are cracks, of course—like when *NME* inadvertently barges in on a member of the Maiden getting their arse massaged pre-show, or when drummer Nicko McBrain, care of some badly planned camera angles throughout 'Die with Your Boots On,' treats the audience to a glimpse of his pulsing, spandex-cocooned scrotum, 10 feet wide on the big screen. Teens—a surprising number are in attendance—avert their eyes in surrogate embarrassment."

Festival appearances included the Rock am Ring and Rock im Park events in Germany, Gods of Metal in Italy, and slots at the coveted Reading and Leeds festivals in England, major coups for the band in exposing their music to a combined mainstream audience of 130,000.

However, the tour was not without controversy.

Maiden was co-headlining that year's American Ozzfest tour with a reunited Black Sabbath (singer Ozzy Osbourne, guitarist Tony Iommi, bassist Geezer Butler, and drummer Bill Ward). Reportedly, Dickinson had criticized Osbourne for using an autocue on stage. On the final night at the Hyundai Pavilion in San Bernardino, California, Sharon Osbourne, Ozzy's wife and manager, and their daughter Kelly, allegedly enticed some members of the crowd to throw eggs at Maiden and run on stage with a flag that said "Don't fuck with Ozzy."

THIS SPREAD: Eddie Rips Up the World tour, Helsinki, July 6, 2005. *All Mick Hutson/Redferns/Getty Images*

SETLIST SELECTIONS

EDDIE RIPS UP
THE WORLD TOUR

THE IDES OF MARCH
KILLERS
THE PROWLER
THE TROOPER
REMEMBER TOMORROW
WHERE EAGLES DARE
RUN TO THE HILLS
REVELATIONS
WRATHCHILD
DIE WITH YOUR BOOTS ON
PHANTOM OF THE OPERA
THE NUMBER OF THE BEAST
HALLOWED BE THY NAME
IRON MAIDEN
RUNNING FREE
DRIFTER
SANCTUARY

The *No More Lies* EP (March 2004) was a fan "thank you" package featuring an orchestral arrangement of "Paschendale," the original take of "Journeyman," and a hidden track, an alternate take of "Age of Innocence" with Nicko McBrain on vocals.

IRON MAIDEN

NO MORE LIES
DANCE OF DEATH SOUVENIR EP

156

Shoreline Amphitheater, Mountain View, California, August 13, 2005. Maiden co-headlined 2005's American Ozzfest tour with a reunited Black Sabbath. The tour would end on a sour note after an incident involving Ozzy's wife, Sharon. *Tim Mosenfelder/Getty Images*

MAIN STAGE PHOTO

ROD SMALLWOOD: MAIDEN'S MANAGER

BY NEIL DANIELS

Peter Grant had Led Zeppelin. Journey had Herbie Herbert. And Iron Maiden had Rod Smallwood. All giants of rock have had in their corners intelligent, dedicated, and fierce managers.

The Yorkshire-born Smallwood has often been dubbed the seventh member of Iron Maiden. As rock promoter Andy Copping told *Classic Rock*, "Why is Iron Maiden still the biggest metal band in the world? It's because of the passion and belief of the people around [Smallwood]." Maiden even penned a song about their manager, "Sheriff of Huddersfield," which was a B-side to the 1986 single "Wasted Years."

Smallwood founded Smallwood-Taylor Enterprises in 1976 with business partner Andy Taylor, and the pair ran the company out of a two-bedroom flat in London. Smallwood-Taylor hooked up with Maiden in 1979 and that

Rod Smallwood backstage in Melbourne, February 6, 2008.
Martin Philbey/Redferns/Gettty Images

year founded the famed Sanctuary Records, named after the Maiden song. The company expanded into the United States in the 1980s and eventually reissued rock classics and inked contracts with a diverse range of artists, including the Who, Destiny's Child, Beyoncé, and Guns N' Roses. In 2006, Smallwood announced he and Maiden were ending their association with Sanctuary and forming a brand-new company called Phantom Music Management.

Sharon also reportedly had the PA system shut off several times during Maiden's performance. By some reports, Sharon then went on stage at the end of the band's set (to boos from the crowd) and called Dickinson a "prick."

The band and their manager Rod Smallwood were appalled. Smallwood issued a statement condemning Sharon Osbourne for her alleged actions. "In thirty years in this business, and after attending hundreds of gigs, I have never seen anything anywhere near as disgusting and unprofessional as what went on that night," the statement read. Smallwood also pointed out hypocritical aspects of Sharon Osbourne's behaviour: "Iron Maiden, like all the bands on Ozzfest, had to sign quite onerous legal documents, part of which was promising not to throw anything into the audience, even wristbands!!! Ironic isn't it."

On their next album, Maiden would include a song about the incident entitled "These Colours Don't Run." The band left it at that and moved on, achieving far greater success with headlining solo tours and album sales than Ozzy would achieve.

Indeed, Maiden was moving ahead, and enthusiastically. Dickinson, in particular, had never sounded or looked better. He kept himself in rigorous shape by fencing and generally looking after himself. Clearly, fans loved having him back, but they still craved the older material rather than the new stuff.

"We literally wouldn't exist without our fans," Dickinson told *The Mirror*. "Press and radio don't give us much of a leg up. Same with MTV. Fortunately, we get a lot of kids saying let's go and see Maiden."

But things would get better. Much better.

2003 *By Ryan LaMar*

Date	Location
05.23	La Coruna, ESP
05.24	Gijon, ESP
05.26	Toulouse, FRA
05.27	Toulon, FRA
05.31	Donington, GBR
06.03	Katowice, POL
06.04	Budapest, HUN
06.06	Nurburgring, GER
06.07	Nurnburg, GER
06.08	Vienna, AUT
06.11	Barcelona, ESP
06.12	Madrid, ESP
06.13	San Sebastian, ESP
06.15	Imola, ITA
06.17	Zagreb, CRO
06.19	Zlin, CZE
06.21	Bergum, NED
06.23	Fribourg, SUI
06.25	Paris, FRA
06.27	Roskilde, DEN
06.28	Stockholm, SWE
06.30	Helsinki, FIN
07.02–03	Oslo, NOR
07.05	Dessel, BEL
07.09	Lisbon, POR
07.11	Jerez, ESP
07.12	Albecete, ESP
07.21	Worcester, USA
07.22	Hartford, USA
07.23	Camden, USA
07.25	Holmdel, USA
07.26	Wantagh, USA
07.29	Washington, D.C., USA
07.30	New York City, USA
08.01	Quebec City, CAN
08.02	Montreal, CAN
08.03	Toronto, CAN
08.05	Cleveland, USA
08.06	Detroit, USA
08.08	Pittsburgh, USA
08.09	Columbus, USA
08.10	Chicago, USA
08.13	Dallas, USA
08.15	San Antonio, USA
08.16	Houston, USA
08.18	El Paso, USA
08.20	Denver, USA
08.22	Phoenix, USA
08.24	Irvine, USA
08.25	Long Beach, USA
08.26	San Diego, USA
08.28	Mountain View, USA
08.29	Concord, USA
08.30	Sacramento, USA
10.19	Debrecen, HUN
10.21	Banska, SVK
10.22	Prague, CZE
10.24	Munich, GER
10.25	Stuttgart, GER
10.27	Milan, ITA
10.28	Firenze, ITA
10.30	Zurich, SUI
11.01	Barcelona, ESP
11.02	Madrid, ESP
11.04	Frankfurt, GER
11.12	Copenhagen, DEN
11.14	Stockholm, SWE
11.15	Gothenburg, SWE
11.17	Hannover, GER
11.18	Berlin, GER
11.20	Leuven, BEL
11.22	Paris, FRA
11.24	Dortmund, GER
11.26	Hamburg, GER
11.27	Leipzig, GER
11.28	Wroclaw, POL (rescheduled from 11.07)
12.01	Dublin, IRE
12.03	Newcastle, GBR
12.04	Nottingham, GBR
12.06	Sheffield, GBR
12.08	Glasgow, GBR
12.09	Manchester, GBR
12.12	London, GBR
12.13	Rotterdam, NED (rescheduled from 11.05)
12.15	Cardiff, GBR
12.16	Birmingham, GBR
12.18	Amneville, FRA (rescheduled from 11.29)
12.21	Helsinki, FIN (rescheduled from 11.10)

2004

Date	Location
01.11	Buenos Aires, ARG
01.13	Santiago, CHI
01.16	Rio de Janeiro, BRA
01.17	Sao Paulo, BRA
01.20	Montreal, CAN
01.21	Quebec City, CAN
01.23–26	New York City, USA
01.30–31	Los Angeles, USA
02.05	Sapporo, JPN
02.07	Osaka, JPN
02.08	Tokyo, JPN

2005

Date	Location
05.28	Prague, CZE
05.29	Chorzow, POL
05.31	Graz, AUT
06.04	Nurburgring, GER
06.05	Nurnburg, GER
06.07	Reykjavik, ISL
06.11	Bologna, ITA
06.12	Zurich, SUI
06.16	Lisbon, POR
06.18	Lorca, ESP
06.21	Athens, GRE

06.25	Paris, FRA	07.21	Darien Lake, USA	08.11	Auburn, USA
06.26	Dessel, BEL	07.23	Burgettstown, USA	08.13	Mountain View, USA
06.28–29	Oslo, NOR	07.24	Bristow, USA	08.15	Marysville, USA
07.02	Lobnitz, GER	07.26–27	Holmdel, USA		(rescheduled from 08.14)
07.03	Weert, NED	07.30	Tinley Park, USA	08.18	Phoenix, USA
07.06–07	Helsinki, FIN	07.31	Noblesville, USA	08.20	San Bernardino, USA
07.09	Gothenburg, SWE	08.02	Columbus, USA	08.26	Leeds, GBR
07.15	Mansfield, USA	08.03	Toronto, CAN	08.28	Reading, GBR
07.16	Quebec City, CAN	08.04	Clarkston, USA	08.31	Dublin, IRE
07.17	Hartford, USA	08.06	East Troy, USA	09.02	London, GBR
07.19	Camden, USA	08.09	Denver, USA	09.02	Hammersmith, GBR

Notes: A scheduled August 21, 2003, show in Albuquerque, New Mexico, was cancelled. Rumor has it that video footage from Death on the Road includes clips from Wroclaw on November 28, 2003.

A fifth New York show scheduled for January 27, 2004, was cancelled.

An August 7, 2005, show in Somerset, Wisconsin, as part of Ozzfest was nixed when Osbourne cancelled due to throat problems. A rescheduled date on August 16 in Salt Lake City, Utah, was also cancelled.

On September 2, 2005, the band performed a live studio session at Maida Vale Studios for rebroadcast on Radio One on September 13.

11 FLIGHT 666

THE BEAST WILL NOT DIE, 2006–2009

"As well as everyone else on our 757 we have now added a seven-man documentary crew . . . so if you see cameras following us around everywhere and around the stage you now know why!! A record of this is something that the band and myself would love to have!"

—Steve Harris, 2008

A new year brought a major change to the Maiden camp—in 2006 they left Sanctuary to form their own company, Phantom Music Management. But it was the release of their new album, *A Matter of Life and Death*, which really made an impact on their legacy. With Kevin Shirley, the band had entered London's Sarm West Studios in September 2005 and came out in July 2006 with a brand-new ten-track, seventy-two-minute album.

After working with Kevin Shirley on *Brave New World* back in 2000, Steve Harris knew that he'd have a lengthy working relationship with the Malibu-based producer. "When

you're stuck in the studio for all that time together you need to have fun," Harris told interviewer Johnny B in 2000. "What I mean is that I'm the one that's in the studio with [Shirley] every day, day in and day out. I am there more so than the others, so I need to get on with him. We got on really well together. It is so important to have a good working relationship. I imagine that there can't be anything worse than going into a studio if you don't like the person that you're working with. We were really lucky because we all got on really well with him and we would definitely work with him again."

With *A Matter of Life and Death*, the band explored their progressive influences more extensively than they had on previous albums, eschewing much of the basic riff-based heavy metal of some of their much earlier work. "This album is a step up on everything else we've ever done, in my opinion,"

Outside Lokomotiv Stadium in Sofia, Bulgaria, June 4, 2007. With *A Matter of Life and Death*, the East End lads cemented their legacy, exploring their progressive influences more extensively than before and proving the band comprised extremely talented musicians. *Mick Hutson/Redferns/Getty Images*

161

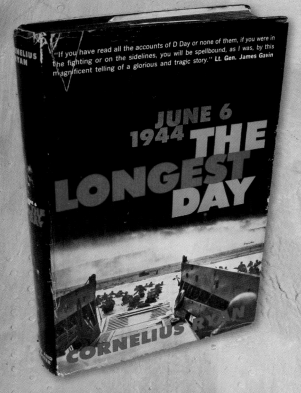

Iron Maiden relied on World War II imagery for *A Matter of Life and Death*, from the cover art to the track "The Longest Day," which takes its name from the landmark D-Day history by Cornelius Ryan.

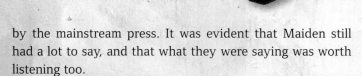

Nicko McBrain told Geoff Martin (*Canada.com*). "I know a few people don't agree with that, but I don't care, you can stuff that up your ass, I don't give a shit."

The swift changes in tempo, multilayered riffs, elaborate production, and overall dynamics of the new album only reinforced that Iron Maiden comprised extremely talented musicians. Indeed, with *A Matter of Life and Death*, the East End lads had outdone themselves. Even lyrically, the album was a significant step forward for the band as they explored such themes as war, religion, and history.

"A lot of it is what happened over the past five hundred years, throughout history really, not just what's happening now," Harris explained to Steve Purcell of *aquarian.com*. "We're basically saying that we haven't learned from our mistakes. It's not really political or anything, it's just stuff that we've been observing, and writing about history as well."

Released in August to overwhelming reviews, the new album peaked at No. 4 in the band's homeland. *Kerrang!* gave the album five out of five rating; *Metal Hammer* gave it ten of ten. Significantly, *A Matter of Life and Death* also became the band's first Top 10 LP in the United States and marked a turning point at which the band began to be taken seriously by the mainstream press. It was evident that Maiden still had a lot to say, and that what they were saying was worth listening too.

Andrew McNiece concluded his review at his esteemed *melodicrock.com* website by saying, "An intense and challenging listen, *A Matter of Life and Death* is a noble effort that quite frankly elevates itself well above its contemporaries and a good portion of the band's very own back catalogue, Maiden having set themselves a new benchmark. It is an album that will stand well next to any Maiden classic and it is the album that has finally cemented the return of the world's number-one metal band. Rejoice!"

"The Reincarnation of Benjamin Breeg" (August 2006).

A MATTER OF LIFE AND DEATH

BY IAN CHRISTE

IRON MAIDEN'S JOURNEY FROM POINTS A TO X is preserved almost night-by-night on a zillion live releases, tour ephemera, DVDs, and the snapshots and war stories of every single heavy metal fan on earth. By 2006, the band had proven themselves more reliable than many nations, yet their quirks kept legions of fans in suspense. For example, twenty-five years and many generations of heavy metal after the band's 1980 debut, Iron Maiden was whittled down to two original members, Steve Harris and Dave Murray, via various avenues of triage and turmoil. Air-raid-siren-in-chief Bruce Dickinson had come and gone and come again, and via an unusual merger in 1999, the band became a six-piece with three guitar players. They were simply too decent to fire replacement player Janick Gers just because veteran Adrian Smith wanted his old job back.

A Matter of Life and Death really is a stubbornly sober sojourn outside the band's normal nonstop jubilance. Starting with cover artwork depicting a sextet of weary skeleton soldiers whose armored tank is decorated with an Eddie insignia, Iron Maiden disarmingly drops the veil and reveals a struggle with their legacy. The speeds are slower, the songs are very moody overall, and the intensity is buried at a respectable depth. No longer the rash firebrands seeking to usurp their elders, Iron Maiden shows grizzled regal paunch as kings of their own domain, titans of a form of music that was only supposed to be greasy kids' stuff. But quite candidly, these are fifty-year-old men with mortality on the mind. Of course, with poise and resolve they tackle this new enemy—actual slow, boring expiration by wear and tear, not the savage violent deaths that once enthralled them. But the resonant message is there: the band that revelled in grisly horror eventually grew wise and became aware of the unavoidable final exit, both personally and for the band.

And so the pace is steady and footsure, as the reformed fantasy heavy metal band navigates weighty material of true importance. Iron Maiden telling their legions to appreciate life and stop and smell the roses in "Different World" was radical; they broke down the illusion and spoke directly to an aging and increasingly nostalgic audience. Rather than digging up a few more valiant tales from old literature and history books, the songs had a strong autobiographical aura. Dwelling on the World War that defined their parents' lives in "The Longest Day" and elsewhere, Iron Maiden seemed preoccupied with very real ghosts. Even the spectres described in "The Reincarnation of Benjamin Bragg" touched close to home for a band that drifted in the 1990s before returning as heavy metal standard bearers in the 2000s.

The upshot of all this introspection and nine-minute songs is that even in their first graying hour, Iron Maiden hit back with a fucking vengeance, with a metal heart beating powerfully to fuel the ongoing fantasy, wanderlust, and bravado. Again keeping fans guessing in their determined way, the band stubbornly played this brand-new material almost exclusively while on tour during this time, refusing to coast down the slope of "Run to the Hills." And the outcome? They played to their largest audiences ever. In Sweden, Iron Maiden performed before nearly 1 percent of the country's entire population during four shows over one long weekend. They still shook seasoned metalheads to the bone and attracted the umpteenth wave of freshly minted teenagers to the curious fracas.

Afterward, with a new breath of creative life, the band would step back from this morbid and introspective precipice and return to inescapable escapism. But the stubborn self-reflective moment that is *A Matter of Life or Death* remains a respectable way marker, a bunch of very long moments of clarity from a crucial point in the band's travels. 🇬🇧

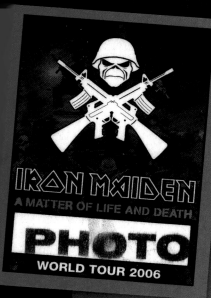

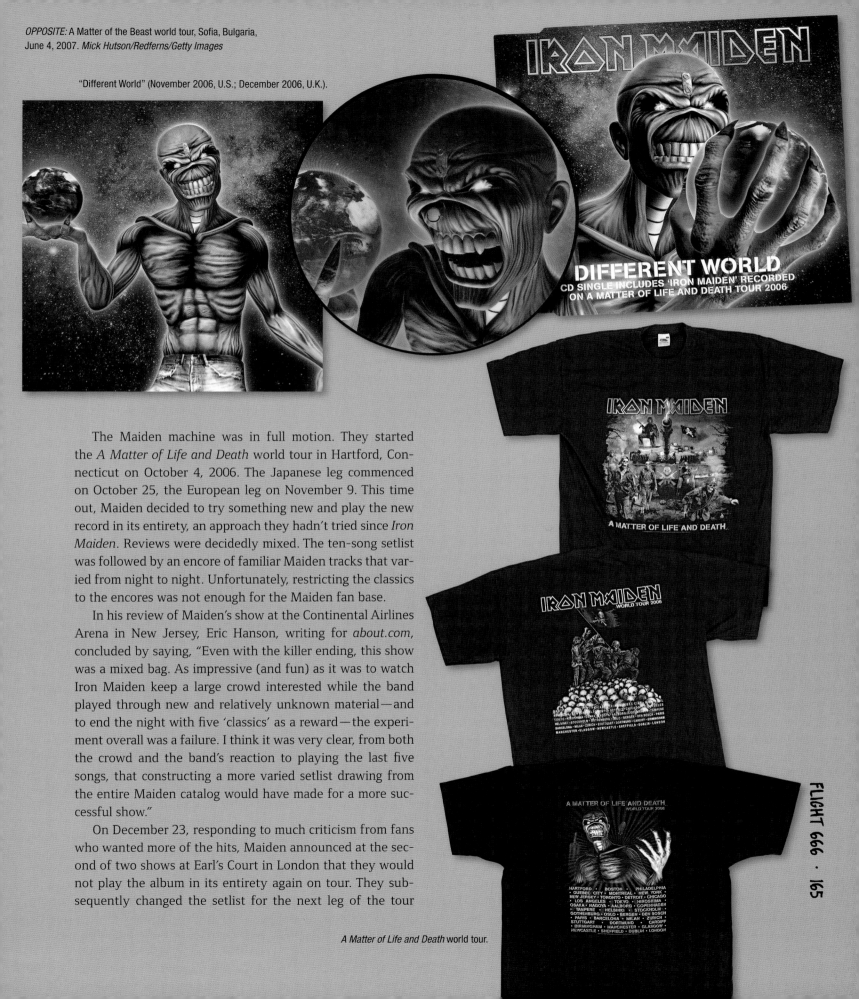

OPPOSITE: A Matter of the Beast world tour, Sofia, Bulgaria,
June 4, 2007. *Mick Hutson/Redferns/Getty Images*

"Different World" (November 2006, U.S.; December 2006, U.K.).

IRON MAIDEN

DIFFERENT WORLD
CD SINGLE INCLUDES 'IRON MAIDEN' RECORDED
ON A MATTER OF LIFE AND DEATH TOUR 2006

The Maiden machine was in full motion. They started
the *A Matter of Life and Death* world tour in Hartford, Connecticut on October 4, 2006. The Japanese leg commenced
on October 25, the European leg on November 9. This time
out, Maiden decided to try something new and play the new
record in its entirety, an approach they hadn't tried since *Iron
Maiden*. Reviews were decidedly mixed. The ten-song setlist
was followed by an encore of familiar Maiden tracks that varied from night to night. Unfortunately, restricting the classics
to the encores was not enough for the Maiden fan base.

In his review of Maiden's show at the Continental Airlines
Arena in New Jersey, Eric Hanson, writing for *about.com*,
concluded by saying, "Even with the killer ending, this show
was a mixed bag. As impressive (and fun) as it was to watch
Iron Maiden keep a large crowd interested while the band
played through new and relatively unknown material—and
to end the night with five 'classics' as a reward—the experiment overall was a failure. I think it was very clear, from both
the crowd and the band's reaction to playing the last five
songs, that constructing a more varied setlist drawing from
the entire Maiden catalog would have made for a more successful show."

On December 23, responding to much criticism from fans
who wanted more of the hits, Maiden announced at the second of two shows at Earl's Court in London that they would
not play the album in its entirety again on tour. They subsequently changed the setlist for the next leg of the tour

A Matter of Life and Death world tour.

Opening night of the *Somewhere Back in Time* world tour, Mumbai, February 1, 2008. © Punit Paranjpe/Reuters/CORBIS

A MATTER OF THE BEAST TOUR

DIFFERENT WORLD
THESE COLOURS DON'T RUN
BRIGHTER THAN A THOUSAND SUNS
WRATHCHILD
THE TROOPER
CHILDREN OF THE DAMNED
THE REINCARNATION OF BENJAMIN BREEG
FOR THE GREATER GOOD OF GOD
THE NUMBER OF THE BEAST
FEAR OF THE DARK
RUN TO THE HILLS
IRON MAIDEN
2 MINUTES TO MIDNIGHT
THE EVIL THAT MEN DO
HALLOWED BE THY NAME

(dubbed A Matter of the Beast), which ran from March 9, 2007, in Dubai, to June 24, 2007. That final night was in aid of The Clive Burr MS Trust Fund and held at Brixton Academy in London. The former Maiden drummer, having been diagnosed with multiple sclerosis, had incurred enormous medical bills.

In 2008, to support the release of the *Live After Death* performance DVD and *Somewhere Back in Time: The Best Of, 1980–1989*, Maiden embarked on the *Somewhere Back in Time* world tour on February 1, in Mumbai, India—with licensed commercial pilot Bruce Dickinson flying the band's Boeing 757, dubbed *Ed Force One*, through the first twenty-one countries. The highly-publicized tour stretched over a year and was completed in four legs. Along the way, the support slots were filled by a number of artists, namely Agora, Anthrax, Atreyu, Avenged Sevenfold, Behind Crimson Eyes, Lauren Harris (Steve's daughter), IRA, Kamelot, Made of Hate, MASACRE, Morbid Angel, Parikrama, Salamandra, Slayer, Tainted Carcass, Trivium, Trooper, Vanishing Point, Witchblade, and Within Temptation.

The *Somewhere Back in Time* tour was a major coup. Maiden had not received as much exposure in the United States and Europe since their mid-1980s heyday. Seemingly, they had won back the fans who deserted them during the Blaze Bayley years—and acquired a younger generation of metalheads who listened to bands like Trivium and InFlames. Iron Maiden was walking on water and there was nothing they could do wrong. The tour's success was documented in the highly acclaimed feature film *Iron Maiden: Flight 666*. It was the first time the band had allowed such access to their inner sanctum.

"As well as everyone else on our 757 we have now added a seven-man documentary crew. . . . This will be such an incredible and exciting tour that we agreed with Scot and Sam's proposal to document this so if you see cameras following us around everywhere and around the stage you now know why!!," Harris said in a statement referring to the film's producers Scot McFayden and Sam Dunn. "A record of this is something that the band and myself would love to have . . . !"

However, the notion of a rock film was not greeted with open arms by everyone in the Maiden camp. "I wasn't really very happy about it," Janick Gers later told *metalhammer.co.uk*. "To me, I don't want to be a film star. Bands should have a bit of mystery about them and I think if you go in with cameras and see how everything works, I think a lot of that is better left unsaid, because once you demystify it it's not as interesting."

Nevertheless, McFayden and Dunn chose a remarkable tour to document. Highlights included Maiden's first shows

Wacken Open Air Festival, Germany, July 31, 2008. © *Friso Gentsch/epa/CORBIS*

in Costa Rica, Colombia, Peru, and Ecuador; they played in Australia for the first time since 1992; they returned to New Zealand after sixteen years away; they'd also been away from western Canada for a long time; they made their first visit to Venezuela in almost twenty years; and, somewhat remarkably, they played their first headlining stadium date in England, at London's Twickenham Stadium on July 5, 2008. The band had come a long way since their first gig at St. Nicholas Hall in Poplar, London, on May 1, 1976.

In *The Times*, David Sinclair observed: "To have filled this 55,000-capacity stadium was a tremendous achievement, not only in terms of scale but also in the credibility it conferred. After thirty years of formation headbanging and dodging cartoon stage monsters, Iron Maiden are finally being taken seriously. . . . Focused firmly on the group's greatest hits and executed with genuine zeal and commitment, the show

offered an escape hatch into a universe where the 'do or die' mentality of comic-book warfare met the fantasy world of ghouls and zombies."

Tony Hampton enthused at *ThrashHits.com*: "To be stronger, tighter, and more at ease with your legacy than ever before must be satisfying but Iron Maiden don't do smug. They like a pint, and the singer is so humble he . . . gets the tube around town. Incomparable, overwhelming genius."

It turned out that the band had an unlikely visitor at the Twickenham show: "I'm still in touch with the lads from Iron Maiden. We went to see them at Twickenham last year," Blaze Bayley confessed to Ian Harvey of the Midlands newspaper *Express & Star* in 2009.

All told, Iron Maiden played to more than two million people on the *Somewhere Back in Time* world tour. "The unique way of touring earlier this year with everyone and all our gear on the plane helped to make 2008 easily one of the most successful, exciting and fun years in the band's career," Bruce Dickinson

(continued on page 173)

At the 2008 Graspop metal festival in Dessel, Belgium, Iron Maiden took top billing from the band they opened for on tour way back in the spring of 1980.

Backstage and photo passes, New York City.

Sziget Festival, Budapest, August 12, 2008. *AP Photo/MTI, Laszlo Beliczay*

MAIDEN ON THE ROAD:
THE LIVE EXPERIENCE

BY NEIL DANIELS

Ed Force One sits on the tarmac at Moscow's Domodedovo International Airport On February 10, 2011. © Serebryakov Dmitry/ITAR-TASS Photo/CORBIS

IRON MAIDEN IS ONE OF THE MOST successful live bands in rock history. Since 1980's *Metal for Muthas* Tour, Iron Maiden has played twenty tours and performed more than two thousand live shows—a staggering achievement that proves Maiden's dedication not only to their craft but also to their enthusiastic fan base. The award-winning documentary *Iron Maiden: Flight 666* followed the band on their 2008–2009 *Somewhere Back in Time* world tour and showed just how incredible the Iron Maiden live experience really is.

Maiden has also headlined such prestigious festivals as England's Monsters of Rock and Download, Brazil's Rock in Rio, the touring Sonisphere festival, and Rock 'N India. On March 15, 2009, Iron Maiden played to 100,000 fans in São Paulo, their biggest ever audience as a headlining solo act.

Maiden concerts defy fickle fashion trends and are usually bombastic and highly energetic events featuring elaborate stage designs, lighting, and pyrotechnics. In other words, everything a rock concert should be.

In 2008 Metallica drummer Lars Ulrich spoke about the Maiden live experience at *metallicablogmagnetic.com*: "We did a few shows with them in Spain back in 1988 and it was us, Anthrax, and Iron Maiden and it was like 'Fuck, we get to play with Iron Maiden' and we got a chance to hang back at the hotel and party with them, dude it was super cool. . . . I got to see them at Long Beach Arena four or five months ago and it was awesome! Steve Harris, I swear to god, I met Steve Harris for the first time in 1981 and it was the last show they ever played with Paul Di'Anno in Copenhagen, Denmark, at a place the size of your living room. Steve Harris, when I saw them back in February of this year, he's the exact same guy, the exact same guy as the guy I met back in '81 except he's got longer hair now!"

One aspect of their live performance that sets Maiden apart is the way they handle setlists. The band has often been brave enough to play a new album in its entirety, as they did with *A Matter of Life and Death*, though they have received a good deal of criticism for it.

In July 2010, Janick Gers told the *Pittsburgh Post-Gazette*: "I think it's really important if you're going to remain a valid band that you play your new stuff. Otherwise you become a parody of what you started out doing. But it's impossible. Back in the early '80s you could probably do it, but now with YouTube and downloading, the songs would all be out before the album was out. . . . You can't go out and play the greatest hits every time—it's important to play the newer songs because we really believe in them."

There is simply no way to stop Iron Maiden once they hit the road. As the Canadian newspaper *Edmonton Journal* printed in a rave review of a June 2010 gig in Alberta: "It's hard to believe that Maiden could have been any more energetic when they were at their peak in the early '80s; truly the metal gods have gifted these six with powers beyond that of mere mortals." 🇬🇧

LEFT: Maiden embarked on the *Somewhere Back in Time* world tour on February 1, 2008, in Mumbai, with Bruce Dickinson flying *Ed Force One* through the first twenty-one countries.

ABOVE AND BELOW: Somewhere Back in Time tour, Fort Lauderdale, April 2, 2009.

LEFT AND CENTER: Somewhere Back in Time tour, Paris, July 1–2, 2008.

TWENTY-FIRST-CENTURY RENAISSANCE MAN

BY NEIL DANIELS

"Bruce is the consummate Renaissance Man," *Flight 666* filmmaker Sam Dunn told the United Kingdom's *Daily Telegraph* in 2009. "He flies planes as a hobby, he's been a professional fencer, he's written a film, and he has a family." Indeed, Dickinson may be metal's most multitalented individual.

As a musician, Dickinson is a tireless artist and one that is not easily categorized. In addition to his work with Maiden, he has released six solo albums: *Tattooed Millionaire* (1990), *Balls to Picasso* (1994), *Skunkworks* (1996), *Accident of Birth* (1997), *The Chemical Wedding* (1998), and *Tyranny of Souls* (2005). As British rock writer and Dickinson biographer Joe Shooman told this author, Dickinson's solo music is "Interesting, varied, sometimes experimental, and more often than not bloody ace!"

But Dickinson is not only a singer, he's also a writer. He started his first book, *The Adventures of Lord Iffy Boatrace*, about an English landlord, during Maiden's 1986–1987 tour, when he was going through a divorce. Published in 1990, the book sold a highly respectable 30,000 copies. A sequel, *The Missionary Position*, was published two years later. Dickson also wrote a screenplay called *Chemical Wedding* that was made in to a film starring the revered British thespian Simon Callow. Speaking about the film, Dickinson told *Digital Spy*, "On several levels, I think it will be nice for [Iron Maiden fans] to see somebody from Maiden doing something else that gets the band's name out there and also potentially gets a bit of respect for heavy metal and all the rest of it. . . . But, in addition, I think they'll just enjoy it. It's a rollicking good story."

Dickinson is also an experienced radio broadcaster—between 2002 and 2010, he hosted a BBC Radio 6 program called *Bruce Dickinson's Friday Rock Show* before going on to present the BBC Radio 2 show *Masters of Rock*—and has been seen on TV—he has hosted television shows about aviation (*Flying Heavy Metal*) and human combustion (*Inside Spontaneous Human Combustion with Bruce Dickinson*).

Finally, Dickinson is also a licensed pilot and regularly flies a Boeing 757—as well as flying his Maiden cohorts and their crew on *Ed Force One*, he has flown the British football clubs Rangers FC and Liverpool FC

Suffice it to say, the Iron Maiden frontman's talents do not lie in just one particular area. 🇬🇧

Rio de Janeiro, March 14, 2009. All told, Iron Maiden played to more than two million people on the *Somewhere Back in Time* world tour. *Monica Imbuzeiro/Globo via Getty Images*

(continued from page 168)

told *Time Out Dubai* in late 2008. "Taking *Ed Force One* around the planet and playing to our fans in so many different countries was an incredible experience for all of us. I personally found that flying and performing was one of the most challenging and satisfying things I've ever done despite the rigors and the many logistical difficulties we encountered."

On March 15, 2009, Iron Maiden played to their biggest ever audience: 100,000 fans at Autodromo de Interlagos in Sao Paulo, Brazil. "Since Bruce has come back, it's gone back like it was in the early '80s, and there's this escalation," McBrain told Geoff Martin. "In the mid-'80s, people said it was the height of our career. Well it was then, but this is the height of our career, really, because we've come full circle, and we're doing it again."

SOMEWHERE BACK IN TIME WORLD TOUR 08

IRON MAIDEN

IRON MAIDEN

FREE WITH ISSUE 181 OF HAMMER

WWW.IRONMAIDEN.COM

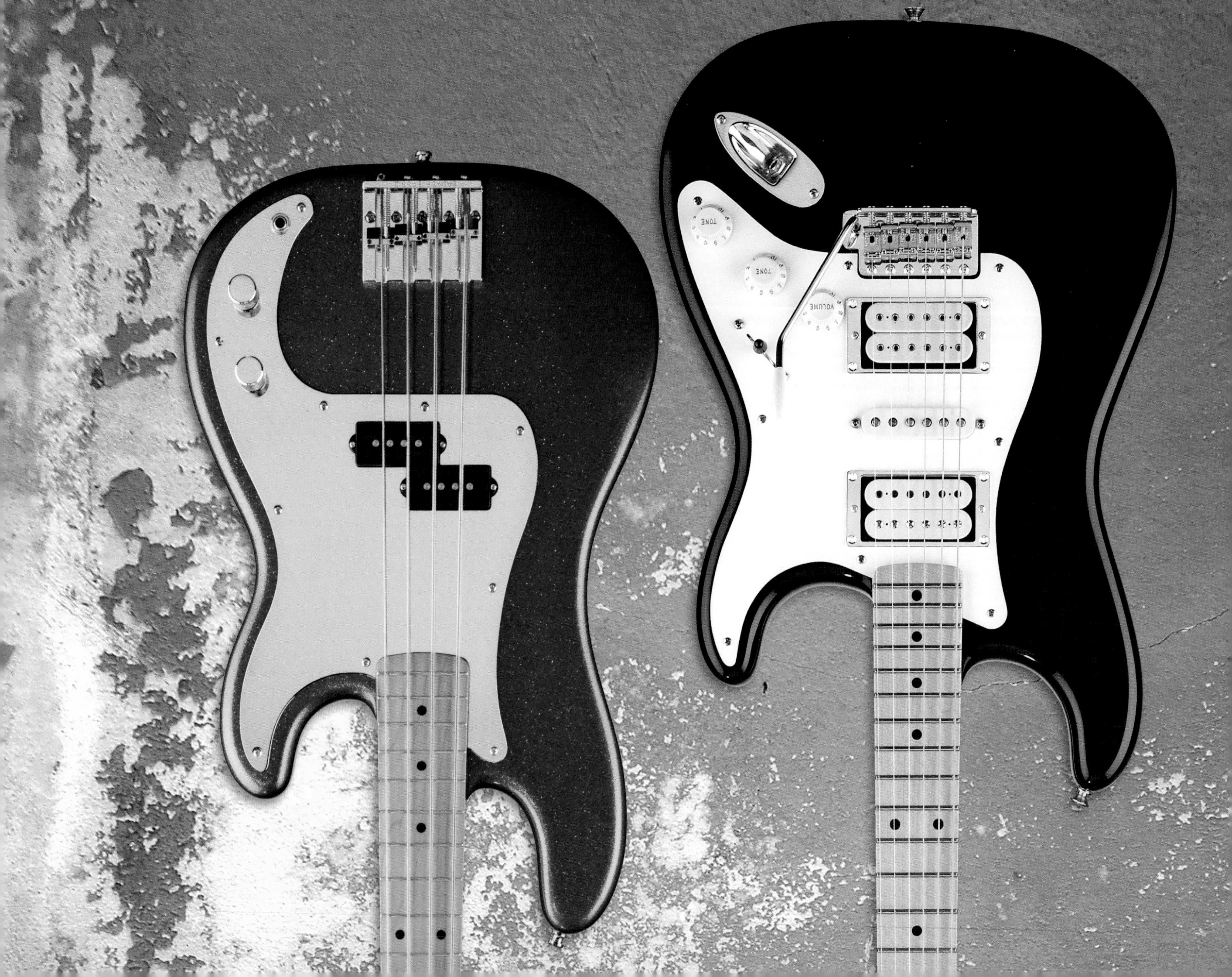

In 2009 Fender unveiled the Steve Harris Precision Bass® and the Dave Murray Stratocaster®. The former sported the blue metalflake paint fans came to associate with Harris' P-Bass. The latter was based on the Stratocaster previously owned by late Free guitarist Paul Kossoff and which Murray snagged in 1976 after answering an ad in *Melody Maker*. Both courtesy Fender Musical Instruments Corporation

SETLIST SELECTIONS

SOMEWHERE BACK IN TIME TOUR

ACES HIGH
2 MINUTES TO MIDNIGHT
REVELATIONS
THE TROOPER
WASTED YEARS
THE NUMBER OF THE BEAST
RUN TO THE HILLS
RIME OF THE ANCIENT MARINER
POWERSLAVE
HEAVEN CAN WAIT
CAN I PLAY WITH MADNESS
FEAR OF THE DARK
IRON MAIDEN
MOONCHILD
THE CLAIRVOYANT
HALLOWED BE THY NAME

The tour proved that Iron Maiden was simply the biggest heavy metal band in the world. Fans revelled in the setlist and a stage design that was an homage to the 1984–1985 World Slavery tour's Egyptian theme. It was exactly what Maiden fans craved.

Since the reunion of Bruce Dickinson, Adrian Smith, and the rest of the band in 1999, and the subsequent album *Brave New World*, Iron Maiden had gone on to dizzying heights of success. The success of *Flight 666* and the press-savvy decision to have Dickinson fly the band around the world in *Ed Force One* gave Iron Maiden a significant amount of mainstream exposure that they had never experienced before. The mainstream press—both the high and low ends—had always

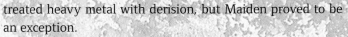

treated heavy metal with derision, but Maiden proved to be an exception.

Apparently, though, not everyone was impressed. At a press conference in Argentina in 2009, Paul Di'Anno levelled some vicious attacks on his former band. "[I]t's Steve Harris' band and all it is is money, money, money, money—nobody else counts," he railed. "And I wrote fuckin' twenty-times better songs than his, but I only got one song on the *Killers* album because it's Steve's—he must have this. Fuckin' Adolf Hitler. I'm not interested. So there you go." Di'Anno continued his rant: "But you need to take drugs when you're with Iron Maiden because they're so fucking boring. And the only drugs were aspirin."

If it really was as bad as all that, Adrian Smith didn't seem to mind. "It's very much right place, right time, with the right management; there are a lot of things involved," he told Chris Vinnicombe of *musicradar.com* when pressed to explain the band's lasting success. "Being a team really helps as a band; a lot of bands have a shelf life because they implode with internal problems."

Various Iron Maiden tribute discs.

CHILDREN OF THE DAMNED

a tribute to IRON MAIDEN

THE PIANO TRIBUTE TO IRON MAIDEN

SOMEWHERE IN HUNGARY

TRIBUTE TO IRON MAIDEN
PART I

NUMBERS FROM THE BEAST
AN ALL STAR SALUTE TO IRON MAIDEN

THE MAIDEN YEARS
VOLUME 2

tribute to Iron Maiden

IRON MAIDNEM
TRIBUTE BAND

10 WASTED YEARS

PIECE OF MADNESS
En honor a Iron Maiden

A Call to Irons

A TRIBUTE TO IRON MAIDEN

2006 *By Ryan LaMar*

Date	City
10.04	Hartford, USA
10.06	Boston, USA
10.07	Camden, USA
10.09	Quebec City, CAN
10.10	Montreal, CAN
10.12	Uniondale, USA
10.13	East Rutherford, USA
10.16	Toronto, CAN
10.17	Auburn Hills, USA
10.18	Rosemont, USA
10.21	Irvine, USA
10.25	Tokyo, JPN
10.26	Hiroshima, JPN
10.28	Tokyo, JPN
10.30	Osaka, JPN
10.31	Nagoya, JPN
11.09	Aalborg, DEN
11.10	Copenhagen, DEN
11.12	Tampere, FIN
11.14–15	Helsinki, FIN
11.17–18	Stockholm, SWE
11.20	Gothenburg, SWE
11.21	Oslo, NOR
11.23	Bergen, NOR
11.25	Stockholm, SWE
11.27	Den Bosch, NED
11.28	Paris, FRA
11.30	Barcelona, ESP
12.02–03	Milan, ITA
12.05	Zurich, SUI
12.07	Stuttgart, GER
12.08	Dortmund, GER
12.10	London, GBR
12.11	Cardiff, GBR
12.12	Birmingham, GBR
12.14	Manchester, GBR
12.15	Glasgow, GBR
12.17	Newcastle, GBR
12.18	Sheffield, GBR
12.20	Dublin, IRE
12.22–23	London, GBR

2007

Date	City
03.09	Dubai, UAE
03.11	Athens, GRE
03.14	Belgrade, SRB
03.17	Bangalore, IND
06.02	Ljubljana, SLO
06.04	Sofia, BUL
06.06	Ostrava, CZE
06.08	Ludwigshafen, GER
06.10	Donington, GBR
06.14	Venice, ITA
06.16	Zwolle, NED
06.17	Dusseldorf, GER
06.20	Rome, ITA
06.21	Bilbao, ESP
06.23	Dessel, BEL
06.24	London, GBR

2008

Date	City
02.01	Mumbai, IND
02.04	Perth, AUS
02.06–07	Melbourne, AUS
02.09–10	Sydney, AUS
02.12	Brisbane, AUS
02.15	Yokohama, JPN
02.16	Tokyo, JPN
02.19	Los Angeles, USA
02.21	Guadalajara, MEX
02.22	Monterrey, MEX
02.24	Mexico City, MEX
02.26	San Jose, CRC
02.28	Bogota, COL
03.02	Sao Paulo, BRA
03.04	Curitiba, BRA
03.05	Porto Allegre, BRA
03.07	Buenos Aires, ARG
03.09	Santiago, CHI
03.12	San Juan, PUR
03.14	East Rutherford, USA
03.16	Toronto, CAN
05.21	San Antonio, USA
05.22	Houston, USA
05.25	Albuquerque, USA
05.26	Phoenix, USA
05.28	Concord, USA
05.30–31	Los Angeles, USA
06.02	Auburn, USA
06.03	Vancouver, CAN
06.05	Calgary, CAN
06.06	Edmonton, CAN
06.08	Regina, CAN
06.09	Winnipeg, CAN
06.11	Rosemont, USA
06.12	Cuyahoga Falls, USA
06.14	Holmdel, USA
06.15	New York City, USA
06.17	Camden, USA
06.18	Columbia, USA
06.20	Mansfield, USA
06.21	Montreal, CAN
06.27	Bologna, ITA
06.29	Dessel, BEL
07.01–02	Paris, FRA
07.05	London, GBR
07.09	Lisbon, POR
07.11	Merida, ESP
07.16	Stockholm, SWE
07.18	Helsinki, FIN
07.19	Tampere, FIN
07.22	Trondheim, NOR
07.24	Oslo, NOR
07.26	Gothenburg, SWE
07.27	Horsens, DEN
07.31	Wacken, GER
08.02	Athens, GRE
08.04	Bucharest, ROU
08.07	Warsaw, POL
08.08	Prague, CZE

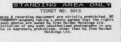

08.10	Split, CRO	02.15	Bangalore, IND		
08.12	Budapest, HUN	02.20	Auckland, NZL		
08.14	Basel, SUI	02.22	Christchurch, NZL	03.14	Rio de Janeiro, BRA
08.16	Assen, NED	02.25	Monterrey, MEX	03.15	Sao Paulo, BRA
08.19	Moscow, RUS	02.26	Guadalajara, MEX	03.18	Belo Horizonte, BRA
		02.28	Mexico City, MEX	03.20	Brasilia, BRA
		03.03	Alajuela, CRC	03.22	Santiago, CHI
		03.05	Caracas, VEN	03.26	Lima, PER

2009

02.10	Belgrade, SRB	03.07	Bogota, COL	03.28	Quilmes, ARG
02.13	Dubai, UAE	03.10	Quito, ECU	03.31	Recife, BRA
		03.12	Manaus, BRA	04.02	Fort Lauderdale, USA

Notes: According to Rod Smallwood, on December 10, 2006, the band performed a live studio session for a C4 TV recording live at Abbey Road for broadcast on April 2, 2007. The band played "Hallowed Be Thy Name" and "Brighter Than a Thousand Suns."

A July 12, 2008, show in Zaragoza, Spain, was cancelled when storms the night before damaged the stage and sound equipment beyond repair.

12. THE 15TH BEAST

THE FINAL FRONTIER AND MAIDEN'S ENDURING LEGACY, 2010–2011

"In ten years time I won't be able to do this and I tell you I don't even want to think about that day."

—Steve Harris, quoted by Paul Morley, *NME*, May 8, 1982

With seemingly nothing left to prove, the notion of slowing down didn't even occur to Iron Maiden. After taking time off during the 2009 holiday season, they wrote and rehearsed new material in Paris the following January. They were ready for album number fifteen. Iron Maiden recorded the follow-up to *A Matter of Life and Death* at the legendary Compass Point Studios in the Bahamas where they had recorded in 1986. The band also recorded at Kevin Shirley's studio in Malibu.

"You always see what comes out really," Adrian Smith told Kelley Simms of the songwriting process (*smnnews.com*). "It's

The band Steve Harris formed back in late 1975 has earned its place in heavy metal history and in popular culture in general. No doubt, whatever the band decides to do in the future, their legacy will endure for generations. *TDC Photography/Shutterstock.com*

a document of where you are at the time. We always set out to come up with the strongest songs possible, melodies, and try and do what Iron Maiden does best. It's difficult to pre-conceive, I mean, I always say that personally, I try and write shorter songs and try to contribute to the more of the rock 'n' roll side. I'm moved into different areas to more progressive pieces, more intricate, which I think is the band's forte."

Despite the running themes, *The Final Frontier*, as the new album was later christened, is not a concept piece. "As with a lot of our albums, you don't really realize when you're doing stuff, but there are common threads," Steve Harris explained to Jon Weiderhorn at *noisecreep.com*. "It's like when we did *Fear of the Dark* [in 1992.] There seemed to be 'fear' mentioned through the album a few times. I just think when you do an album, whatever train of thought you're in at the time, there does seem to be a loose thing going through that ties it all together somehow."

Shirley and Maiden continued to explore the fundamentals of their working relationship and to try new approaches to the music. "Iron Maiden never do demos. Some of the songs were written in the studio and recorded in sections—with no click track, either, because they don't go in for that," the producer revealed to *musicradar.com*'s Joe Bosso. "In fact, 'Where the Wild Wind Blows' was Steve playing and singing parts to us—we didn't know where he was going, but he did, and it came together in the end. Still, I have to say, I much prefer it when a band plays live in the studio instead of layering and doing things in sections. If you can get a great take of a song out of a band, it makes doing any overdubs and embellishments so much easier."

"We just learned parts and then did them and we saw where it went to a certain degree, or how many parts we did," Harris said (Weiderhorn). "Nobody knew which order they were coming in, and nobody except me knew where I wanted to take it. So I just thought it was good to play with a bit of spontaneity like that. We got some really interesting takes for that."

For drummer Nicko McBrain, the making of *The Final Frontier* brought back some bouts of nostalgia. "In terms of figuring out the progressions on the album, it was very much like it was in the old days," he told Bosso. "It was us together in one room going, 'Okay, how are we going to get from this bit to that bit?' You know what I mean? It was natural, a band working as one. We were all looking at one another and communicating and feeling at home, if you like."

The Final Frontier runs a total of seventy-six minutes and thirty-four seconds, the longest Maiden album ever. It is the length of a feature film. The band soaked up their progressive rock influences from the '70s, with influences such as Jethro Tull, Pink Floyd, Yes, ELP, and Genesis peaking through. "Some of the songs are very proggy, especially the ones toward the end of the album," Harris admitted to Weiderhorn. "It's weird because if you talk about one song, it doesn't really represent what's on the rest of the album. It's so diverse, which I think is good. It's one of the things that make the album enjoyable for me."

Given the album's title and the fact that the band had released a total of fifteen studio albums, rumors were rife that Maiden would retire.

"Well, it's not really a numbers game. Not for us, anyway," Bruce Dickinson was quoted by the *Toronto Sun*'s Darryl Sterdan. "Every album you put out is important because it could

"Satellite 15 . . . the Final Frontier" (August 2010).

"Coming Home" (October 2010).

be the last one—especially when you get up to fifteen. I'd like to think this album would be a great starting point for our next album, or an equally great finishing point if we decide never to make another one. Not that we think of it as our last album. But never say never at this point."

The critically acclaimed *The Final Frontier* was released in August 2010 and, incredibly, peaked at No. 1 in over twenty countries. In the United States, where the band basked in the limelight for the first time since the mid-'80s, it topped out at No. 4. Maiden made more headlines and got more press exposure than they had at any time in their lengthy career. Their hard work had paid off. They also stayed true to their musical roots.

J. Edward Keyes wrote in *Rolling Stone*, "Maiden have long had a knack for the lung-busting chorus, but what impresses here are the complicated arrangements." Metal

THE FINAL FRONTIER

BY MICK WALL

FOR AN ALBUM THAT WAS initially hyped as possibly the very last that Iron Maiden would ever record, *The Final Frontier*, released in August 2010, sounds surprisingly alive with ideas and musical invention. Indeed, it may be the most daringly different Maiden album since their empire-building days of the early '80s.

At over seventy-six minutes in length, *The Final Frontier* is also their longest—ever. Casual listeners may find this challenging, but longtime Maiden fanatics will feel justly rewarded by it, given the four-year gap between its release and their previous studio album.

The fourth album of the revitalized Maiden era that ensued with the return of both Bruce Dickinson and Adrian Smith more than a decade before, perhaps the most astonishing aspect of *The Final Frontier* is the sheer audacity of its execution. Six of its ten tracks are more than seven minutes long. Of the remaining four, only one is under five minutes. None are even remotely close to what used to pass as Maiden singles like "Run to the Hills" or "Can I Play with Madness." Instead, they all come from the creative wellspring that gave us first-time-around Maiden epics like "Phantom of the Opera," "Hallowed Be Thy Name," and "Rime of the Ancient Mariner." That is to say, monumental metal classics meant for no one other than Maiden adepts.

The sheer force of will exhibited on *The Final Frontier* leaves the listener almost exhausted by journey's end, yet exhilarated at the same time that a band this old, carrying this much baggage, can still do musical battle with such ferocity. The only modern equivalent that bears comparison is Metallica, and for some years even they have not produced anything as uncompromising as this.

Highlights of an unrelentingly top-heavy set include the moody, mid-paced "Mother of Mercy," the arena-friendly power-ballad "Coming Home," and the battering ram that is "The Alchemist." All are examples of classic, sabre-rattling Iron Maiden. The real excitement, though, is reserved for the latter half of the album, where the changes of timing and tone move at the speed of light, from the thought-provoking "Isle of Avalon" to the unnervingly ominous finale, "When the Wild Wind Blows." The latter, based on author Raymond Briggs' famous post-nuclear graphic novel of almost the same title, while lyrically bleak, is brought to exciting life by music that is so deeply layered it impels you to listen over again almost as soon as it rumbles to a close.

An album that both embraces the band's musical past and reaches out to the file-sharing future, a free download of the track "El Dorado" preceded its release by some two months, while the album was simultaneously released as a regular CD, an iTunes LP, a digital download, and a limited "Mission Edition" containing interviews and a computer game, *Mission II: Rescue & Revenge*.

Although there has been no official single released from the album, a video was produced featuring the latter half of opening track "Satellite 15 . . . The Final Frontier." An edited version of "Coming Home" was also later issued to radio.

The Final Frontier, then, is the twenty-first-century Iron Maiden living their dream, despite the setbacks, the previous triumphs, the dark moments, and the bright lights.

And, no, it is definitely not their final album.

The Final Frontier world tour, Denver, Colorado, June 14, 2010. © Scott D. Smith/CORBIS

The Final Frontier world tour included a headlining slot at Knebworth's Sonisphere Festival.

guru Dom Lawson reviewed the album for *bravewords.com*, writing, "The good news (for everyone else, that is) is that the fifteenth Iron Maiden album is a stunning piece of work that expands on the band's recent progressive explorations, takes them into new textural and melodic areas and does new and intriguing things with that instantly recognisable compositional formula."

Arwa Haider gushed about Dickinson's voice in the United Kingdom's free daily *Metro*: "Classic vocalist and sometime pilot Bruce Dickinson has always functioned best as a master storyteller. Here he has plenty of florid scope, on the fire-and-brimstone atmospheres of 'Mothers of Mercy,' the baroque-inflected 'The Talisman' and eleven-minute closer 'When the Wild Wind Blows,' where he sounds like a rather jaunty harbinger of the apocalypse."

That's not to say the album didn't have its detractors. "*The Final Frontier* becomes less an exercise in experimentation than old-fashioned endurance, and the hushed-intro-bombastic-chorus dynamic begins to grate a little," Jamie Thompson wrote in *The Guardian*. "A shame, because with a bit of judicious editing and a couple more excursions to the edges of their comfort zone, this could have been something special."

One of the U.K.'s top music writers, Simon Price, wrote in the *Independent*, "Business as usual, then, with trademark riffs. Lucky for them the world will never run out of 14 year-old boys."

On December 1, 2010, Maiden learned they had been nominated for a Grammy Award for Best Metal Performance for "El Dorado." It was the band's third such nomination (following "Fear of the Dark" and "The Wicker Man"). "I had the music to the track and I think Bruce wrote the lyrics," Adrian Smith told Kelley Simms. "'El Dorado,' I think, is a comment on people's expectations of a better life. . . . People who are borrowing money so they can have the latest fancy car or the big TV and all that. A lot of people got the rug pulled out from under them with the recession and stuff. So I suppose it's loosely based on that."

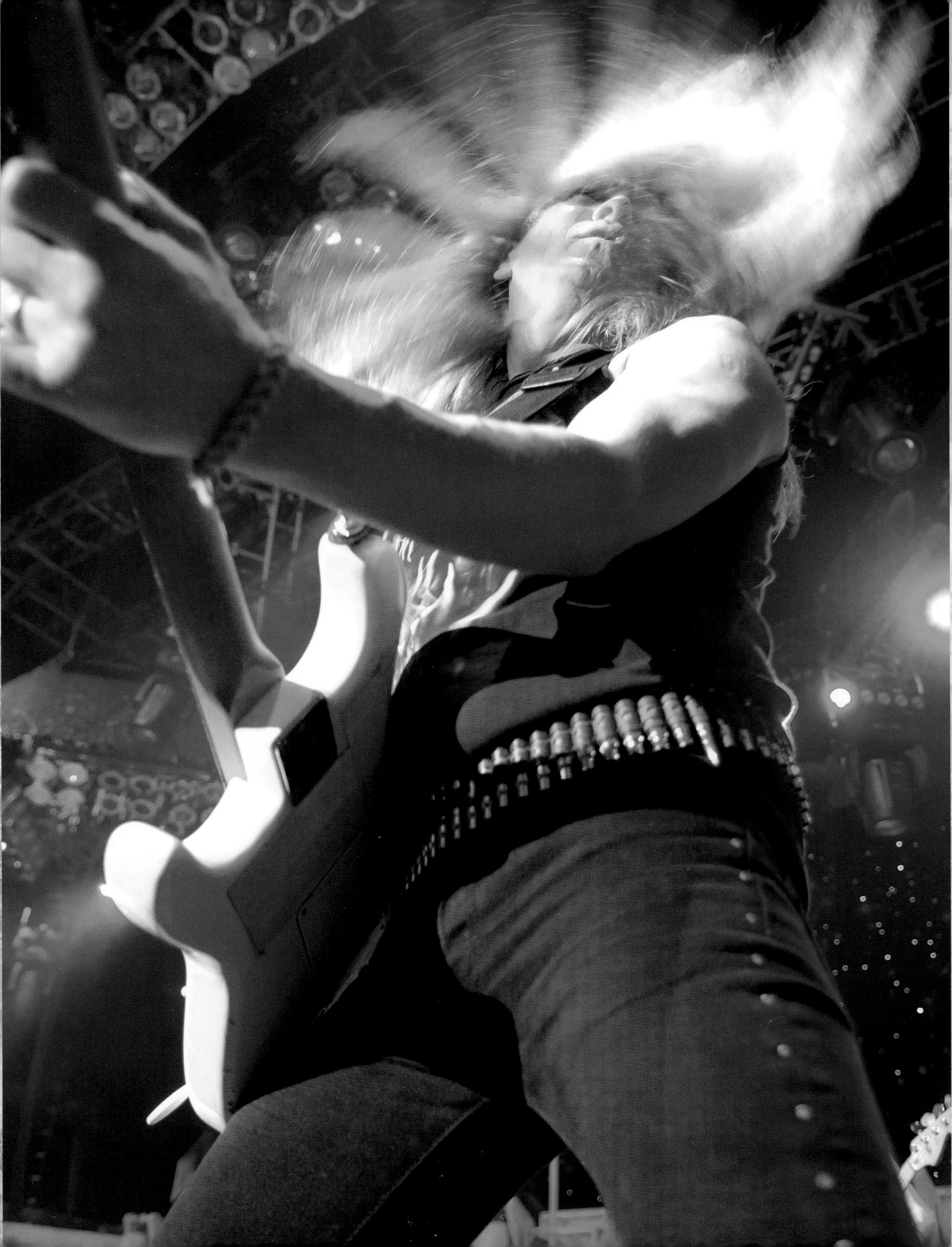

MAIDEN ABROAD

BY NEIL DANIELS

TO REALIZE JUST HOW STAGGERINGLY popular Iron Maiden is outside of the United States and their native United Kingdom, all you have to do is watch the award-winning documentary *Iron Maiden: Flight 666*, which follows the band on the first leg of their *Somewhere Back in Time* world tour in early 2008. Consider, too, that this award-winning film eventually screened in forty-four countries.

In addition to the English-speaking world, Iron Maiden has enjoyed tremendous success in East Asia and, of course, all over heavy-metal-lovin' Europe, where they have played some of the continent's most famous stadiums. But as *Flight 666* shows, Maiden has also brought heavy metal to countries and continents that for whatever reasons had previously shunned the genre. They've played to thousands in Dubai, for example, and have an enormous fan base in India, where heavy metal is not especially popular. In 2008, they opened the *Somewhere* tour in Mumbai, and on the last leg of the tour in 2009 played to an audience of 30,000 at the Palace Grounds in Bangalore as part of the Rock 'N India festival. (Maiden had also previously headlined India in 2007, becoming the first metal band to play that country.)

Maiden has played throughout Latin America, including Brazil, Costa Rica, Colombia, Ecuador, Peru, and Venezuela. In 2008, Adrian Smith told CNN, "In South America, it's like verging on hysteria. . . . We got here to the hotel yesterday and there were 2,300 people screaming. They were screaming up until sort of midnight last night. I could hear them chanting 'Maiden, Maiden.'"

In 2010, *The Final Frontier* peaked at No. 1 in more than two dozen countries. On that tour (as well as the *Somewhere Back in Time* tour in 2008–2009), Bruce Dickinson flew the band and their crew around the world in a Boeing 757 christened *Ed Force One*.

Iron Maiden has come a long way from their unassuming East End roots, to be sure. From the Middle East to the Far East, from South America to the subcontinent, they are, in essence, heavy metal missionaries. 🏴󠁧󠁢󠁥󠁮󠁧󠁿

The Final Frontier world tour had kicked off on June 9, 2010, in Dallas, Texas, and included a number of headlining performances at festivals around the world, including Quebec City Summer Festival in Canada, Sonisphere in England, Sweden, and Finland, and Wacken Open Air Festival in Germany.

Reviewing Maiden's gig at Toronto's Molson Canadian Amphitheatre on July 3, for *Canoe Jam!*, Jason McNeil observed, "[T]he band—who brought along with them a *Star Trek*–like stage design with towers, spaceships, and a backdrop of stars—began the sixteen-song evening with 'The Wicker Man,' a fast, fist-pumper fuelled by the tireless singer Bruce Dickinson. . . . The seemingly all-ages crowd seemed to separate themselves, though, the longer the show went on. As Iron Maiden tossed out oldies such as 'Wrathchild' from 1981's *Killers* quite sparingly, the energy hit another level."

James Gill reviewed the band's show in Denver, Colorado, for U.K. metal rag *Metal Hammer*: "Everyone was in top form. It was evident they would show no mercy on this night. . . . If you have never had the good fortune to witness the greatest heavy metal band of all time, what the fuck are you waiting for?"

The tour continued well in to 2011 and included a healthy number of dates at major U.K. arenas, including those in Manchester, Birmingham, and London. Iconic Maiden mascot Eddie has been featured in a number of incarnations over the

(continued on page 194)

The Final Frontier world tour, Denver, Colorado, June 14, 2010.
TDC Photography/Shutterstock.com

JAPAN 2011
THE FINAL FRONTIER

12TH + 13TH MARCH
TOKYO, JAPAN

SETLIST SELECTIONS

THE FINAL FRONTIER TOUR

THE WICKER MAN
GHOST OF THE NAVIGATOR
WRATHCHILD
EL DORADO
DANCE OF DEATH
THE REINCARNATION OF BENJAMIN BREEG
THESE COLOURS DON'T RUN
BLOOD BROTHERS
WILDEST DREAMS
NO MORE LIES
BRAVE NEW WORLD
FEAR OF THE DARK
IRON MAIDEN
THE NUMBER OF THE BEAST
HALLOWED BE THY NAME
RUNNING FREE

THE FINAL FRONTIER
WORLD TOUR 2011

6TH JUL - TELENOR ARENA, OSLO, NORWAY

IN MEMORY OF THE FALLEN IN OSLO
22.7.11
R.I.P

The Final Frontier world tour, Tokyo (left) and Mexico City (right). The Tokyo dates were cancelled after the March 11 earthquake.

The Final Frontier world tour, Mexico City, March 18, 2011. *Pablo Salazar/Clasos.com/ LatinContent/Getty Images*

THE FINAL FRONTIER
WORLD TOUR

NORTH AMERICA 2010

IRON MAIDEN

VERY SPECIAL GUESTS
DREAM THEATER

FRIDAY, JUNE 11TH   PAVILION

ON SALE THIS SATURDAY AT 10AM!

BUY TICKETS AT LIVEnation.com   CHARGE BY PHONE AT 800-745-3000 OR ONLINE AT LIVENATION.COM.

WWW.IRONMAIDEN.COM

IRON MAIDEN

THE FINAL FRONTIER

WORLD TOUR - 2011

IRON MAIDEN
DOMINGO 20 MARZO
C.E.C. SOPÓ

BOLETAS A LA VENTA
DESDE NOVIEMBRE 12

MÁS INFORMACIÓN:
WWW.EVENPRO.CO

BOLETAS:

Tuboleta.com

DOMICILIOS - CONTACT CENTER
593-6300
 # 593 Desde tu celular

*Cargos Tu boleta en todos los canales de venta.

OTRO CONCIERTO:

Evenpro
www.evenpro.co

(continued from page 186)

years, and on *The Final Frontier* world tour he appeared as an alien mutant during the song "Iron Maiden."

"You see it in how the fans react, how our shows sell out, the whole climate that surrounds us," Nicko McBrain observed of the band's renewed success (Bosso). "We're just at the crest of that new cycle right now. Hopefully, we can make it last longer than the others."

Iron Maiden had earned their place in heavy metal history and in pop culture in general. Would 2011 really mark the final frontier for the band? Would they at least take a well-deserved rest and come back with another masterful album?

"No, it ain't gonna be the last record," McBrain confessed to *metalhammer.co.uk* in 2010. "Not as far as I'm concerned. The general feeling is that is if we want to make another record, we will. You can never say never."

"I think I would say that the band, since its inception up to now, hasn't changed a great deal in essence," Smith told *Review Magazine*'s Ed McArdle. "Iron Maiden never sold out—that's the bottom line. We've always toured—always taken our music to the fans. We've had to because of no radio play. And I think when you've achieved success that way it's more long-lasting than when you have a couple of radio hits. I could never figure out this phenomenon, but I've been around a while now and I think that's what it is."

Indeed, there is no doubt that whatever the band decides to do in the future their legacy will endure for many years to come. As Bruce

Dickinson told *The Mirror* in 2008, "With the Internet, bands can come and go every five minutes and the music looks disposable. Maiden represents something that's not disposable."

Whatever Maiden decides to do, they'll never lose sight of their roots. They'll stay true to their fans, themselves, and their art. 🇬🇧

The Final Frontier world tour visits the thirtieth International Motorcycling Meeting in Faro, Portugal, July 14, 2011. © Luis Forra/epa/CORBIS

194 · IRON MAIDEN

2010
By Ryan LaMar

06.09	Dallas, USA
06.11	Houston, USA
06.12	San Antonio, USA
06.14	Denver, USA
06.16	Albuquerque, USA
06.17	Phoenix, USA
06.19	San Bernardino, USA
06.20	Concord, USA
06.22	Auburn, USA
06.24	Vancouver, CAN
06.26	Edmonton, CAN
06.27	Calgary, CAN
06.29	Saskatoon, CAN
06.30	Winnipeg, CAN
07.03	Toronto, CAN
07.06	Ottawa, CAN
07.07	Montreal, CAN
07.09	Quebec City, CAN
07.11	Holmdel, USA
07.12	New York City, USA
07.14	Pittsburgh, USA
07.15	Cleveland, USA
07.17	Detroit, USA
07.18	Chicago, USA
07.20	Bristow, USA

07.30	Dublin, IRE
08.01	Knebworth, GBR
08.05	Wacken, GER
08.07	Stockholm, SWE
08.08	Pori, FIN
08.11	Bergen, NOR
08.14	Budapest, HUN
08.15	Cluj-Napoca, ROU
08.17	Codroipo, ITA
08.19	Kiewit, BEL
08.21	Valencia, ESP

2011

02.11	Moscow, RUS
02.15	Kallang, SIN
02.17	Jakarta, INA
02.20	Bali, INA
02.23	Melbourne, AUS
02.24	Sydney, AUS
02.26	Brisbane, AUS
02.27	Sydney, AUS
03.04	Melbourne, AUS
03.05	Adelaide, AUS
03.07	Perth, AUS
03.10	Seoul, KOR
03.17	Monterrey, MEX
03.18	Mexico City, MEX
03.20	Bogota, COL
03.23	Lima, PER
03.26	Sao Paulo, BRA
03.28	Rio de Janeiro, BRA (rescheduled from 03.27)
03.30	Brasilia, BRA
04.01	Belem, BRA
04.03	Recife, BRA
04.05	Curritiba, BRA

04.08	Buenos Aires, ARG
04.10	Santiago, CHI
04.14	San Juan, PUR
04.16	Sunrise, USA
04.17	Tampa, USA
05.28	Frankfurt, GER
05.29	Oberhausen, GER
05.31	Munich, GER
06.02	Hamburg, GER
06.03	Berlin, GER
06.07	Stuttgart, GER
06.08	Arnhem, NED
06.10	Warsaw, POL
06.11	Milovice, CZE
06.12–13	Nickelsdorf, AUT
06.17	Athens, GRE
06.19	Istanbul, TUR
06.24	Basel, SUI
06.25	Imola, ITA
06.27–28	Paris, FRA
06.30	Roskilde, DEN
07.01	Gothenburg, SWE
07.03	Werchter, BEL
07.06	Oslo, NOR
07.08	Helsinki, FIN
07.10	St. Petersburg, RUS
07.14	Faro, POR
07.16	Madrid, ESP
07.20	Glasgow, GBR
07.21	Aberdeen, GBR
07.23	Newcastle, GBR
07.24	Sheffield, GBR
07.27	Nottingham, GBR
07.28	Manchester, GBR
07.31	Birmingham, GBR
08.01	Cardiff, GBR
08.03	Belfast, GBR
08.05–06	London, GBR

Note: The March 12–13, 2011, dates in Tokyo were cancelled due to the March 11 earthquake.

SELECTED DISCOGRAPHY

BY NEIL DANIELS

As of this publication, Iron Maiden has released fifteen studio albums as well as several live albums and collections with global sales of 85 million. Discounting the many tribute albums and bootlegs, the official Maiden discography is still pretty extensive. What follows is a selective yet detailed discography of original U.K. and U.S. releases. While all studio albums are included, as well as selected official compilations, not every Iron Maiden song ever issued is represented. Further, in the interest of space and curbing repetition, standard quotation marks are omitted from song titles in album, compilation, and DVD/VHS track listings, and songwriting credits are noted only on the first reference to each song (except in the case of covers).

Studio Albums

IRON MAIDEN

Labels: EMI (U.K.); Harvest/Capitol (U.S.)
Released: April 1980 (U.K.); August 1980 (U.S.)
Recorded: Kingsway Studios, London
Producer: Will Malone

1. Prowler (Harris); 2. Remember Tomorrow (Harris/Di'Anno); 3. Running Free (Harris/Di'Anno); 4. Phantom of the Opera (Harris); 5. Transylvania (Harris); 6. Strange World (Harris); 7. Sanctuary (Iron Maiden)*; 8. Charlotte the Harlot (Murray); 9. Iron Maiden (Harris)

Note: "Sanctuary" originally appeared on the American release only.

KILLERS

Labels: EMI (U.K.); Harvest/Capitol (U.S.)
Released: February 1981 (U.K.); June 1981 (U.S.)
Recorded: Battery Studios, London
Producer: Martin Birch

1. The Ides of March (Harris); 2. Wrathchild (Harris); 3. Murders in the Rue Morgue (Harris); 4. Another Life (Harris); 5. Genghis Khan (Harris); 6. Innocent Exile (Harris); 7. Killers (Di'Anno/Harris); 8. Twilight Zone (Harris/Murray); 9. Prodigal Son (Harris); 10. Purgatory (Harris); Drifter (Harris)

Notes: "Twilight Zone" originally appeared on the American release only. Release marked the Maiden debut of guitarist Adrian Smith, who replaced Dennis Stratton.

THE NUMBER OF THE BEAST

Labels: EMI (U.K.); Harvest/Capitol (U.S.)
Released: March 1982
Recorded: Battery Studios, London
Producer: Martin Birch

1. Invaders (Harris); 2. Children of the Damned (Harris); 3. The Prisoner (Smith/Harris); 4. 22 Acacia Avenue (Smith/Harris); 5. The Number of the Beast (Harris); 6. Run to the Hills (Harris); 7. Gangland (Smith/Burr); 8. Hallowed Be Thy Name (Harris)

Note: Release marked the Maiden debut of vocalist Bruce Dickinson, who replaced Paul Di'Anno.

PIECE OF MIND

Labels: EMI (U.K.); Harvest/Capitol (U.S.)
Released: May 1983
Recorded: Compass Point Studios, Nassau, Bahamas
Producer: Martin Birch

1. Where Eagles Dare (Harris); 2. Revelations (Dickinson); 3. Flight of Icarus (Smith/Dickinson); 4. Die with Your Boots On (Smith/Dickinson/Harris); 5. The Trooper (Harris); 6. Still Life (Murray/Harris); 7. Quest for Fire (Harris); 8. Sun and Steel (Dickinson/Smith); 9. To Tame a Land (Harris)

Note: Release marked the Maiden debut of drummer Nicko McBrain, who replaced Clive Burr.

POWERSLAVE

Labels: EMI (U.K.); Harvest/Capitol (U.S.)
Released: September 1984
Recorded: Battery Studios, London
Producer: Martin Birch

1. Aces High (Harris); 2. 2 Minutes to Midnight (Smith/Dickinson); 3. Losfer Words (Big 'Orra) (Harris); 4. Flash of the Blade (Dickinson); 5. The Duellists (Harris); 6. Back in the Village (Smith/Dickinson); 7. Powerslave (Dickinson); 8. Rime of the Ancient Mariner (Harris)

Note: "Rime of the Ancient Mariner" excerpted from Samuel Taylor Coleridge's epic poem of the same name.

SOMEWHERE IN TIME

Labels: EMI (U.K.); Harvest/Capitol (U.S.)
Released: September 1986
Recorded: Compass Point Studios, Nassau, Bahamas; Wisseloord Studios, Hilversum, Netherlands
Producer: Martin Birch

1. Caught Somewhere in Time (Harris); 2. Wasted Years (Smith); 3. Sea of Madness (Smith); 4. Heaven Can Wait (Harris); 5. The Loneliness of the Long Distance Runner (Harris); 6. Stranger in a Strange Land (Smith); 7. Deja-Vu (Murray/Harris); 8. Alexander the Great (Harris)

SEVENTH SON OF A SEVENTH SON

Labels: EMI (U.K.); Harvest/Capitol (U.S.)
Released: April 1988
Recorded: Musicland Studios, Munich
Producer: Martin Birch

1. Moonchild (Smith/Dickinson); 2. Infinite Dreams (Harris); 3. Can I Play with Madness (Smith/Dickinson/Harris); 4. The Evil That Men Do (Smith/Dickinson/Harris); 5. Seventh Son of a Seventh Son (Harris); 6. The Prophecy (Murray/Harris); 7. The Clairvoyant (Harris); 8. Only the Good Die Young (Harris/Dickinson)

Note: This was the first studio album to feature the work of the band's touring keyboardist Michael Kenney, who would appear on the band's next four studio releases. Kenney was still a touring member at the time of publication.

NO PRAYER FOR THE DYING

Labels: EMI (U.K.); Epic (U.S.)
Released: October 1990
Recorded: Barnyard Studios, Essex, England
Producer: Martin Birch

1. Tailgunner (Harris/Dickinson); 2. Holy Smoke (Harris/Dickinson); 3. No Prayer for the Dying (Harris); 4. Public Enema Number One (Murray/Dickinson); 5. Fates Warning (Murray/Harris); 6. The Assassin (Harris); 7. Run Silent, Run Deep (Harris/Dickinson); 8. Hooks in You (Dickinson/Smith); 9. Bring Your Daughter . . . to the Slaughter (Dickinson); 10. Mother Russia (Harris); 11. Listen with Nicko! Part XI

Notes: "Listen with Nicko! Part XI" was a hidden track on the U.S. release only. Release marked the Maiden debut of guitarist Janick Gers, who replaced Adrian Smith. It was also the band's first album on Epic in the United States.

FEAR OF THE DARK

Labels: EMI (U.K.); Epic (U.S.)
Released: May 1992
Recorded: Barnyard Studios, Essex, England
Producers: Martin Birch and Steve Harris

1. Be Quick or Be Dead (Dickinson/Gers); 2. From Here to Eternity (Harris); 3. Afraid to Shoot Strangers (Harris); 4. Fear Is the Key (Dickinson/Gers); 5. Childhood's End (Harris); 6. Wasting Love (Dickinson/Gers); 7. The Fugitive (Harris); 8. Chains of Misery (Dickinson/Murray); 9. The Apparition (Harris/Gers); 10. Judas Be My Guide (Dickinson/Murray); 11. Weekend Warrior (Harris/Gers); 12. Fear of the Dark (Harris)

Notes: Fear of the Dark was the first Maiden album to feature sleeve art by someone other than Derek Riggs. The cover's Eddie-like creature was illustrated by Melvyn Grant. The album was also notable in that it would be the last with longtime producer Martin Birch at the helm and the last featuring Bruce Dickinson until his return in 1999.

THE X FACTOR

Label: EMI (U.K.); CMC International (U.S.)
Released: October 1995
Recorded: Barnyard Studios, Essex, England
Producers: Steve Harris and Nigel Green

1. Sign of the Cross (Harris); 2. Lord of the Flies (Harris/Gers); 3. Man on the Edge (Bayley/Gers); 4. Fortunes of War (Harris); 5. Look for the Truth (Harris/Bayley/Gers); 6. The Aftermath (Harris/Bayley/Gers); 7. Judgement of Heaven (Harris); 8. Blood on the World's Hands (Harris); 9. The Edge of Darkness (Harris/Bayley/Gers); 10. 2 A.M. (Harris/Bayley/Gers); 11. The Unbeliever (Harris/Gers)

Note: Release marked the Maiden debut of vocalist Blaze Bayley, who replaced Bruce Dickinson.

VIRTUAL XI

Label: EMI (U.K.); CMC International (U.S.)
Released: March 1998
Recorded: Barnyard Studios, Essex, England
Producers: Steve Harris and Nigel Green

1. Futureal (Bayley/Harris); 2. The Angel and the Gambler (Harris); 3. Lightning Strikes Twice (Murray/Harris); 4. The Clansman (Harris); 5. When Two Worlds Collide (Bayley/Murray/Harris); 6. The Educated Fool (Harris); 7. Don't Look to the Eyes of a Stranger (Harris); 8. Como Estais Amigos (Bayley/Gers)

BRAVE NEW WORLD

Labels: EMI (U.K.); Sony Portrait (U.S.)
Released: May 2000
Recorded: Guillaume Tell Studios, Paris
Producers: Steve Harris and Kevin Shirley

1. The Wicker Man (Dickinson/Smith/Harris); 2. Ghost of the Navigator (Dickinson/Gers/Harris); 3. Brave New World (Dickinson/Murray/Harris); 4. Blood Brothers (Harris); 5. The Mercenary (Gers/Harris); 6. Dream of Mirrors (Gers/Harris); 7. The Fallen Angel (Smith/Harris); 8. The Nomad (Murray/Harris); 9. Out of the Silent Planet (Dickinson/Gers/Harris); 10. The Thin Line Between Love & Hate (Murray/Harris)

Notes: Brave New World officially marked the end of the Blaze Bayley era, with Bruce Dickinson returning to the fold. Also returning to Maiden for this album was guitarist Adrian Smith, the band instituting a three-guitar line-up. Finally, the album cover (the band's first on Sony's Portrait imprint) was the first studio LP since No Prayer for the Dying *to feature the work of Derek Riggs, who illustrated the Eddie head at the top of the sleeve.*

DANCE OF DEATH

Label: EMI
Released: September 2003
Recorded: Sarm West Studios, London
Producer: Kevin Shirley
Co-producer: Steve Harris

1. Wildest Dreams (Smith/Harris); 2. Rainmaker (Murray/Harris/Dickinson); 3. No More Lies (Harris); 4. Montségur (Gers/Harris/Dickinson); 5. Dance of Death (Gers/Harris); 6. Gates of Tomorrow (Gers/Harris/Dickinson); 7. New Frontier (McBrain/Smith/Dickinson); 8. Paschendale (Smith/Harris); 9. Face in the Sand (Smith/Harris/Dickinson); 10. Age of Innocence (Murray/Harris); 11. Journeyman (Smith/Harris/Dickinson)

Notes: The only Iron Maiden album to date to feature a Nicko McBrain songwriting credit. Illustrator David Patchett asked for his credit to be removed from the album when the band decided to use an unfinished concept illustration that he provided to the band.

A MATTER OF LIFE AND DEATH

Label: EMI
Released: August 2006 (worldwide); September 2006 (U.S., Canada, and Japan)
Recorded: Sarm West Studios, London
Producer: Kevin Shirley
Co-producer: Steve Harris

1. Different World (Smith/Harris); 2. These Colours Don't Run (Smith/Harris/Dickinson); 3. Brighter Than a Thousand Suns (Smith/Harris/Dickinson); 4. The Pilgrim (Gers/Harris); 5. The Longest Day (Smith/Harris/Dickinson); 6. Out of the Shadows (Dickinson/Harris); 7. The Reincarnation of Benjamin Breeg (Murray/Harris); 8. For the Greater Good of God (Harris); 9. Lord of Light (Smith/Harris/Dickinson); 10. The Legacy (Gers/Harris)

Note: A Matter of Life and Death was released in Italy and Finland on August 25 and worldwide on August 28, except in the United States, Canada, and Japan, where it was released September 5.

THE FINAL FRONTIER

Labels: EMI (U.K.); Sony, UME (U.S.)
Released: August 2010
Recorded: Compass Point Studios, Nassau, Bahamas; The Cave Studios, Malibu, California
Producer: Kevin Shirley
Co-producer: Steve Harris

1. Satellite 15 . . . The Final Frontier (Smith/Harris); 2. El Dorado (Smith/Harris/Dickinson); 3. Mother of Mercy (Smith/Harris); 4. Coming Home (Smith/Harris/Dickinson); 5. The Alchemist (Gers/Harris/Dickinson); 6. Isle of Avalon (Smith/Harris); 7. Starblind (Smith/Harris/Dickinson); 8. The Talisman (Gers/Harris); 9. The Man Who Would Be King (Murray/Harris); 10. When the Wild Wind Blows (Harris)

Note: The Final Frontier reached No. 1 on the album charts in an astounding thirty countries.

Live Albums

LIVE AFTER DEATH

Labels: EMI (U.K.); Harvest/Capitol (U.S.)
Released: October 1985
Producer: Martin Birch
Recorded: Arena, Long Beach, California, March 14–17, 1985
Personnel: Dickinson, Murray, Smith, Harris, and McBrain

1. Intro: Churchill's Speech; 2. Aces High; 3. 2 Minutes to Midnight; 4. The Trooper; 5. Revelations; 6. Flight of Icarus; 7. Rime of the Ancient Mariner; 8. Powerslave; 9. The Number of the Beast; 10. Hallowed Be Thy Name; 11. Iron Maiden; 12. Run to the Hills; 13. Running Free

Note: Reissues in 1995 and 1998 featured additional material recorded at Hammersmith Odeon, London, on October 8–10 and 12, 1985.

A REAL LIVE ONE

Label: EMI

Released: March 1993

Producer: Steve Harris

Personnel: Dickinson, Murray, Gers, Harris, McBrain, and Kenney

Recorded: Track 1, Monsters of Rock, Donington, England, August 22, 1992; Track 2, Valby Hallen, Copenhagen, August 25, 1992; Track 3, Brabanthallen, Den Bosch, Netherlands, September 2, 1992; Track 4, La Grande Halle de la Villette, Paris, September 5, 1992; Track 5, La Patinoire de Malley, Lausanne, Switzerland, September 4, 1992; Track 6, Forest National, Brussels, August 17, 1992; Track 7, The Globe, Stockholm, August 29, 1992; Tracks 8 and 10–11, the Ice Hall, Helsinki, August 27, 1992; Track 9, unknown.

1. Be Quick or Be Dead; 2. From Here to Eternity; 3. Can I Play with Madness; 4. Wasting Love; 5. Tailgunner; 6. The Evil That Men Do; 7. Afraid to Shoot Strangers; 8. Bring Your Daughter . . . to the Slaughter; 9. Heaven Can Wait; 10. The Clairvoyant; 11. Fear of the Dark

A REAL DEAD ONE

Label: EMI

Released: October 1993

Producer: Steve Harris

Personnel: Dickinson, Murray, Gers, Harris, McBrain, and Kenney

Recorded: Track 1, Valby Hallen, Copenhagen, August 25, 1992; Tracks 2 and 11, the Ice Hall, Helsinki, August 27, 1992; Track 3, the Palaghiaccio, Rome, April 30, 1993; Tracks 4 and 5, Grugahalle, Essen, Germany, April 17, 1993; Track 6 unknown; Tracks 7 and 8, La Patinoire de Malley, Lausanne, Switzerland, September 4, 1992; Track 9, Vitkovice Sports Hall, Ostrava, Czech Republic, April 5, 1993; Track 10, La Grande Halle de la Villette, Paris, September 5, 1992; Track 12, Olympic Arena, Moscow, June 2 or 3, 1993.

1. The Number of the Beast; 2. The Trooper; 3. Prowler; 4. Transylvania; 5. Remember Tomorrow; 6. Where Eagles Dare; 7. Sanctuary; 8. Running Free; 9. Run to the Hills; 10. 2 Minutes to Midnight; 11. Iron Maiden; 12. Hallowed By Thy Name

Note: A Real Live One and A Real Dead One were released together in September 1998 as a two-disc package entitled A Real Live Dead One.

LIVE AT DONINGTON

Label: EMI

Released: November 1993 (U.K.); October 1998 (U.S.)

Producer: Steve Harris

Personnel: Dickinson, Murray, Gers, Harris, McBrain, and Kenney

Recorded: Monsters of Rock, Donington, England, August 22, 1992

(CD1) 1. Be Quick or Be Dead; 2. The Number of the Beast; 3. Wrathchild; 4. From Here to Eternity; 5. Can I Play with Madness; 6. Wasting Love; 7. Tailgunner; 8. The Evil That Men Do; 9. Afraid to Shoot Strangers; 10. Fear of the Dark (CD2) 1. Bring Your Daughter . . . to the Slaughter; 2. The Clairvoyant; 3. Heaven Can Wait; 4. Run to the Hills; 5. 2 Minutes to Midnight; 6. Iron Maiden; 7. Hallowed Be Thy Name; 8. The Trooper; 9. Sanctuary; 10. Running Free

ROCK IN RIO

Labels: EMI (U.K.); Sony (U.S.)

Released: March 2002

Producer: Kevin Shirley

Personnel: Dickinson, Murray, Gers, Smith, Harris, McBrain, and Kenney

Recorded: Rock in Rio, Rio de Janeiro, January 19, 2001

(CD1) 1. Intro: Arthur's Farewell (Jerry Goldsmith); 2. The Wicker Man; 3. Ghost of the Navigator; 4. Brave New World; 5. Wrathchild; 6. 2 Minutes to Midnight; 7. Blood Brothers; 8. Sign of the Cross; 9. The Mercenary; 10. The Trooper (CD2) 1. Dream of Mirrors; 2. The Clansman; 3. The Evil That Men Do; 4. Fear of the Dark; 5. Iron Maiden; 6. The Number of the Beast; 7. Hallowed Be Thy Name; 8. Sanctuary; 9. Run to the Hills

Note: Over the years, dramatic entrance music (and speeches, as in the case of "Churchill's Speech") became a Maiden staple. In this case "Arthur's Farewell" was culled from the 1995 Sean Connery and Richard Gere film First Knight. The performance from which this release was recorded took place before a quarter-million fans.

BBC ARCHIVES

Label: EMI

Released: November 2002

Producer: Tony Wilson

Personnel: (CD1) Di'Anno, Murray, Tony Parsons, Harris, Doug Sampson, Dickinson, Smith, and Burr; (CD2) Di'Anno, Murray, Stratton, Harris, Burr, Dickinson, Smith, and McBrain

Recorded: (CD1) Tracks 1–4, BBC's Friday Rock Session Show, London, likely November 14, 1979; Tracks 5–14, Reading Festival, Reading, England, August 28, 1982 (CD2) Tracks 1–6, Reading Festival, Reading, England, August 23, 1980; Tracks 7–14, Monsters of Rock, Donington, England, August 20, 1988

(CD1) 1. Iron Maiden; 2. Running Free; 3. Transylvania; 4. Sanctuary; 5. Wrathchild; 6. Run to the Hills; 7. Children of the Damned; 8. The Number of the Beast; 9. 22 Acacia Avenue; 10. Transylvania; 11. The Prisoner; 12. Hallowed Be Thy Name; 13. Phantom of the Opera; 14. Iron Maiden
(CD2) 1. Prowler; 2. Remember Tomorrow; 3. Killers; 4. Running Free; 5. Transylvania; 6. Iron Maiden; 7. Moonchild; 8. Wrathchild; 9. Infinite Dreams; 10. The Trooper; 11. Seventh Son of a Seventh Son; 12. The Number of the Beast; 13. Hallowed Be Thy Name; 14. Iron Maiden

BEAST OVER HAMMERSMITH

Label: EMI

Released: November 2002

Producers: Doug Hall and Steve Harris

Personnel: Dickinson, Murray, Smith, Harris, and Burr

Recorded: Hammersmith Odeon, London, March 20, 1982

(CD1) 1. Murders in the Rue Morgue; 2. Run to the Hills; 3. Children of the Damned; 4. The Number of the Beast; 5. Another Life; 6. Killers; 7. 22 Acacia Avenue; 8. Total Eclipse (CD2) 1. Transylvania; 2. The Prisoner; 3. Hallowed Be Thy Name; 4. Phantom of the Opera; 5. Iron Maiden; 6. Sanctuary; 7. Drifter; 8. Running Free; 9. Prowler

DEATH ON THE ROAD

Label: EMI

Released: August 2005

Producers: Kevin Shirley and Steve Harris

Personnel: Dickinson, Murray, Smith, Gers, Harris, McBrain, and Kenney

Recorded: Westfalenhalle, Dortmund, Germany, November 24, 2003

(CD1) 1. Wildest Dreams; 2. Wrathchild; 3. Can I Play with Madness; 4. The Trooper; 5. Dance of Death; 6. Rainmaker; 7. Brave New World; 8. Paschendale; 9. Lord of the Flies (CD2) 1. No More Lies; 2. Hallowed Be Thy Name; 3. Fear of the Dark; 4. Iron Maiden; 5. Journeyman; 6. The Number of the Beast; 7. Run to the Hills

IRON MAIDEN: FLIGHT 666

Label: EMI; Universal Music (U.S.)

Released: May 2009 (U.K.); June 2009 (U.S.)

Producers: Kevin Shirley and Steve Harris

Personnel: Dickinson, Murray, Smith, Gers, Harris, McBrain, and Kenney

Recorded: (CD1) Tracks 1–2, Bandra-Kurla Complex, Mumbai, February 1, 2008; Track 3, Rod Laver Arena, Melbourne, February 7, 2008; Track 4, Acer Arena, Sydney, February 9, 2008; Track 5, Makuhari Messe, Chiba, Japan, February 16, 2008; Track 6, Arena Monterrey, Monterrey, Mexico, February 22, 2008; Track 7, The Forum, Inglewood, California, February 19, 2008; Track 8, Foro Sol Stadium, Mexico City, February 24, 2008; Track 9, Izod Center, Meadowlands, New Jersey, March 14, 2008 (CD2) Track 1, Saprissa Stadium, San José, Costa Rica, February 26, 2008; Track 2, Palmeiras Stadium, São Paulo, March 2, 2008; Track 3, Simón Bolívar Park, Bogotá, February 28, 2008; Track 4, Ferrocaril Oeste Stadium, Buenos Aires, March 7, 2008; Track 5, Pista Atletica, Santiago, Chile, March 9, 2008; Track 6, Coliseo de Puerto Rico, San Juan, March 12, 2008; Track 7, Pedreira Paulo Leminski, Curitiba, Brazil, March 4, 2008; Track 8, Air Canada Centre, Toronto, March 16, 2008

(CD1) 1. Intro: Churchill's Speech; 2. Aces High; 3. 2 Minutes to Midnight; 4. Revelations; 5. The Trooper; 6. Wasted Years; 7. The Number of the Beast; 8. Can I Play with Madness; 9. Rime of the Ancient Mariner (CD2) 1. Powerslave; 2. Heaven Can Wait; 3. Run to the Hills; 4. Fear of the Dark; 5. Iron Maiden; 6. Moonchild; 7. The Clairvoyant; 8. Hallowed Be Thy Name

Collections

BEST OF THE BEAST

Released: September 1996

1. The Number of the Beast; 2. Can I Play with Madness; 3. Fear of the Dark (live); 4. Run to the Hills; 5. Bring Your Daughter . . . to the Slaughter; 6. The Evil That Men Do; 7. Aces High; 8. Be Quick or Be Dead; 9. 2 Minutes to Midnight; 10. Man on the Edge; 11. Virus (Bayley/Murray/Gers/Harris); 12. Running Free (live); 13. Wasted Years; 14. The Clairvoyant; 15. The Trooper; 16. Hallowed Be Thy Name

Notes: "Fear of the Dark" was culled from A Real Live One. *"Virus" was previously unreleased and recorded for this compilation. "Running Free" was taken from* Live After Death. *A deluxe two-CD edition contained twenty-seven tracks including two songs from the 1979 demo.*

ED HUNTER

Released: July 1999

(CD1) 1. Iron Maiden (live); 2. The Trooper; 3. The Number of the Beast; 4. Wrathchild; 5. Futureal; 6. Fear of the Dark; 7. Be Quick or Be Dead; 8. 2 Minutes to Midnight; 9. Man on the Edge; 10. Aces High; 11. The Evil That Men Do; 12. Wasted Years; 13. Powerslave; 14. Hallowed Be Thy Name; 15. Wrathchild (1999 Version) (CD2) 1. Run to the Hills; 2. The Clansman; 3. Phantom of the Opera; 4. Killers; 5. Stranger in a Strange Land; 6. Tailgunner

Notes: Released in conjunction with the video game of the same name. "Wrathchild (1999 Version)" was a hidden track appearing on the American release only.

EDWARD THE GREAT

Released: November 2002

1. Run to the Hills; 2. The Number of the Beast; 3. Flight of Icarus; 4. The Trooper; 5. 2 Minutes to Midnight; 6. Wasted Years; 7. Can I Play with Madness; 8. The Evil That Men Do; 9. The Clairvoyant; 10. Infinite Dreams; 11. Holy Smoke; 12. Bring Your Daughter . . . to the Slaughter; 13. Man on the Edge; 14. Futureal; 15. The Wicker Man; 16. Fear of the Dark (live)

Notes: "Fear of the Dark" was taken from the Rock in Rio *live release. A revised and resequenced edition released in 2005 featured the live version of "Fear of the Dark" for* Death on the Road. *It also dropped "The Clairvoyant," "Infinite Dreams," and "Holy Smoke" (which appeared on 2005's* The Essential Iron Maiden*) and added "Brave New World," "Wildest Dreams," and "Rainmaker."*

THE ESSENTIAL IRON MAIDEN

Released: July 2005

(CD1) 1. Paschendale; 2. Rainmaker; 3. The Wicker Man; 4. Brave New World; 5. Futureal; 6. The Clansman; 7. Sign of the Cross; 8. Man on the Edge; 9. Be Quick or Be Dead; 10. Fear of the Dark (live); 11. Holy Smoke; 12. Bring Your Daughter . . . to the Slaughter; 13. The Clairvoyant (CD2) 1. The Evil That Men Do; 2. Wasted Years; 3. Heaven Can Wait; 4. 2 Minutes to Midnight; 5. Aces High; 6. Flight of Icarus; 7. The Trooper; 8. The Number of the Beast; 9. Run to the Hills; 10. Wrathchild; 11. Killers; 12. Phantom of the Opera; 13. Running Free (live); 14. Iron Maiden (live)

Notes: Live tracks were taken from the following releases: "Fear of the Dark," Rock in Rio*; "Running Free,"* Live After Death*; and "Iron Maiden,"* Death on the Road.

SOMEWHERE BACK IN TIME: THE BEST OF, 1980–1989

Released: May 2008

1. Intro: Churchill's Speech; 2. Aces High (live); 3. 2 Minutes to Midnight; 4. The Trooper; 5. Wasted Years; 6. Children of the Damned; 7. The Number of the Beast; 8. Run to the Hills; 9. Phantom of the Opera (live); 10. The Evil That Men Do; 11. Wrathchild (live); 12. Can I Play with Madness; 13. Powerslave; 14. Hallowed Be Thy Name; 15. Iron Maiden (live)

Note: Released in conjunction with the Somewhere Back in Time world tour, this disc features two Di'Anno-era tracks ("Iron Maiden" and "Phantom of the Opera") recorded live with Bruce Dickinson and also released on Live After Death.

FROM FEAR TO ETERNITY: THE BEST OF, 1990–2010

Released: June 2011

(CD1) 1. The Wicker Man; 2. Holy Smoke; 3. El Dorado; 4. Paschendale; 5. Different World; 6. Man on the Edge (live); 7. The Reincarnation of Benjamin Breeg; 8. Blood Brothers; 9. Rainmaker; 10. Sign of the Cross (live); 11. Brave New World; 12. Fear of the Dark (live) (CD2) 1. Be Quick or Be Dead; 2. Tailgunner; 3. No More Lies; 4. Coming Home; 5. The Clansman (live); 6. For the Greater Good of God; 7. These Colours Don't Run; 8. Bring Your Daughter . . . to the Slaughter; 9. Afraid to Shoot; 10. Dance of Death; 11. When the Wild Winds Blows

Notes: This version of "Man on the Edge" was a B-side to "The Wicker Man" and was recorded at Milano, Italy, September 23, 1999. "Sign of the Cross," "Fear of the Dark," and "The Clansman" are taken from Rock in Rio.

Box Sets

THE FIRST TEN YEARS

Released: February–April 1990

(CD1) 1. Running Free; 2. Burning Ambition (Harris); 3. Sanctuary; 4. Drifter (live); 5. I've Got the Fire (live) (Ronnie Montrose); 6. Listen with Nicko! Part I (CD2) 1. Women in Uniform (Greg Macainsh); 2. Invasion (Harris); 3. Phantom of the Opera (live); 4. Twilight Zone; 5. Wrathchild; 6. Listen with Nicko! Part II (CD3) 1. Purgatory; 2. Genghis Khan; 3. Running Free (live); 4. Remember Tomorrow (live); 5. Killers (live); 6. Innocent Exile (live); 7. Listen with Nicko! Part III (CD4) 1. Run to the Hills; 2. Total Eclipse; 3. The Number of the Beast; 4. Remember Tomorrow (live); 5. Listen with Nicko! Part IV (CD5) 1. Flight of Icarus; 2. I've Got the Fire (Montrose); 3. The Trooper; 4. Cross-Eyed Mary (Ian Anderson); 5. Listen with Nicko! Part V (CD6) 1. 2 Minutes to Midnight; 2. Rainbow's Gold (Terry Slesser/Kenny Mountain); 3. Mission from 'Arry (Harris/McBrain); 4. Aces High; 5. King of Twilight (Nektar); 6. The Number of the Beast (live); 7. Listen with Nicko! Part VI (CD7) 1. Running Free (live); 2. Sanctuary (live); 3. Murders in the Rue Morgue (live); 4. Run to the Hills (live); 5. Phantom of the Opera (live); 6. Losfer Words (Big 'Orra) (live); 7. Listen with Nicko! Part VII (CD8) 1. Wasted Years; 2. Reach Out (Dave Colwell); 3. Sheriff of Huddersfield (Iron Maiden); 4. Stranger in a Strange Land; 5. That Girl (Andy Barnett/Merv Goldsworthy/Pete Jupp); 6. Juanita (Steve Barnacle/Derek O'Neil); 7. Listen with Nicko! Part VIII (CD9) 1. Can I Play with Madness; 2. Black Bart Blues (Harris/Dickinson); 3. Massacre (Phil Lynott/Scott Gorham/Brian Downey); 4. The Evil That Men Do; 5. Prowler '88; 6. Charlotte the Harlot '88; 7. Listen with Nicko! Part IX (CD10) 1. The Clairvoyant (live); 2. The Prisoner (live); 3. Heaven Can Wait (live); 4. Infinite Dreams (live); 5. Killers (live); 6. Still Life (live); 7. Listen with Nicko! Part X

Notes: (CD1) *"I've Got the Fire" was a cover of Montrose's "I Got the Fire," recorded at the Marquee, London, April 3, 1980. It appeared as B-side to "Sanctuary" that year.* (CD2) *The band's cover of Skyhooks' "Women in Uniform" was their third single and first video. To date it's been issued just twice on CD—here and on a deluxe issue of* Killers. (CD3) *The four live tracks were recorded at Nagoya, Japan, May 23, 1981.* (CD5) *Maiden's cover of Jethro Tull's "Cross-Eyed Mary" was the B-side to "The Trooper."* (CD6) *"Rainbow's Gold" was the B-side to "2 Minutes to Midnight." Co-writer Slesser was best known as the vocalist in Back Street Crawler with former Free guitarist Paul Kossoff (later amended to Crawler after Kossoff's death). Slesser is rumored to have been considered as the replacement vocalist for both Iron Maiden and AC/DC. "Mission from 'Arry" was an argument Harris and McBrain clandestinely recorded by Dickinson backstage at a show on the World Piece tour. Nektar was a German prog-rock band; Maiden covered their "King of Twilight" as a B-side to "Aces High."* (CD7) *"Running Free" was released in 1985 as a live single b/w live versions of "Sanctuary" and "Murders in the Rue Morgue." Likewise, "Run to the Hills" was released as a 1985 live single b/w live versions of "Phantom of the Opera" and "Losfer*

Words (Big 'Orra)." **(CD8)** "Reach Out" was a B-side of "Wasted Years." Colwell did stints in Bad Company and Samson. The cover FM's "That Girl" was a B-Side to "Stranger in a Strange Land." Goldsworthy and Jupp had previously comprised the rhythm section of Samson. The other B-side to "Stranger. . ." was "Juanita," a cover of the band Marshall Fury, which featured Barnett. **(CD9)** "Black Bart Blues," a non album track and a paean to a suit of armor that rode in the band's tour bus, along with a cover of Thin Lizzy's "Massacre" were the B-sides to "Can I Play with Madness." "Prowler '88" and "Charlotte the Harlot '88" were 1988 re-recordings that backed the single "The Evil That Men Do." **(CD10)** The live cuts of "The Prisoner" and "Heaven Can Wait" were recorded at the 1988 Monsters of Rock and appeared on various 7- and 12-inch-single releases of the studio version of "The Clairvoyant." The live version of "Infinite Dreams," as well as its live B-sides, "Killers" and "Still Life," can also be found on Maiden England.

The "Listen with Nicko" spoken-word segments feature McBrain providing a history of each track on the disc.

EDDIE'S HEAD

Released: December 1998

(CD1) *(Iron Maiden)* 1. Prowler; 2. Sanctuary; 3. Remember Tomorrow; 4. Running Free; 5. Phantom of the Opera; 6. Transylvania; 7. Strange World; 8. Charlotte the Harlot; 9 Iron Maiden **(CD2)** *(Killers)* 1. The Ides of March; 2. Wrathchild; 3. Murders in the Rue Morgue; 4. Another Life; 5. Genghis Khan; 6. Innocent Exile; 7. Killers; 8. Prodigal Son; 9. Purgatory; 10. Twilight Zone; 11. Drifter **(CD3)** *(The Number of the Beast)* 1. Invaders; 2. Children of the Damned; 3. The Prisoner; 4. 22 Acacia Avenue; 5. The Number of the Beast; 6. Run to the Hills; 7. Gangland; 8. Total Eclipse; 9. Hallowed Be Thy Name **(CD4)** *(Piece of Mind)* 1. Where Eagles Dare; 2. Revelations; 3. Flight of Icarus; 4. Die with Your Boots On; 5. The Trooper; 6. Still Life; 7. Quest for Fire; 8. Sun and Steel; 9. To Tame a Land **(CD5)** *(Powerslave)* 1. Aces High; 2. 2 Minutes to Midnight; 3. Losfer Words (Big 'Orra); 4. Flash of the Blade; 5. The Duellists; 6. Back in the Village; 7. Powerslave; 8. Rime of the Ancient Mariner **(CD6)** *(Live After Death)* 1. Intro: Churchill's Speech (live); 2. Aces High (live); 3. 2 Minutes to Midnight (live); 4. The Trooper (live); 5. Revelations (live); 6. Flight of Icarus (live); 7. Rime of the Ancient Mariner (live); 8. Powerslave (live); 9. The Number of the Beast (live); 10. Hallowed Be Thy Name (live); 11. Iron Maiden (live); 12. Run to the Hills (live); 13. Running Free (live) **(CD7)** *(Live After Death)* 1. Wrathchild (live); 2. 22 Acacia Avenue (live); 3. Children of the Damned (live); 4. Die with Your Boots On (live); 5. Phantom of the Opera (live) **(CD8)** *(Somewhere in Time)* 1. Caught Somewhere in Time; 2. Wasted Years; 3. Sea of Madness; 4. Heaven Can Wait; 5. The Loneliness of the Long Distance Runner; 6. Stranger in a Strange Land; 7. Deja-Vu; 8. Alexander the Great **(CD9)** *(Seventh Son of a Seventh Son)* 1. Moonchild; 2. Infinite Dreams; 3. Can I Play with Madness; 4. The Evil That Men Do; 5. Seventh Son of a Seventh Son; 6. The Prophecy; 7. The Clairvoyant; 8. Only the Good Die Young **(CD10)** *(No Prayer for the Dying)* 1. Tailgunner; 2. Holy Smoke; 3. No Prayer for the Dying; 4. Public Enema Number One; 5. Fates Warning; 6. The Assassin; 7. Run Silent Run Deep; 8. Hooks in You; 9. Bring Your Daughter . . . to the Slaughter; 10. Mother Russia **(CD11)** *(Fear Of The Dark)* 1. Be Quick or Be Dead; 2. From Here to Eternity; 3. Afraid to Shoot Strangers; 4. Fear Is the Key; 5. Childhood's End; 6. Wasting Love; 7. The Fugitive; 8. Chains of Misery; 9. The Apparition; 10. Judas Be My Guide; 11. Weekend Warrior; 12. Fear of the Dark **(CD12)** *(A Real Dead One)* 1. The Number of the Beast (live); 2. The Trooper (live); 3. Prowler (live); 4. Transylvania (live); 5. Remember Tomorrow (live); 6. Where Eagles Dare (live); 7. Sanctuary (live); 8. Running Free (live); 9. Run to the Hills (live); 10. 2 Minutes to Midnight (live); 11. Iron Maiden (live); 12. Hallowed Be Thy Name (live) **(CD13)** *(A Real Live One)* 1. Be Quick or Be Dead (live); 2. From Here to Eternity (live); 3. Can I Play with Madness (live); 4. Wasting Love (live); 5. Tailgunner (live); 6. The Evil That Men Do (live); 7. Afraid to Shoot Strangers (live); 8. Bring Your Daughter . . . to the Slaughter (live); 9. Heaven Can Wait (live); 10. The Clairvoyant (live); 11. Fear of the Dark (live) **(CD14)** *(Live at Donington)* 1. Be Quick or Be Dead; 2. The Number of the Beast; 3. Wrathchild; 4. From Here to Eternity; 5. Can I Play with Madness; 6. Wasting Love; 7. Tailgunner; 8. The Evil That Men Do; 9. Afraid to Shoot Strangers; 10. Fear of the Dark; 11. Bring Your Daughter . . . to the Slaughter; 12. The Clairvoyant; 13. Heaven Can Wait; 14. Run to the Hills **(CD15)** *(Live at Donington)* 1. 2 Minutes to Midnight; 2. Iron Maiden; 3. Hallowed Be Thy Name; 4. The Trooper; 5. Sanctuary; 6. Running Free

Notes: This deluxe package features remasters of the first twelve releases— each containing bonus multimedia content, and all packaged in a "box" shaped like Eddie's head. A sixteenth disc, In Profile, *features audio interviews with Harris, Murray, Bayley, and manager Rod Smallwood.*

EDDIE'S ARCHIVE

Released: November 2002

BBC ARCHIVES (CD1) 1. Iron Maiden (live); 2. Running Free (live); 3. Transylvania (live); 4. Sanctuary (live) **(CD2)** 1. Wrathchild (live); 2. Run to the Hills (live); 3. Children of the Damned (live); 4. The Number of the Beast (live); 5. 22 Acacia Avenue (live); 6. Transylvania (live); 7. The Prisoner (live); 8. Hallowed Be Thy Name (live); 9. Phantom of the Opera (live); 10. Iron Maiden (live) · **BEAST OVER HAMMERSMITH (CD1)** 1. Murders in the Rue Morgue (live); 2. Run to the Hills (live); 3. Children of the Damned (live); 4. The Number of the Beast (live); 5. Another Life (live); 6. Killers (live); 7. 22 Acacia Avenue (live); 8. Total Eclipse (live) **(CD2)** 1. Transylvania (live); 2. The Prisoner (live); 3. Hallowed By Thy Name (live); 4. Phantom of the Opera (live); 5. Iron Maiden (live); 6. Sanctuary (live); 7. Drifter (live); 8. Running Free (live); 9. Prowler (live) · **BEST OF THE 'B' SIDES (CD1)** 1. Burning Ambition; 2. Drifter (live); 3. Invasion; 4. Remember Tomorrow; 5. I've Got the Fire (Montrose); 6. Cross-Eyed Mary (Anderson); 7. Rainbow's Gold (Terry Slesser/Kenny Mountain); 8. King of Twilight (Nektar); 9. Reach Out (Colwell); 10. That Girl (Barnett/Goldsworthy/

Jupp); 11. Juanita (Barnacle/O'Neil); 12. Sheriff of Huddersfield; 13 .Black Bart Blues; 14. Prowler '88; 15. Charlotte the Harlot '88 (CD2) 1. All in Your Mind (Del Bromham); 2. Kill Me Ce Soir (George Kooymans/Barry Hay/John Fenton); 3. I'm a Mover (Andy Fraser/ Paul Rodgers); 4. Nodding Donkey Blues (Iron Maiden); 5. Space Station No. 5 (Ronnie Montrose); 6. I Can't See My Feelings (Tony Bourge/Burke Shelley); 7. Roll over Vic Vella (Chuck Berry); 8. Justice of the Peace (Harris/Murray); 9. Judgement Day (Bayley/Gers); 10. My Generation (Pete Townshend); 11. Doctor Doctor (Michael Schenker/Phil Mogg); 12. Blood on the World's Hands (live); 13. The Aftermath (live); 14. Futureal (live); 15. Wasted Years (live)

Notes: Packaged in an embossed casket, box set features three previously released double-CDs: BBC Archives, Beast over Hammersmith *(both already covered here), and* Best of the 'B' Sides. *The B-sides on disc one of* The Best of the 'B' Sides *are discussed under* The First Ten Years *release. Of note on disc two, the covers of "All in Your Mind" by British band Stray and Golden Earring's "Kill Me Ce Soir" appeared on the flip of "Holy Smoke" (9/90); Free's "I'm a Mover" was a B-side of "Bring Your Daughter . . ." (12/90) (along with Led Zeppelin's "Communication Breakdown," not included here); Montrose's "Space Station No. 5" was a B-side of "Be Quick or Be Dead" (4/92) (along with "Nodding Donkey Blues," a straight-up blues rocker); Budgie's "I Can't See My Feelings" was on the reverse of "From Here to Eternity" (6/92), as was "Roll Over Vic Vella," a bastardization of the Chuck Berry classic with spoken-word segments from longtime Maiden roadie Vella; The Who's "My Generation" and UFO's "Doctor Doctor" were the B-sides of "Lord of the Flies" (4/96).*

As for the live tracks on Best of the 'B' Sides, *"Drifter" was a B-side of "Sanctuary" (5/80) and was recorded at the Marquee on April 3, 1980. "Blood on the World's Hands" and "The Aftermath" were recorded at Gothenburg, Sweden, on November 1, 1995 and released as B-sides to "The Angel and the Gambler" (3/98); "Futureal," with Bayley on vocals, was recorded at Helsinki on September 15, 1999 and issued as a B-side to "The Wicker Man" (4/00); and "Wasted Years" was recorded at Milano on September 23, 1999 and released as a B-side to "Out of the Silent Planet" (10/00).*

EPs

THE SOUNDHOUSE TAPES

Label: Rock House Records
Released: November 1979
Producers: Iron Maiden

1. Iron Maiden; 2. Invasion; 3. Prowler

Note: U.K.-only release culled from the band's first demo featured Harris, Murray, and Di'Anno, with Doug Sampson on drums.

LIVE!! + ONE

Label: EMI
Released: November 1980
Producer: Doug Hall

1. Sanctuary; 2. Phantom of the Opera; 3. Drifter; 4. Women in Uniform

Notes: Recorded July 4, 1980 at the Marquee. The Greek pressing, not issued until 1984, featured tracks from Maiden Japan *and the LP version of "Prowler."*

MAIDEN JAPAN

Label: EMI
Released: August 1981
Producers: Doug Hall and Iron Maiden

1. Running Free; 2. Remember Tomorrow; 3. Killers; 4. Innocent Exile

Notes: Di'Anno's final recording with the band was made May 23, 1981, at Kosei Nenkin Hall in Nagoya, Japan. The sleeve of Venezuelan pressings featured Eddie holding the singer's severed head. Pressings later issued in the U.S., Canada, New Zealand, Australia, Argentina, and Brazil also featured "Wrathchild."

NO MORE LIES

Label: EMI
Released: March 2004
Producers: Kevin Shirley and Steve Harris

1. No More Lies; 2. Paschendale; 3. Journeyman/Age of Innocence (How Old?)

Notes: A fan "thank you" package featuring an orchestral arrangement of "Paschendale," the original take of "Journeyman," and a hidden track, an alternate take of "Age of Innocence" with McBrain on vocals.

Singles

The following is a list of Iron Maiden's U.K. and U.S. single releases, along with peak chart positions in those countries (an "—" indicates that the release did not chart). Due to the proliferation of multiple B-sides as the band's career (and live catalog) prospered, only the A-side releases are noted. Because specific days of release (i.e., "street dates") are often points of contention, and in fact sometimes vary between the United Kingdom and the United States, only months and years are noted.

"Running Free" (February 1980); U.K. No. 34
"Sanctuary" (May 1980); U.K. No. 29
"Women in Uniform" (October 1980); U.K. No. 35

"Twilight Zone" (March 1981); U.K. No. 31
"Purgatory" (June 1981); U.K. No. 52

"Run to the Hills" (February 1982); U.K. No. 7; U.S. No. 100
"The Number of the Beast" (April 1982); U.K. No. 18

"Flight of Icarus" (April 1983); U.K. No. 7
"The Trooper" (June 1983); U.K. No. 12

"2 Minutes to Midnight" (August 1984); U.K. No. 11
"Aces High" (October 1984); U.K. No. 20

"Running Free" (live) (September 1985); U.K. No. 9
"Run to the Hills" (live) (December 1985); U.K. No. 26

"Wasted Years" (September 1986); U.K. No. 9; U.S. No. 35
"Stranger in a Strange Land" (November 1986); U.K. No. 22

"Can I Play with Madness" (March 1988); U.K. No. 3
"The Evil That Men Do" (August 1988); U.K. No. 5
"The Clairvoyant" (November 1988); U.K. No. 6

"Infinite Dreams" (live) (November 1989); U.K. No. 6

"Holy Smoke" (September 1990); U.K. No. 3
"Bring Your Daughter . . . to the Slaughter" (December 1990); U.K.
  No. 1

"Be Quick or Be Dead" (April 1992); U.K. No. 2
"From Here to Eternity" (June 1992); U.K. No. 21
"Wasting Love" (September 1992); —

"Fear of the Dark" (live) (March 1993); U.K. No. 5
"Hallowed Be Thy Name" (live) (October 1993); U.K. No. 9

"Man on the Edge" (September 1995); U.K. No. 10

"Lord of the Flies" (April 1996); —
"Virus" (September 1996); U.K. No. 16

"The Angel and the Gambler" (March 1998); U.K. No. 18
"Futureal" (July 1998); —

"The Wicker Man" (April 2000); U.K. No. 9
"Out of the Silent Planet" (October 2000); U.K. No. 20

"Run to the Hills" (live) (March 2002); U.K. No. 9

"Wildest Dreams" (September 2003); U.K. No. 6
"Rainmaker" (November 2003); U.K. No. 13

"The Number of the Beast" (live) (January 2005); U.K. No. 2
"The Trooper" (live) (August 2005); U.K. No. 5; U.S. No. 67

"The Reincarnation of Benjamin Breeg" (August 2006); —
"Different World" (November 2006, U.S.; December 2006, U.K.);
  U.K. No. 3

"El Dorado" (June 2010); —
"Satellite 15 . . . the Final Frontier" (August 2010); —
"Coming Home" (October 2010); —

VHS/DVD

LIVE AT THE RAINBOW (CONCERT)
Released: May 1981
Recorded: Rainbow Theatre, London, December 21, 1980

1. The Ides of March; 2. Wrathchild; 3. Killers; 4. Remember Tomorrow; 5. Transylvania; 6. Phantom of the Opera; 7. Iron Maiden

VIDEO PIECES (PROMO VIDEOS)
Released: July 1983

1. Run to the Hills; 2. The Number of the Beast; 3. Flight of Icarus; 4. The Trooper

BEHIND THE IRON CURTAIN (PROMO VIDEOS/CONCERT)
Released: October 1984
Recorded: Track 3: Katowice, Poland, August 14, 1984; Track 4: Budapest, Hungary, August 17, 1984

1. 2 Minutes to Midnight (promo video); 2. Aces High (promo video); 3. Hallowed Be Thy Name; 4. Run to the Hills

Note: An expanded edition featuring seven tracks was issued as a part of disc two of the Live After Death *DVD release in 2008.*

LIVE AFTER DEATH (CONCERT)
Released: October 1985; February 2008
Recorded: Arena, Long Beach, California, March 15, 1985

1. Intro: Churchill's Speech; 2. Aces High; 3. 2 Minutes to Midnight; 4. The Trooper; 5. Revelations; 6. Flight of Icarus; 7. Rime of the Ancient Mariner; 8. Powerslave; 9. The Number of the Beast; 10. Hallowed Be Thy Name; 11. Iron Maiden; 12. Run to the Hills; 13. Running Free; 14. Sanctuary

Note: DVD release includes a second disc featuring, among other things, a band documentary, concert footage from the Eastern Bloc in 1984, the 1985 Rock in Rio appearance, and a soundcheck filmed in San Antonio, Texas, in 1983.

12 WASTED YEARS (DOCUMENTARY)

Released: October 1987

1. Stranger in a Strange Land (video); 2. Charlotte the Harlot (live); 3. Running Free (live); 4. Women in Uniform (video); 5. Murders in the Rue Morgue (live); 6. Children of the Damned (live); 7. The Number of the Beast (live); 8. Total Eclipse (live); 9. Iron Maiden (live); 10. Sanctuary (live); 11. The Prisoner (live); 12. 22 Acacia Avenue (live); 13. Wasted Years (live); 14. The Trooper (live)

Note: Most live tracks on this release were later included on The Early Days *DVD release in 2004 (see following page).*

MAIDEN ENGLAND (CONCERT)

Released: November 1989
Recorded: NEC, Birmingham, England, November 27–28, 1988

1. Moonchild; 2. The Evil That Men Do; 3. The Prisoner; 4. Still Life; 5. Die with Your Boots On; 6. Infinite Dreams; 7. Killers; 8. Can I Play with Madness; 9. Heaven Can Wait; 10. Wasted Years; 11. The Clairvoyant; 12. Seventh Son of a Seventh Son; 13. The Number of the Beast; 14. Hallowed Be Thy Name; 15. Iron Maiden

THE FIRST TEN YEARS: THE VIDEOS (PROMO VIDEOS)

Released: November 1990

1. Women in Uniform; 2. Wrathchild (live); 3. Run to the Hills; 4. The Number of the Beast; 5. Flight of Icarus; 6. The Trooper; 7. 2 Minutes to Midnight; 8. Aces High; 9. Running Free (live); 10. Wasted Years; 11. Stranger in a Strange Land; 12. Can I Play with Madness; 13. The Evil That Men Do; 14. The Clairvoyant; 15. Infinite Dreams (live); 16. Holy Smoke

Note: A 1992 U.S. reissue entitled From There to Eternity *also featured videos for "Tailgunner," "Bring Your Daughter . . . to the Slaughter," "Be Quick or Be Dead," "From Here to Eternity," and "Wasting Love."*

DONINGTON LIVE 1992 (CONCERT)

Released: November 1993
Recorded: Monsters of Rock, Donington, England, August 22, 1992

1. Be Quick or Be Dead; 2. The Number of the Beast; 3. Wrathchild; 4. From Here to Eternity; 5. Can I Play with Madness; 6. Wasting Love; 7. Tailgunner; 8. The Evil That Men Do; 9. Afraid to Shoot Strangers; 10. Fear of the Dark; 11. Bring Your Daughter . . . to the Slaughter; 12. The Clairvoyant; 13. Heaven Can Wait; 14. Run to the Hills; 15. 2 Minutes to Midnight; 16. Iron Maiden; 17. Hallowed Be Thy Name; 18. The Trooper; 19. Sanctuary; 20. Running Free

RAISING HELL (CONCERT)

Released: May 1994
Recorded: Pinewood Studios, London, August 28, 1993

1. Be Quick or Be Dead; 2. The Trooper; 3. The Evil That Men Do; 4. The Clairvoyant; 5. Hallowed Be Thy Name; 6. Wrathchild; 7. Transylvania; 8. From Here to Eternity; 9. Fear of the Dark; 10. The Number of the Beast; 11. Bring Your Daughter . . . to the Slaughter; 12. 2 Minutes to Midnight; 13. Afraid to Shoot Strangers; 14. Heaven Can Wait; 15. Sanctuary; 16. Run to the Hills; 17. Iron Maiden

Note: Broadcast on a pay-per-view basis prior to the release of the VHS and DVD, this concert also featured performance by magician Simon Drake.

CLASSIC ALBUMS: THE NUMBER OF THE BEAST (DOCUMENTARY)

Released: December 2001

1. Children of the Damned; 2. Run to the Hills; 3. The Prisoner

Note: Installment in the Eagle Rock Entertainment "Classic Albums" series documents the making of The Number of the Beast.

ROCK IN RIO (CONCERT)

Released: July 2002
Recorded: Rock in Rio, Rio de Janeiro, January 19, 2001

1. Intro: Arthur's Farewell; 2. The Wicker Man; 3. Ghost of the Navigator; 4. Brave New World; 5. Wrathchild; 6. 2 Minutes to Midnight; 7. Blood Brothers; 8. Sign of the Cross; 9. The Mercenary; 10. The Trooper; 11. Dream of Mirrors; 12. The Clansman; 13. The Evil That Men Do; 14. Fear of the Dark; 15. Iron Maiden; 16. The Number of the Beast; 17. Hallowed Be Thy Name; 18. Sanctuary; 19. Run to the Hills

VISIONS OF THE BEAST (PROMO VIDEOS)

Released: June 2003

(DVD1) 1. Women in Uniform; 2. Wrathchild (live); 3. Run to the Hills; 4. The Number of the Beast; 5. Flight of Icarus; 6. The Trooper; 7. 2 Minutes to Midnight; 8. Aces High; 9. Wasted Years; 10. Stranger in a Strange Land; 11. Can I Play with Madness; 12. The Evil That Men Do; 13. The Clairvoyant (live); 14. Infinite Dreams (live); 15. Holy Smoke; 16. Tailgunner; 17. Aces High (Camp Chaos version); 18. The Number of the Beast (Camp Chaos version); 19. Futureal (football version); 20. Fear of the Dark (live); 21. Man on the Edge (fun version; Easter egg) (DVD2) 1. Bring Your Daughter . . . to the Slaughter; 2. Be Quick or Be Dead; 3. From Here to Eternity; 4. Wasting Love; 5. Fear of the Dark (live); 6. Hallowed Be Thy Name (live); 7. Man on the Edge; 8. Afraid to Shoot Strangers (live); 9. Lord of the Flies; 10. Virus; 11. The Angel and the Gambler; 12. Futureal; 13. The Wicker Man; 14. Out of the Silent Planet; 15. Brave New World (live); 16. The Wicker Man (Camp Chaos version); 17. Run to the Hills (Camp Chaos version); 18. Flight of Icarus (Camp Chaos version); 19. The Trooper (Camp Chaos version; Easter egg)

Notes: Essentially the updated version of The First Ten Years, *this set includes every promo video through* Rock in Rio. *Camp Chaos versions are animated videos. "Afraid to Shoot Strangers" features Bayley on vocals.*

THE EARLY DAYS (DOCUMENTARY/CONCERT)

Released: November 2004

Recorded: (DVD1) *Tracks 1–7, the Rainbow Theatre, December 21, 1980; Tracks 8–16, Hammersmith Odeon, March 20, 1982; Tracks 19–23, Dortmund, December 18, 1983* (DVD2) *Tracks 1–9, the Ruskin Arms, London, April 1980* (Extras) *Tracks 1–2,* Top of the Pops, *1980; Track 3,* Rock and Pop, *1980*

(DVD1) 1. The Ides of March; 2. Wrathchild; 3. Killers; 4. Remember Tomorrow; 5. Transylvania; 6. Phantom of the Opera; 7. Iron Maiden; 8. Murders in the Rue Morgue; 9. Run to the Hills; 10. Children of the Damned; 11. The Number of the Beast; 12. 22 Acacia Avenue; 13. Total Eclipse; 14. The Prisoner; 15. Hallowed Be Thy Name; 16. Iron Maiden; 17. Sanctuary; 18. The Trooper; 19. Revelations; 20. Flight of Icarus; 21. 22 Acacia Avenue; 22. The Number of the Beast; 23. Run to the Hills (DVD2) 1. Sanctuary; 2. Wrathchild; 3. Prowler; 4. Remember Tomorrow; 5. Running Free; 6. Transylvania; 7. Another Life; 8. Phantom of the Opera; 9. Charlotte the Harlot (Extras) 1. Running Free; 2. Women in Uniform; 3. Running Free; 4. Women in Uniform (promo video); 5. Run to the Hills (promo video); 6. The Number of the Beast (promo video); 7. Flight of Icarus (promo video); 8. The Trooper (promo video)

Notes: Directed by Matthew Amos, this essential document of the band's early history includes interviews with a slew of former members, including Di'Anno, Burr, Sampson, and Stratton. The Ruskin Arms performance is the earliest live footage of the band.

DEATH ON THE ROAD (CONCERT)

Released: August 2005

Recorded: Westfalenhalle, Dortmund, Germany, November 24, 2003

1. Wildest Dreams; 2. Wrathchild; 3. Can I Play with Madness; 4. The Trooper; 5. Dance of Death; 6. Rainmaker; 7. Brave New World; 8. Paschendale; 9. Lord of the Flies; 10. No More Lies; 11. Hallowed Be Thy Name; 12. Fear of the Dark; 13. Iron Maiden; 14. Journeyman; 15. The Number of the Beast; 16. Run to the Hills

IRON MAIDEN: FLIGHT 666 (DOCUMENTARY/CONCERT)

Released: May 2009, U.K.; June 2009, U.S.

Music Videos

"Women in Uniform" (1980) Dir.: Doug Smith

"Wrathchild" (1981) Dir.: Dave Hillier
"Run to the Hills" (1981) Dir.: David Mallet

"The Number of the Beast" (1982) Dir.: David Mallet
"The Prisoner" (1982) Dir.: David Mallet
"Flight of Icarus" (1982) Dir.: Jim Yukich

"The Trooper" (1983) Dir.: Jim Yukich
"2 Minutes to Midnight" (1983) Dir.: Tony Halton

"Aces High" (1984) Dir.: Jim Yukich

"Wasted Years" (1986) Dir.: Jim Yukich
"Stranger in a Strange Land" (1986) Dir.: Julian Caidan

"Can I Play with Madness" (1988) Dir.: Julian Doyle
"The Evil That Men Do" (1988) Dir.: Toby Philips and Steve Harris
"The Clairvoyant" (1988) Dir.: Julian Caidan and Steve Harris

"Infinite Dreams" (1989) Dir.: Steve Harris

"Holy Smoke" (1990) Dir.: Steve Harris
"Tailgunner" (1990) Dir.: Steve Harris
"Bring Your Daughter . . . to the Slaughter" (1990) Dir.: Steve Harris

"Be Quick or Be Dead" (1992) Dir.: Wing Ko
"From Here to Eternity" (1992) Dir.: Ralph Ziman
"Wasting Love" (1992) Dir.: Samuel Bayer

"Hallowed Be Thy Name" (1993) Dir.: Samuel Bayer

"Man on the Edge" (1995) Dir.: Wing Ko

"Afraid to Shoot Strangers" (1996) Dir.: Steve Lazarus and Steve Harris
"Lord of the Flies" (1996) Dir.: Steve Lazarus and Steve Harris
"Virus" (1996) Dir.: Steve Lazarus and Steve Harris

"The Angel and the Gambler" (1998) Dir.: Simon Hilton
"Futureal" (1998) Dir.: Steve Lazarus

"The Wicker Man" (2000) Dir.: Dean Karr
"Out of the Silent Planet" (2000) Dir.: David Pattenden and Trevor Thompson
"Brave New World" (2000) Dir.: Dean Karr

"Wildest Dreams" (2003) Dir.: Howard Greenhalgh
"Rainmaker" (2003) Dir.: Howard Greenhalgh

"No More Lies" (2004) Dir.: Matthew Amos

"The Reincarnation of Benjamin Breeg" (2006) Dir.: Matthew Amos
"Different World" (2006) Dir.: Howard Greenhalgh

"Satellite 15 . . . the Final Frontier" (2010) Dir.: Dirk Maggs

TOUROGRAPHY METHODOLOGY

BY RYAN LAMAR

In researching and compiling the tour dates found at the end of each chapter, I used several primary sources, listed here in order of precedence and reliability:

Reliable Primary Sources

1. MEDIA-REPORTED CONCERT REVIEWS. Concert reviews coming from newspapers, magazines, and major media websites tend to be the most reliable source of information. This is because these media groups have earned a reputation for accuracy by using control measures such as fact-checking, and they provide the "trifecta" necessary to confirm that a concert did happen: date, location, and event details. Media groups also usually publish their concert reviews shortly after the concert occurred, thus reducing the likelihood of incorrect date and location information while, at the same time, establishing for fact that the concert did happen. The closer the review's publication date is to the date of the concert, the better, which means that daily publications tend to be more reliable than those published less frequently. One caveat: No matter how good the control measures are that these groups implement, they do sometimes make mistakes. The most common error is publishing a review after its originally intended publication date without correcting the date-related language of the review. For example, when a review that reads "last night. . ." is held back from publication until a later date without being edited, the date-related language becomes misleading. Such examples are obvious when the "last night" error wrongly refers to a date and location already established to be another date and location by other evidence.

2. FAN CONCERT REVIEWS. A fan review is a reliable source as long as the fan writes in a journal or publishes on a website his or her account of a concert shortly after the event occurred, preferably within a week. Several things have to be taken into consideration, however. The fan must have the "trifecta" listed in his or her review. Without all three key pieces of information tied together in one source, a tour date and location has not been listed as verified unless there is corroborating evidence from another source to support it. Also keep in mind that a fan review can be misleading. Many fans dig up old journal entries and post them on their own blogs or websites, and in the absence of any component of the trifecta, they research information from another website and list the researched information as part of the original journal entry. In most cases of an online fan source, an email to the individual can help to determine the authenticity and reliability of the source. Many fans do not realize the historical value of their online expositions; fortunately, when confronted with this information and how it is valuable to conducting research about the band, most are honest and willing to help.

Primary Sources of Questionable Reliability

3. MULTIPLE ISOLATED FAN ACCOUNTS, LONG AFTER THE EVENT OCCURRED. If several fans with intimate knowledge of the event recount the same dates, locations, and other details (i.e., the aforementioned trifecta) months or years afterward, then this can very well be considered a reliable source. However, there is one major issue with collective memory that makes the reliability of this type of source questionable. Psychological tests have revealed that memory can be manipulated even on a massive scale: If enough people are exposed to the same piece of misinformation over a period of time, they will remember that misinformation as part of their original experience. This was the case with the Moscow 1993 shows. Several fans, having believed the dates listed by the band in the multimedia reissue of *A Real Live Dead One* to be correct, actually *remembered* those dates despite a Moscow newspaper review that listed different information. Still, because collective memory mishaps such as this are rare, and because most collective memories can be corroborated by other evidence, this type of source usually can be of benefit.

4. PUBLICIZED INDIVIDUAL TOUR DATES. Print publications and institutional websites receive press releases from management and report tour dates as they are informed of them, yet they rarely, if ever, make corrections to these dates and locations as itinerary changes occur. However, if a local newspaper announces a concert date within approximately a week of that date, then this resource tends to be reliable because of the proximity of the report to the actual date. The greater the span of time between the announcement and the planned date, the less reliable the report is. See "Tour itineraries" below for more information on publicized tour dates.

5. CONCERT FLYERS. While these are very good resources indicating city, date, and venue, they can cause quite a bit of confusion when the band is forced to cancel and/or reschedule dates. One thing to note: They have a slight edge over concert tickets because concert flyers sometimes are reprinted for a rescheduled date, whereas new tickets are rarely, if ever, reissued for a rescheduled date. Concert flyers also pose an additional problem: Because they have no publication dates on them, it can be difficult to determine which one has the correct date when there exists a flyer with a conflicting date. In cases such as this, other resources must be used to help determine which flyer is the original and which is for the rescheduled date.

6. CONCERT TICKETS. While these are very good resources indicating city, date, and venue, because they are not printed unless final arrangements have been made between management and the venue, they can cause quite a bit of confusion if the band is forced to cancel and/or reschedule dates. Tickets with the original date and location are usually used for the new date and location as a convenience and cost-cutting measure by the venue and/or promoter. This is why it is not uncommon to come across a ticket stub with the wrong date, and in some cases, with the wrong date crossed out by a fan who attended the concert and the correct date written in its place. This was the very case with the Portsmouth gig originally scheduled for June 3, 1980. Two tickets were discovered with the date crossed out and "1 July"

written in its place. The mystery was solved by an account from a fan who attended the show, and it was further corroborated by a *Sounds* article establishing that the band had rescheduled the date.

7. OFFICIAL IRON MAIDEN PUBLICATIONS AND MERCHANDISE. This category is not to be confused with tour-related merchandise. This is, instead, regular merchandise unrelated to concerts, such as DVDs, CDs, and books. While one would think that these kinds of merchandise would have accurate information, they tend to be fraught with inaccuracies. Management has made it clear that tour dates and locations are considered bonus material to merchandise and not worthy of being thoroughly checked for accuracy. For example, when the band rereleased all of their CDs in the *Eddie's Head* box set, tour dates were included in the multimedia section that propagated the same longstanding errors bootleg traders have known to be incorrect. However, it is clear that these dates go through at least minimal checking because some errors listed on tour merchandise have been corrected. On the other hand, sometimes merchandise includes band interviews or quotes from the band, management, or tour support crew that occasionally provide a few nuggets of reliable information.

8. IRON MAIDEN BIOGRAPHIES AND COLLECTOR BOOKS. These things tend to be hit or miss. One would expect an author to do a good deal of research before presenting anything as fact, yet many authors print incorrect tour dates and locations because they either borrowed them from other authors or they took them directly from tour programs or tour itineraries without checking for accuracy. Nonetheless, biographies and collector books can and often do provide a good amount of fairly reliable information in the form of band interviews and tour narrations. Any date or location written about with detail can be considered potentially accurate, but dates and locations merely listed without commentary should be suspect. It should also be noted that biographies and collector books make for excellent resources when they feature reproductions of concert flyers, tickets, tour shirts, programs, etc., such as Marco Gamba's *Iron Maiden Collectibles*.

9. TOUR SHIRTS. Tour shirts are problematic as a resource because they are sometimes printed before the band's management has the tour arrangements finalized. Additionally, plans do change mid-tour for various reasons, and it is too expensive to reprint shirts with the correct dates. Therefore, many tour shirts have the wrong information on them. However, some tour shirts prove to be more beneficial than others. Localized "event" shirts, i.e. those specialized for just a specific portion of the tour, tend to be more reliable because management does not print them as early in the tour as the rest of the shirts. It's quite difficult, or at least quite embarrassing, to sell a shirt specific for one concert location (e.g., Chicago Mutants, September 30, 1983) with an incorrect date or location, but it still happens—the band printed a shirt for Essen, dated July 9, 2000, but they had to reschedule for November 6 after Janick's accident the night before in Mannheim.

10. TOUR PROGRAMS. Tour programs are questionable for the same reason tour shirts are questionable: They are usually printed before the tour starts and are never reprinted to reflect midtour changes. These are also considered less accurate than tour shirts due to the fact that management does not normally print programs specialized for just one concert or one region, although management does print separate programs for separate tour legs. This is important to note because the band traditionally has played Japan at the end of their tours, and

management has waited as late as possible before printing programs for that particular leg. As a result, Japanese tour programs usually reflect more accurate dates—not just for the Japanese leg, but for the entire tour since these programs tend to reflect the previous changes in the tour itinerary.

11. TOUR ITINERARIES. As a source coming from the band and/or reputable media outlets, one would expect tour itineraries to be a great way to verify dates and locations, especially since they list the whole tour. The problem is that these are usually published before the tour begins. While updated tour itineraries are commonplace on the Internet, older media sources rarely published updates. As such, tour itineraries have no more value than providing a baseline from which to work to corroborate or negate individual dates and locations through other resources. The No Prayer on the Road Tour presents a great example of the problems with tour itineraries. The band released several different itineraries before starting the tour, but because none have a publication date on them, it is difficult to discern which dates and locations are correct without using other resources.

12. ISOLATED FAN ACCOUNTS. Any single fan account that comes months or years after the fact tends not to be reliable because of the nature of the human mind to forget details over time. Fans who did not attend the event are especially not reliable because they base their information on other accounts and not on firsthand knowledge. However, if a fan reveals an associative memory, such as a concert date coinciding with a birthday or some other notable personal experience, then this source should be considered potentially reliable. It should also be noted that any information about primary sources (e.g., ticket stubs, programs, etc.) coming from another party that is not considered authoritative or scholarly should not be accepted as fact unless that party provides verifiable proof of the source. In other words, it is not prudent to take someone's word for it that "such and such piece of evidence exists because my friend told me about it" or "such and such piece of evidence exists because I saw it with my own eyes!" While Iron Maiden fans have proved to be mostly honest and very helpful, their memories can betray their good intentions.

13. FAN-CREATED TOUROGRAPHIES. This is the bottom of the barrel—and for a valid reason. Most fansite tourographies propagate the same errors from other fansites by copying information and accepting it as fact without making any serious effort to check its accuracy. However, not all fansites are like this, and some prove to be of value because the authors conduct their own research and publish their sources and findings. Nonetheless, because of the problems inherent in many fansites, and because these sites are secondary sources of information, most should be disregarded.

WHERE ARE THEY NOW?

BY NEIL DANIELS

As with most bands, there have been several line-up changes throughout Iron Maiden's extensive history. The following selections trace what each of the more prominent former members has been up to since they last performed with the "Great Beast," and offers a listing of nearly all past and current members, along with the years of their tenure.

BLAZE BAYLEY (vocalist, 1994–1998)

Bayley suffered a lot of harsh criticism during his tenure in Iron Maiden. After leaving Maiden, he formed his own band, Blaze, and released *Silicon Messiah* in 2000. *Tenth Dimension* followed in 2002, and *Blood & Belief* in 2004 (all three were released on the German metal label SPV).

The band has seen a number of line-up changes and was revised again for *The Man Who Would Not Die*, released in 2008 under the name Blaze Bayley.

Bayley spoke to the author in 2009 for an interview with the British rock magazine *Fireworks*: "I originally wanted to call [the band] Blaze Bayley, but I had some bad advice from management and stuff like that. The other guys in the previous band Blaze didn't want to change it. I just explained to everybody, 'Well, I really think that people don't know.' They don't associate the name with me. If you Google 'Blaze' you'll come up with thousands of things that have nothing to do with me. But if you Google 'Blaze Bayley'. . . . I managed to persuade everybody to do it, so the first time we went out as Blaze Bayley we played to twice as many people as we did as Blaze.'

The Man Who Would Not Die was a personal album for the singer, as he told the author in the same interview: "It means that people told me to give up and people said that all my ideas were wrong and that I couldn't make it. . . . So *The Man Who Would Not Die* is saying, 'Well, I'm going to get you back and I'm not going to give my career. I'm not going to give up singing because you think I should. Because you think I should go away. Fuck you. The fans are the people that know. I'm going to prove it and I'm going to get you all back. I'm going to show you.'"

Bayley self-published his official biography, *At the End of the Day*, by Lawrence Paterson in 2009.

In 2010, Bayley's previous band Wolfsbane officially reunited after sixteen years. In 2011 the band toured and released a new EP. Visit *blazebayley.net*.

CLIVE BURR (drummer, 1980–1982)

After leaving Maiden in 1982 due to the band's hectic touring schedule and pressing personal issues, Burr played with a number of low-key rock bands throughout the '80s, including the French band Trust, the American band Alcatrazz, and the obscure New Wave Of British Heavy Metal band Gogmagog with former Maiden singer Paul Di'Anno and guitarist Janick Gers, who of course went on to join Maiden. Burr also hooked up with some former members of Praying Mantis and formed Clive Burr's Escape (also known as Stratus), which produced one album, *Throwing Shapes* in 1984. Burr even went on to work with Twisted Sister frontman Dee Snider and guitarist Bernie Torme in the failed project Desperado. Subsequent drumming gigs included brief stints in Elixir and Praying Mantis.

However, the biggest challenge that Burr has faced in his life is living with multiple sclerosis, which has left him not only in severe financial difficulty but also bound to a wheelchair. Iron Maiden acknowledged Burr's importance in the band's history—after all he did played drums on Maiden's first three albums, including the seminal *The Number of the Beast*—and helped co-found the Clive Burr MS Trust Fund. The band has held a number of fundraising concerts dubbed Clive Aid in honor of Burr, and many Maiden fans have come out in support of Burr. Visit *cliveaid.com*.

PAUL DAY (vocalist, 1975–1976)

Besides his brief stint as Iron Maiden's first singer, Paul Day is probably best known for recording a live album as the lead singer of seminal British glam rock band The Sweet in 1986. He had previously formed a band called More that played at the famed Monsters of Rock festival at Donington in 1981, and he was also the frontman for a now long-forgotten band called Wildlife between 1983 and 1984. Day has lived in Australia since the mid-'80s and sings with the band Crimzon Lake. He is also a designer and video producer. Visit *paulmarioday.com*.

PAUL DI'ANNO (vocalist, 1978–1981)

The most famous former member of Iron Maiden, Di'Anno is obviously best known as Maiden's vocalist on the band's first two albums. Di'Anno has been involved in a number of projects post–Iron Maiden. The first of these was the unoriginally named Di'Anno, a six-piece project with a brief shelf life. In 1985 he worked with the short-lived rock project Gogmagog with former Maiden drummer Clive Burr and future Maiden guitarist Janick Gers, which produced the EP *I Will Be There*. From there, Di'Anno formed Battlezone and released *Fighting Back* in 1986 and a second, more successful, album, *Children of Madness*, in 1987.

Battlezone folded due to internal difficulties, though Di'Anno did briefly bring the name back in 1998. After a brief association with Praying Mantis in 1990, Di'Anno formed the band Killers in the early '90s. They released *Murder One* in 1992, followed by more releases, a break in 1997, and a reformation in 2001. Killers finally fell apart in 2003. In 2000, Di'Anno lived in São Paulo, where he teamed with some Brazilian musicians to form Nomad, which released a self-produced album later reissued as *The Living Dead*. Since 2008, Di'Anno has been involved in a project called RockFellas, also with Brazilian musicians.

Di'Anno has struggled with addiction and wrote about his drug problems in his frank autobiography, *The Beast*. In March 2011 he was sentenced to nine months in a British prison for benefit fraud to the tune of £45,000. He was released after serving two months.

Visit *pauldianno.com*.

BARRY PURKIS (drummer, 1977)

Also known as Thunderstick and Barry Graham, drummer Barry Purkis was reportedly often drunk when playing in Maiden, which made it impossible for him to continue with the band. He was briefly involved in the band Samson following his departure from Maiden. He is famous for wearing a mask onstage and often playing drums inside a cage. It was a very bizarre sight at the time; less so these days, with bands like Slipknot playing to millions of fans around the world. Purkis' own band, Thunderstick, is still playing music.

Visit *thunderstick.co.uk*.

DOUG SAMPSON (drummer, 1977–1979)

Sampson had to leave Maiden prior to their debut album because he was ill at the time and the stressful touring schedule proved too much for him. His drums can be heard on the now-legendary Maiden release *Soundhouse Tapes* and on "Burning Ambition" the B-side to Maiden's first single, "Running Free." Next to nothing is known about his current whereabouts or any recent music activities.

DENNIS STRATTON (guitarist, 1979–1980)

After Stratton's departure from Iron Maiden in October 1980, he joined the British rock band Lionheart for their excellent 1984 album *Hot Tonight*. But he is best known for playing in Praying Mantis throughout the 1990s. His guitars can be heard on a number of Praying Mantis live releases and albums, including *Live at Last* (1990), *A Cry for the New World* (1993), and *Captured Alive in Tokyo City* (1996). He officially left Praying Mantis in 1996. In 1995, Stratton even hooked up with Paul Di'Anno for a project called the Original Iron Men. These days Stratton plays in pubs in and around London area and collaborates with other musicians.

DENNIS WILCOCK (vocalist, 1976–1977)

The second singer in Iron Maiden, Dennis Wilcock—like drummer Doug Sampson—is one of the former Maiden players to have faded into obscurity. Nothing is known about his current location and he hasn't been heard of musically in a long time. He is, however, featured on the comprehensive, highly acclaimed Iron Maiden DVD *The Early Years*.

Line-up History

CURRENT "CLASSIC" LINE-UP

Steve Harris (bass and backing vocals, 1975–present)
Dave Murray (guitar, 1976–present)
Adrian Smith (guitar and backing vocals, 1980–1990 and 1999–present)
Bruce Dickinson (lead vocals, 1981–1993 and 1999–present)
Nicko McBrain (drums and percussion, 1982–present)
Janick Gers (guitar, 1990–present)

TOURING MEMBER

Michael Kenney (keyboards, 1986–present)

PAST MEMBERS

Paul Day (lead vocals, 1975–1976)
Ron Matthews (drums, 1975–1976)
Terry Rance (guitar, 1975–76)
Dave Sullivan (guitar, 1975–76)
Dennis Wilcock (lead vocals, 1976–1977)
Rob Sawyer (guitar, 1976)
Terry Wapram (guitar, 1977)
Tony Moore (keyboards, 1977)
Barry "Thunderstick" Purkis (drums and percussion, 1977)
Doug Sampson (drums and percussion, 1977–1979)
Paul Cairns (guitar, 1979)
Paul Todd (guitar, 1979)
Tony Parsons (guitar, 1979)
Paul Di'Anno (lead vocals, 1978–1981)
Dennis Stratton (guitar and backing vocals, 1979–1980)
Clive Burr (drums and percussion, 1980–1982)
Blaze Bayley (lead vocals, 1994–1998)

BIBLIOGRAPHY & SOURCES

The following books, magazines, and websites were integral in the writing of this book:

IRON MAIDEN BOOKS

Brown, Jake. *Iron Maiden: In the Studio: The Stories Behind Every Album*. London: John Blake, 2011.

Di'Anno, Paul. *The Beast: Singing with Iron Maiden—The Drugs, the Groupies . . . the Whole Story*. London: John Blake, 2010.

Halfin, Ross. *Iron Maiden: A Photo History*. London: Omnibus Press, 2006.

Paterson, Lawrence. *Blaze Bayley: At the End of the Day*. West Midlands, U.K.: Blaze Bayley Recordings, 2009.

Popoff, Martin. *Run for Cover: The Art of Derek Riggs*. Salt Lake City, Utah: Aardvark Global Publishing, 2006.

Shooman, Joe. *Bruce Dickinson: Flashing Metal with Maiden and Flying Solo*. Shropshire, U.K.: Independent Music Press, 2007.

Stenning, Paul. *Iron Maiden: 30 Years of the Beast*. Surrey, U.K.: Chrome Dreams, 2006.

Wall, Mick. *Run to the Hills: The Authorised Biography of Iron Maiden, Rev. Ed*. London: Sanctuary Publishing, 2001.

HEAVY METAL BOOKS

Baddeley, Gavin. *Lucifer Rising: Sin, Devil Worshipping & Rock 'n' Roll*. London: Plexus Publishing, 1999.

Christe, Ian. *Sound of the Beast: The Complete Headbanging History of Heavy Metal*. London: Allison & Busby, 2004.

Konow, David. *Bang Your Head: The Rise and Fall of Heavy Metal*. London: Plexus Publishing, 2004.

MacMillan, Malc. *The New Wave of British Heavy Metal Encyclopedia*. Berlin: IP Verlag, 2001.

Tucker, John. *The New Wave of British Heavy Metal: Suzie Smiled*. Shropshire, U.K.: Independent Music Press, 2006.

REFERENCE BOOKS

Betts, Graham. *Complete British Hit Albums*. London: Collins, 2004.

—————. *Complete UK Hit Singles 1952–2005, Rev. Ed*. London: Collins, 2005.

Larkin, Colin. *The Virgin Illustrated Encyclopedia of Rock, New Ed*. London: Virgin Books, 1999.

Roberts, David, Editor. *British Hit Singles & Albums, 19th Ed*. London: Guinness World Records, 2006.

Strong, Martin C. *The Great Rock Discography, 6th Ed*. London: Canongate, 2002.

MAGAZINES

Artist Magazine; BW&BK (Brave Words & Bloody Knuckles); Classic Rock; Fireworks; Guitarist; Hard Rock; Hard Roxx; Hit Parader; Kerrang!; Mega Metal; Melt Down; Metal Edge; Metal Forces; Metal Hammer; Metal Maniacs; Modern Drummer; Modern Recording; NME; Powerplay; RAW; Record Collector; Rock Hard; Rock Magazine!; Rolling Stone; Soundcheck!; and Sounds

NEWSPAPERS AND NON-MUSIC PUBLICATIONS

The Daily Mirror; Express & Star; The Sun (U.K.); and *The Times* (London)

IRON MAIDEN ONLINE

blazebayley.net
ironmaiden.com (official)
ironmaidencommentary.com (fan site)
ironmaidenheaven.com (fan site)
maidencentral.com (fan site)
maidenfans.com (fan site)
pauldianno.com (official)
paulmarioday.com (official)

MUSIC WEBSITES

allmusic.com
angelfire.com/rock2/rockinterviews
aquarian.com
battlehelm.com
blasting-zone.com
blistering.com
blogcritics.org/music
bookofhours.net
bravewords.com
classicrockmagazine.com
exclaim.ca
fanpop.com

getreadytorock.com
getreadytoroll.com
hardradio.com
heavymetal.about.com
jam.canoe.ca
junkonline.net
kaos2000.net
metalhammer.co.uk
metallicablogmagnetic.com
metal-observer.com
metal-rules.com
metalstorm.net
metalunderground.com
mixonline.com
moshville.com
musicradar.com
musicrooms.net
noisecreep.com
review-mag.com
rockzone.com
sputnikmusic.com
storyofthestars.com
stylusmagazine.com
thequietus.com
thrashhits.com
ultimate-guitar.com

NEWS, ENTERTAINMENT, AND NON MUSIC WEBSITES

bbc.co.uk
canada.com
digitalspy.co.uk
edition.cnn.com
edmontonjournal.com
examiner.com
guardian.co.uk
harbinger.net
independant.co.uk
metro.co.uk
mirror.co.uk
scritube.com
skynews.com
smnnews.com
timeoutdubai.com
timesofindia.com
torontosun.com

SECONDARY SOURCES

In addition to the above types of primary sources, I have in various instances used the following secondary sources:

Bowler, Dave and Brian Dray. *Infinite Dreams: Iron Maiden*. London: Boxtree, 1996.

"Bridge House Diaries." *thebridgehousee16.com*.

Bushell, Gary. *Running Free: The Official Story of Iron Maiden, 2nd Ed.* London: Zomba Books, 1987.

Gamba, Marco and Nicola Visintini. *Iron Maiden Collectibles*. Genoa, Italy: Moving Sound Books, 1997.

———. *Iron Maiden Companion*. Genoa, Italy: Moving Media & Arts, 2001.

———. *Iron Maiden Companion: Update 1*. Genoa, Italy: Moving Media & Arts, 2004.

Gooch, Curt and Jeff Suhs. *KISS Alive Forever: The Complete Touring History*. New York: Billboard Books, 2002.

Heavy Metal Soundhouse, The. *hmsoundhouse.com*.

Iron Maiden. *The History of Iron Maiden, Part 1: The Early Years*. Columbia Music Video, 2004.

Iron Maiden Commentary, The. *ironmaidencommentary.com*.

Judas Priest Info Pages. Website no longer in service.

New Wave of British Heavy Metal Online Encyclopedia, The. *nwobhm.com* no longer in service.

Skoog, Robert. "Iron Maiden Tour Index." *hem.passagen.se/davemurray/tour_index.htm?*.

Stenning, Paul. *Iron Maiden: 30 Years of the Beast*. Surrey, U.K.: Chrome Dreams, 2006.

ACKNOWLEDGMENTS

THE AUTHOR WOULD LIKE TO THANK THE FOLLOWING:

Robert Alford, Al "The Metallian", Johnny B, Gavin Baddeley, John Barnett,
Blaze Bayley, Joe Bosso, Dan Bukszpan, Garry Bushell, Ian Christe,
Andy Copping, Jess Cox, Michael Dregni, Joe Geesin, Gueniviere, Ian Harvey,
Arwa Haider, Scott Hefflon, Gary James, Ryan LaMar, Bob Leafe, Alan Lewis,
Matthias and Henrik, Matthias Mader, Geoff Martin, Joe Matera, Ed McArdle,
Meghan McGivern, Joel McIver, Mark Morton, Bob Nalbandian, Todd Newton,
Robyn Orsini at Fender, Dennis Pernu, Steven Poole, Martin Popoff,
Kevin Purcell, Bryan Reesman, Derek Riggs, Jason Ritchie, Steven Rosen,
Cindy Samargia Laun, Ram Samudrala, Linda Serck, Joe Shooman,
Kelley Simms, Shan Siva, Darryl Sterdan, Eamon Sweeney, Marko Syri,
Brian Tatler, Ron "Bumblefoot" Thal, Kevin Thompson, John Tucker,
Catherine Turner, Chris Vinnicombe, Mick Wall, Jeff Waters, Jon Weiderhorn,
Frank White, Mark Wilkinson, David Lee Wilson, and Joshua Woods.

CONTRIBUTORS

Detroit-based **Robert Alford** is a rock 'n' roll photographer of thirty-five-plus years who has photographed more than five hundred acts, from AC/DC to ZZ Top. His work has featured prominently in magazines such as *CREEM*, *People*, *Rolling Stone*, and on album covers, in liner notes, on television, and in books and documentaries.

Gavin Baddeley is an English journalist and author specializing in ghoulish pop culture and macabre history. He is perhaps best known for his 1999 book, *Lucifer Rising: A Book of Sin, Devil Worship and Rock 'n' Roll*, an acclaimed study of Satanism, though his 2010 "bible of decadence and darkness," *The Gospel of Filth*, is now fast becoming a cult tome. He first discovered Iron Maiden's debut album at the impressionable age of fourteen, and has been a fan ever since.

Daniel Bukszpan is the author of *The Encyclopedia of Heavy Metal*. He has been a freelance writer since 1994, and he has written for such publications as the *New York Post*, *Pop Smear*, *Guitar World*, the *Pit Report*, and *Hails and Horns*. He lives in Brooklyn with his wife, Asia, and his son, Roman.

The son of a London fireman, **Garry Bushell** (*garry-bushell. co.uk*) began his career as a rock writer in *Sounds* in 1975, and in 1984 wrote Iron Maiden's authorized biography, *Running Free*. In addition, Garry managed the Cockney Rejects and the Blood, discovered Twisted Sister in a West Chester County bar, and travelled the world with the likes of Ozzy Osbourne, the Specials, and Motörhead. Dubbed "the Godfather of Street-Punk," he compiled the original Oi! albums and still sings with punk band the Gonads. He currently writes pulp fiction novels and bad jokes about TV in the U.K. nationals. Howard Stern once dubbed him "my ambassador in England."

Ian Christe is the author of *Sound of the Beast: The Complete Headbanging History of Heavy Metal* and *Everybody Wants Some: The Van Halen Saga*. He is also the publisher of Bazillion Points Books (*bazillionpoints.com*), home to *Swedish Death Metal* by Daniel Ekeroth, *Hellbent for Cooking* by Annick Giroux, *Sheriff McCoy* by Andy McCoy, *Dirty Deeds* by Mark Evans, *Touch and Go: The Complete Hardcore Punk Zine '79–'83* by Tesco Vee and Dave Stimson, and *Mellodrama: The Mellotron Movie* DVD.

Ryan LaMar has been an Iron Maiden fan since he was nine. He currently serves as a captain in the U.S. Army and holds a degree in history from Washington State University. He also studied at the graduate school at Western Washington University where he undertook researching Iron Maiden's tourography as a graduate project. He continues to refine it as new historical evidence comes to light.

Bob Leafe (*bobleafe.com*) has photographed more than fifteen hundred music performers, from Led Zeppelin to Liberace. He has been the house photographer for major concert venues, radio stations, TV shows, and for MTV, where he shot the first Video Music Awards and the 1984 New Year's Eve Ball. He's been published in more than one hundred U.S. magazines and all over the world.

Martin Popoff (*martinpopoff.com*) is the author of twenty-eight books on hard rock and heavy metal. Additionally, he has written more record reviews than anyone living or dead. His band bios include works on Black Sabbath, Deep Purple, Judas Priest, UFO, Rainbow, Dio, Rush, and the mighty Blue Öyster Cult.

Derek Riggs is the sole creator of Eddie, Iron Maiden's ubiquitous mascot. He designed the monster as a specimen artwork for his portfolio in the late 1970s, and the first "Eddie picture," entitled Electric Matthew Says Hello, appeared on the first Iron Maiden album cover. The piece was conceived as a cover for a punk album, thus the character's mohawk (longer hair was later added at the request of Iron Maiden). Riggs showed the artwork to several record companies and as a result was thrown out of many art directors' offices. After ten years or so, Riggs grew bored of Eddie and became a freelancer so that he could expand into other styles. He remains a freelance artist today, and a book of his illustrations entitled *Run for Cover: The Art of Derek Riggs* can be purchased from his website, *www.derekriggs.com.*

John Tucker (*johntuckeronline.com*) is an acknowledged authority on the New Wave of British Heavy Metal. As a fanzine writer and photographer at the time—as well as a massive fan of the music—Tucker was perfectly placed to watch the NWOBHM unfold around him. He has written three books, including *The New Wave of British Heavy Metal: Suzie Smiled* (2006), contributed to countless metal magazines, and worked with various record labels.

Mick Wall (*mickwall.com*) is one of Britain's best-known music journalists, broadcasters, and authors. His most recent book is the critically acclaimed biography of Metallica, *Enter Night* (2011). Formerly editor-in-chief of *Classic Rock* magazine and a founding father of *Kerrang!*, his work has also appeared in *The Times* (London), *Mojo*, *Guitar World*, and numerous other newspapers and magazines around the world. His thirty-five-year career has also included stints as a high-profile PR exec, artist manager, TV and radio presenter, and record company executive.

Frank White began his photography career on February 12, 1975, shooting Led Zeppelin at Madison Square Garden. He began selling his images in 1982, first to *Relix* and then to several other music publications, including *Guitar World*, *Circus*, *CREEM*, *Kerrang!*, *Hit Parader*, *Rock Scene*, and others. His images have also been licensed to record companies, MTV, and VH1. In 1986, he began the Frank White Photo Agency. He continues to photograph music and other subjects.

ABOUT THE AUTHOR

Neil Daniels (*neildaniels.com* and *neildanielsbooks.wordpress.com*) has written about classic rock and heavy metal for a wide range of magazines, fanzines, and websites. He has written books on Judas Priest, Robert Plant, Bon Jovi, Linkin Park, and Journey. He also co-authored *Dawn of the Metal Gods: My Life in Judas Priest & Heavy Metal* with original Judas Priest singer/co-founder Al Atkins. His acclaimed series, *All Pens Blazing: A Rock & Heavy Metal Writer's Handbook, Vols. I and II*, collects more than a hundred original and exclusive interviews with some of the world's most famous rock and heavy metal scribes. His other duel collection, *Rock 'n' Roll Mercenaries: Interviews with Rock Stars, Vols. I and II*, compiles sixty interviews with many well-known rock stars.

Neil's reviews, articles, and interviews have been published in *The Guardian*, *Classic Rock Presents AOR*, *Classic Rock Presents Let It Rock*, *Rock Sound*, *Record Collector*, *Big Cheese*, *Powerplay*, *Fireworks*, *MediaMagazine*, *rocktopia.co.uk*, *getreadytorock.com*, *musicOMH.com*, *drownedinsound.com*, *BBCnewsonline.co.uk*, *carling.com*, *unbarred.co.uk*, and *Planet Sound* on Channel4's Teletext service.

First published in 2012 by Voyageur Press, an imprint of MBI Publishing Company, 400 First Avenue North, Suite 300, Minneapolis, MN 55401 USA

Voyageur Press titles are also available at discounts in bulk quantity for industrial or sales-promotional use. For details write to Special Sales Manager at MBI Publishing Company, 400 First Avenue North, Suite 300, Minneapolis, MN 55401 USA.

To find out more about our books, visit us online at www.voyageurpress.com.

Library of Congress Cataloging-in-Publication Data

Daniels, Neil.
 Iron Maiden : the ultimate unauthorized history of the beast / Neil Daniels.
    p. cm.
 Includes bibliographical references and index.
 ISBN 978-0-7603-4221-3 (plc)
 1. Iron Maiden (Musical group) 2. Rock groups–England–Pictorial works. 3. Rock musicians–England–Biography. I. Title.
 ML421.I76D36 2012
 782.42166092'2–dc23
                    2011037352

Speakermouth Eddie, endpaper: Derek Riggs, 2011. www.derekriggs.com
Torturous frontispiece, page 1: pandapaw/Shutterstock.com
Headbangin' title, page 3: © Bob Leafe
Cracked contents, page 4: Mick Hutson/Redferns/Getty Images

Acquisitions and Project Editor: Dennis Pernu
Design Manager: Cindy Samargia Laun
Interior Design and Layout: John Barnett/4 Eyes Design
Cover Design: John Barnett/4 Eyes Design

Printed in China

10 9 8 7 6 5 4 3 2 1

INDEX

Iron Maiden flight cases, circa 2000. *Mick Hutson/Redferns/Getty Images*